China's Investment Laws: New Directions

To

Yishui

China's Investment Laws: New Directions

Guiguo Wang
JSD (Yale), LL M (Columbia),
Diploma (Peking Foreign Languages Institute)

Butterworths
Singapore – UK – Australia – Canada
New Zealand – USA
1988

THE BUTTERWORTH GROUP OF COMPANIES

SINGAPORE	BUTTERWORTH & CO (ASIA) PTE LTD 30 Robinson Road #12-01 Tuan Sing Towers, Singapore 0104
UK	BUTTERWORTH & CO (PUBLISHERS) LTD London, Edinburgh
AUSTRALIA	BUTTERWORTH (PTY) LIMITED Sydney, Melbourne, Brisbane, Adelaide and Perth
CANADA	BUTTERWORTH & CO (CANADA) LTD Toronto and Vancouver
NEW ZEALAND	BUTTERWORTHS OF NEW ZEALAND LTD Wellington and Auckland
UNITED STATES OF AMERICA	BUTTERWORTH LEGAL PUBLISHERS St Paul, Minnesota Seattle, Washington Boston, Massachusetts Austin, Texas D & S PUBLISHING COMPANY Clearwater, Florida

ISBN 0-409-99560-6

Typeset in Singapore by Times Graphics and printed in Hong Kong by Astros Printing Limited

Preface

The year 1986 saw a considerable evolution in China's policy on foreign investment. Having enjoyed a foreign-trade surplus for three consecutive years, China suffered a huge trade deficit in 1985. In order to stop the drain on its valuable foreign exchange reserves, China began from 1986 to encourage foreign investment in export-oriented, import-substitution and technology-intensive projects. Foreign investors had also complained about red tape, slow decision-making, overlapping controls over joint venture management, insufficient working capital and borrowing powers, operating costs, labour, infrastructure, and treatment by Customs authorities. As a result, the flow of foreign capital into China slowed down.

The Chinese government conducted a series of studies on the foreign-investment environment in mid-1986 and concluded that improvements had to be made in order to attract overseas funds and advanced technology. In October 1986, the State Council of China promulgated a set of regulations, known as the '22 Articles', to tackle the problems of foreign investment. Thereafter, ministries under the State Council, local governments at provincial and city levels, and the Special Economic Zones issued a number of detailed regulations to implement and supplement the 22 Articles.

The enactment of these new laws has been warmly welcomed by foreign businesses. After interviewing 121 executives from 70 joint ventures from the United States, Hong Kong, Japan and Europe in early 1987, AT Kearney, an international management consulting firm, concluded that China was on the threshold of a new era in foreign investment and that the time was ripe for Western firms to make strategic commitments there. 'From extensive interviews with joint venture investors, we recommend serious consideration of immediate investment in China. . . . Although some commentators speculate about political change, we believe that the economic environment for foreign investors will continue to be positive,' stated Philip Banks, vice-president international for AT Kearney.

The intention of this book is to summarize the experiences of the Chinese government, Chinese enterprises and overseas businesses with respect to investment in China; to analyze the new laws and their practical significance to foreign investors; and to forecast future trends.

In order to examine effectively the new laws, Chapter one of this book, which serves as an introduction, will outline China's legal system in its application to foreign investment. Chapter two will examine the issues and problems arising from the development of foreign investment in China.

Chapters three to seven will analyze the new laws adopted by the central government, the provincial governments, cities and the Special Economic Zones. In addition to the supplementary provisions adopted by the local governments, corporate laws and regulations on foreign banks, which are exclusively applicable to the Special Economic Zones, will be surveyed briefly.

Chapter eight will compare the new laws with the existing statutes adopted by the central government, and with the supplementary rules enacted by the various coastal cities, provinces and the Special Economic Zones. Chapter nine will focus on the practical significance of the new foreign-investment mechanism, including the extent to which this new legal regime can resolve foreign-investment difficulties, such as land use fees, utilities costs, labour costs, and red tape etc. The impact of an emerging domestic entrepreneurial spirit, and the competition to attract foreign capital, will also be discussed.

Chapter ten will explore possible solutions for the better operation of foreign-investment enterprises in China.

This book is aimed at legal practitioners and academics and will trace the social, economic and political elements contributing to the Chinese legal system and its economic reforms. In addition, an equal emphasis has been placed on an analysis of the practical effect that the current Chinese legal framework will have on foreign enterprises.

The author wishes to extend his sincere gratitude to Professor Robert E Lutz II of Southwestern University School of Law, in the United States, for his invaluable assistance in the preparation of this book. The author also gratefully thanks Miss Telly Tang, his former secretary, for her dedication in preparing the manuscript, and the Editorial Department of Butterworths Asia for its professionalism. Needless to say, the author remains solely responsible for what is said in this book.

Guiguo Wang
January 1988

Contents

Chapter one

China's investment environment

China has embarked on a policy of opening itself to the outside world ie an 'open policy'. This is sometimes referred to by foreigners as an 'open-door policy'. The avoidance by the Chinese of the term 'open-door policy' has a strong basis, for the term is linked to China's semi-colonial past when she was reluctant to have economic or commercial relations with Western countries. China's open policy reflects its recognition of economic interdependence among nations in the world and its desire to cooperate with other members of the international community by inviting foreign investment and expanding commercial relations and exchanges.

The open policy has also an internal dimension. It expresses the need for China's domestic economy to be reformed, for example, through the introduction of contract responsibility systems, private farming (the State Government owns the land, while farmers have the right to use it and in turn pay an agricultural tax to the State Government), leasing and sales of State-owned enterprises in urban areas to individuals or collectives etc.

In short, China's open policy is intended to invigorate the domestic economy and, moreover, as an extension of domestic economic policy, to boost economic exchanges with other countries. This chapter will briefly examine the formation of China's open policy, its effect on both domestic economic structure and foreign trade and investment, the rapid building up of China's legal systems since the late 1970s, and the basic characteristics of Chinese laws and the legal system.

I. The open policy and its significance

Domestic reforms

The communique of the 3rd Plenary Session of the 11th Central Committee of the Communist Party of China, adopted on 22 December 1978, marked the beginning of China's open policy.[1] It put an end to the large-scale nationwide political movements which were very common in China during the previous three decades, and declared that China would

1 *People's Daily*, 24 December 1978.

focus on economic development by opening itself to the outside world and revitalizing the domestic economy. In implementing this policy, the Chinese government first abolished the People's Commune system in rural areas, and gave farmers full freedom in decision-making with respect to production and distribution of their products. Thereafter, rapid changes took place in domestic pricing and wage systems. The market has begun to play a more important role in the domestic economic system.

Another change in the domestic economic system was the introduction of a tax system in the early 1980s which has replaced the previous system under which the government was directly and effectively responsible for the profits and losses of State-owned enterprises. Traditionally, Chinese enterprises had to submit all their profits to the State Government in lieu of taxation. The State Government would bear all the losses of these enterprises. Under the new system, both State-owned enterprises and collectively-owned enterprises are taxed by the State Government on the basis of the net income of each of the enterprises. The enterprises themselves are permitted to withhold a portion of their profits and can therefore manage their funds more effectively. In order to implement this tax system successfully, the Chinese government has delegated substantial powers in respect of production and distribution to the management of the enterprises. The general manager and assistant general managers of each enterprise are, at least in theory, exclusively responsible for the business activities of the enterprise.

In addition, vigorous reforms have been introduced to small-sized enterprises. By early 1987, 50,395 of the existing 94,963 small enterprises had been reorganized.[2] Among the reorganized enterprises, the power of business decision-making and management of 42,261 enterprises was handed over to the workers themselves, while the State Government retained ownership. Under this arrangement, the management and the workers have full power of decision-making in connection with the operation of their enterprise. They are obligated to submit a certain amount of profit to the State Government annually. If the actual profit made in the year is higher than that agreed upon, the State Government will take a certain portion of the net income exceeding the agreed level while the workers keep the rest. If the actual net profit is lower than the quota set up, the income of the workers and the State Government must also be reduced based on the formula agreed upon.

By early 1987, the ownership of 4,540 enterprises, or about 7.91% of the reorganized small enterprises, had been changed from the State Government to the employees. The nature of this reform is to convert the enterprise in question from a State-owned one to a collectively-owned one. The workers of these enterprises, sometimes together with other institutions, own the enterprises.

2 *Wen Wei Po*, 4 March 1987, p. 3.

Leasing is another method of reforming small enterprises. By March 1987, 10,436 small enterprises had been let to individuals or collective enterprises. Under the lease, the lessee retains full power of management of the enterprise in question and has to submit a fixed amount of rent to the owner, the State Government, regardless of how much profit he may make or the loss he may suffer.[3] The practice of leasing has developed very quickly since the lessee does not have to purchase the property of the enterprise to gain management control. The status of the employees remains unchanged too.

In addition, by early 1987, 95 small enterprises had been sold by the State Government to individuals for cash.[4] These enterprises were usually very small in size or located in remote areas.

Undoubtedly, both the Chinese central and local governments are in favour of the reforms. They have adopted measures such as tax exemption and reduction for reorganized enterprises. These internal economic reforms have created a more conducive climate for foreign investment. They have introduced into the domestic economy market elements which are conventional in Western countries.

In addition, China's open policy has forged horizontal economic links and cooperation among the domestic enterprises. Such cooperation has introduced systematic changes to the traditional vertical structure of China's planned economy. Under the new economic system, a number of new large conglomerates have been established. They include Dongfeng and Liberation Truck Makers, The Great Wall Computers Companies Group, and several export-oriented integrated enterprises for the production of brand-name bicycles.

SEZs and coastal cities

China's open policy commenced in 1980 with the establishment of four special economic zones along the south-eastern coast: Shenzhen, Zhuhai and Shantou in Guangdong Province and Xiamen in Fujian Province (hereinafter referred to singularly as the 'SEZ' and collectively as the 'SEZs'). Three years later, Hainan Island was declared open to foreign investors.

In late 1984, the Central Committee of the Communist Party of China further committed China to the expansion of economic and technological exchanges and cooperation with foreign countries.[5] The decision proclaimed that the need to use foreign funds and establish Sino-foreign joint ventures, Sino-foreign cooperative ventures or wholly foreign-owned enterprises was necessary for the development of China's

3 *Id.*
4 *Id.*
5 'Decision on Reform of Economic Structure' adopted at the 3rd Plenary Session of the 12th Central Committeee of the Communist Party of China on 20 October 1984.

economy. It called for further Sino-foreign economic cooperation, particularly in the special economic zones and other coastal cities, so as to make the best use of China's domestic and foreign resources, organize domestic construction and strengthen economic ties with foreign countries and enterprises.[6]

As a result, 14 coastal cities and ports, which were opened in mid-1984 for foreign investment, have, except for Wenzhou and Beihai, established adjacent economic and technological development zones ('ETDZ') where large-scale infrastructure has been developed to create basic conditions for foreign investment.[7] The ETDZs and Hainan Island administrative region enjoy a status similar to that of the SEZs. Foreign investors in these zones are not limited to any particular industry or industries and are entitled to preferential treatment.

China's open policy was further implemented in early 1985 when the central government opened up the country's three most fertile river delta areas, famed as China's 'land of rice and fish', namely, the Yangtse River Delta in Shanghai, Hangzhou and Nanjing forming three triangular points; the Zhujiang (Pearl) River Delta centering on Guangzhou; and the Xiamen-Zhangzhou-Quanzhou Delta in southern Fujian Province.

The application of the open policy, however, is not limited to regions designated as SEZs or open coastal cities etc. Sino-foreign economic cooperation has also spread to China's vast hinterland. Joint ventures and cooperative ventures have been set up in all the provinces and autonomous regions.[8]

Achievements in foreign investment

During the eight years from the beginning of 1979 to the end of 1986, foreign investment totalling US$7.43 b was made in China. By the end of 1986, the number of foreign-investment enterprises had reached 7,783, including 138 with exclusively foreign funds.[9] In other words, in one year, on average, about US$928.75 m worth of foreign investment was made and 973 enterprises with foreign participation were established in China (see Table 1):

As indicated in Table 2, over the eight-year period (1979–1986), foreign investment was made largely in property areas such as hotels and residential and office complexes.

Foreign investment in the property area accounts for 44% of the total foreign investment in China. Of these property enterprises, 45% are cooperative ventures, 10% wholly foreign-owned enterprises, with the

6 *Id.*
7 These 14 coastal cities include, from north to south, Dalian, Qinghuangdao, Tianjin, Yantai, Qindao, Lianyungang, Nantong, Shanghai, Ningbo, Wenzhou, Fuzhou, Guangzhou, Zhanjiang and Beihai.
8 *South China Morning Post*, 9 March 1987, p. BN9.
9 *Id.*

Table 1: Foreign investment statistics (1979–1986)

Year	July 1979–1983	1984	1985	1986	Total
Number of ventures approved	1392	1856	3073	1462	7783
Foreign investment made (US$ billion)	2.69	1.42	1.96	1.37	7.44

Source: Ministry of Foreign Economic Relations and Trade of China, *Wen Wei Po*, 4 April 1987, p. BN2.

Table 2: Foreign investment by sector (1979–1986 (%))

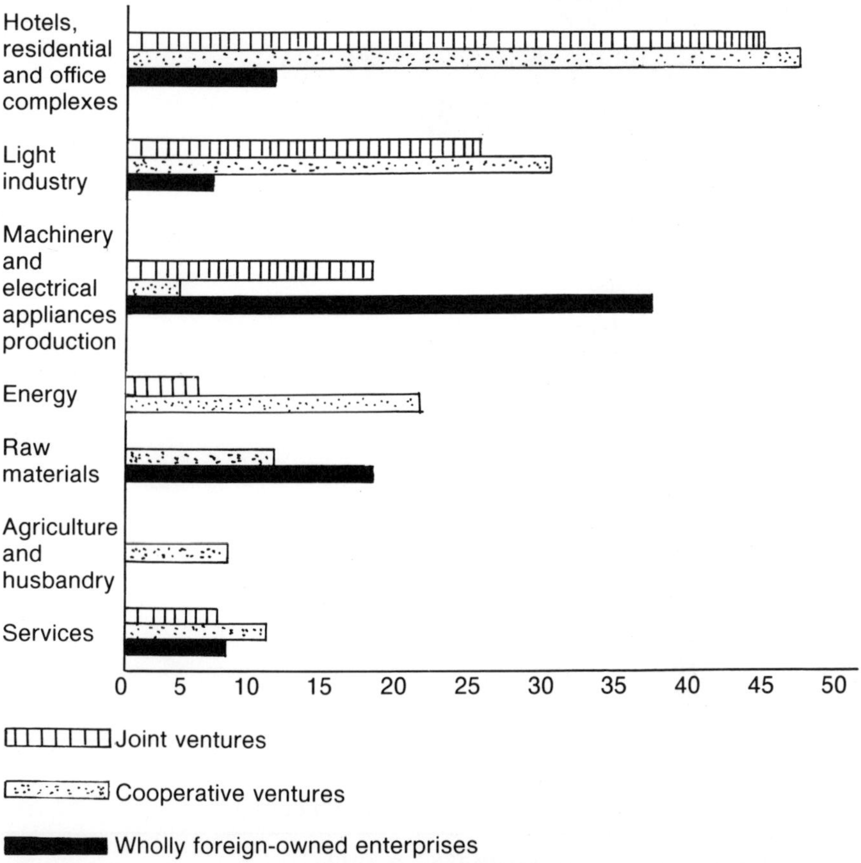

Source: Wen Wei Po, 25 February 1987, p. BN2.

rest being joint ventures. By the end of 1986, 431 hotel projects had been approved by the Chinese government.[10]

Most of the hotels and residential and office complexes have been built in large cities and coastal areas where foreign investment is concentrated (see Table 3).

Table 3: Property projects with foreign funds (1979–1986)

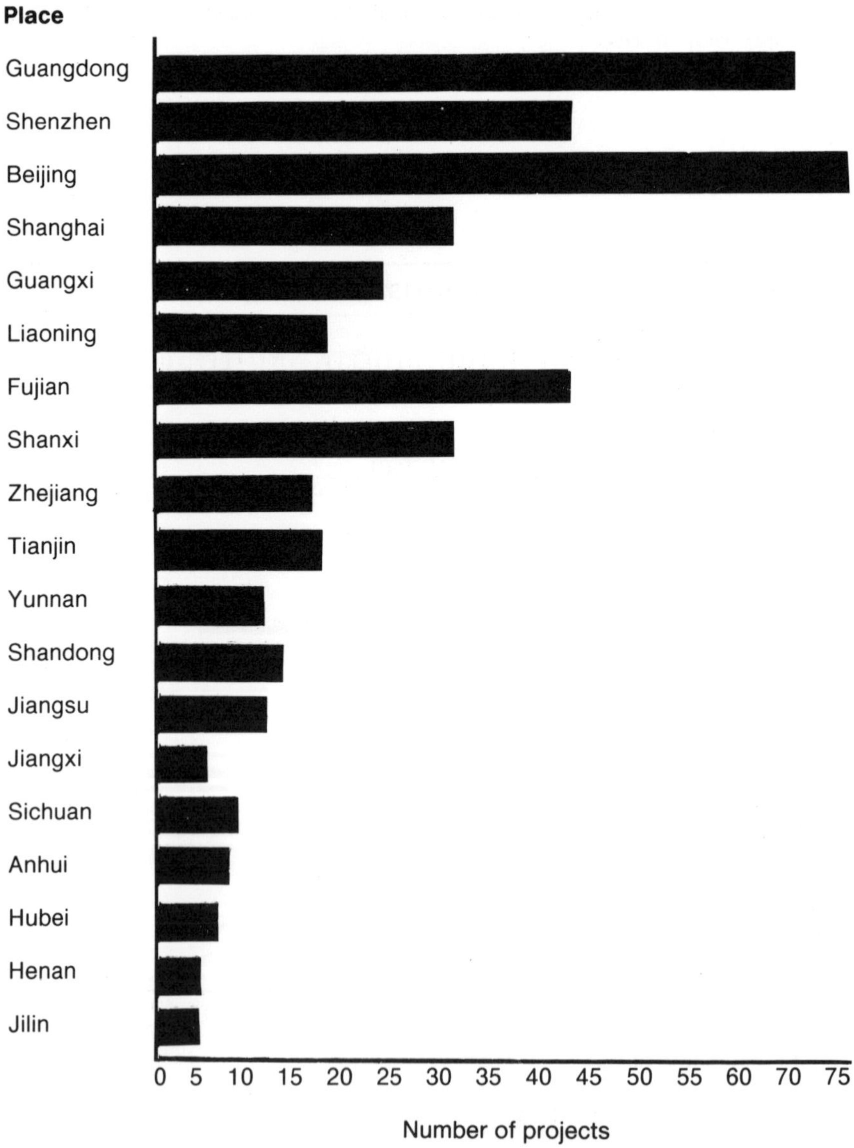

Source: Wen Wei Po, 25 February 1987, p. BN2.

10 *Wen Wei Po*, 25 February 1987, p. BN2.

From a historical point of view, the fast growth of the hotel business was a direct market response to China's economic situation in the late 1970s. At that time, the hotels in China were too few to accommodate the foreign businessmen and tourists who were arriving in large numbers. As a result, both China and foreign investors were keen to build more hotels and restaurants as well as residential and office complexes to meet the demands of foreign investors and tourists. The boost in the hotel business has in effect provided an example of collaboration between enterprises from market economy countries and their counterparts from planned economy countries.

Foreign investment in the energy and natural resources sector, transportation, machinery and electronics as well as raw materials is also substantial. The best known projects include the Daya Bay Nuclear Power Plant, Pingshuo Open Coal Mine (with the investment from Occidental Petroleum Company), the 37 offshore petroleum co-development ventures, the Beijing Jeep Joint Venture, the Schindler Elevator Venture, and the Wang Laboratories Computer Venture etc.[11]

In addition, Ecolaire, a US-based supplier of electricity-generating equipment, has set up its Asian regional headquarters in Beijing, China. Ecolaire's decision is in contrast to the approach of most other European and US companies who usually establish their Asian regional offices in Hong Kong, Tokyo or Singapore.[12] Ecolaire's Beijing office is responsible for coordinating the company's extensive activities in South Korea, Japan, Thailand, Singapore, Malaysia, Indonesia, India and the Philippines.[13]

Transfer of technology

In the area of technology transfer, China has also achieved great success.[14] In 1986 alone, enterprises in China imported 744 items of technology, valued at US$4.45 b, equivalent to 7% of the total imports by China for the same year.[15] According to the statistics released by the Ministry of Foreign Economic Relations and Trade, from 1981 when

11 *Wen Wei Po*, 25 February 1987, p. BN2.
12 *South China Morning Post*, 7 March 1987, p. BN8.
13 *Id.*
14 The transfer of technology under the Chinese system includes importation of technical know-how, productive technology, productive and managerial skills, and the machinery, equipment and instruments for the application of the imported technology and know-how. In addition, importation of key equipment, raw materials or equipment for the production of certain products or services is also regarded as a transfer of technology. Nevertheless, importation of pure equipment without the transfer of know-how is not regarded as a transfer of technology. In other words, the transfer of technology in China is importation by Chinese companies, joint ventures or cooperative ventures of systematic knowledge or skills in connection with the production of certain products, the application of productive methods or the provision of services. See Research Department, Hong Kong Trade Development Council, *China's Procedure for Transfer of Technology*, 1987, p. 2.
15 *Id.*

China started importing technology in considerable quantities to 1986, a total of 2,141 contracts involving importation of technology and equipment worth US$9.4 b in value, were approved by the Ministry.[16]

In recent years, West European countries have been the most active in the transfer of technology to China. They account for 45% of the contracts signed by China. In terms of contract value, they account for 48% or US$4.5 b.

As indicated in Table 4, West Germany, France, the United Kingdom and Italy are the main suppliers of technology to China. Technology and equipment imported by China from European countries have been used in such industries as machinery, electronics, metallurgy, electricity, light industrial products, textiles, construction materials and petro-chemicals.

Table 4: Transfer of technology by West European countries to China (1981–1986)

Country	% in terms of no. of contracts	% in terms of investment
West Germany	39.6	28.0
United Kingdom	12.8	12.8
France	8.3	35.6
Italy	14.9	11.0
Belgium	1.7	1.2
Holland	1.7	0.4
Denmark	2.5	2.5
Switzerland	7.1	2.8
Sweden	6.8	3.5
Austria	3.1	1.8
Others	1.5	0.4
Total	100	100

Source: China Economic News, 2 March 1987, p. 5.

The transfer of technology, cooperative production, technological consultancy services and service contracts account for a large proportion of the economic exchanges between China and West European countries. From 1983 to 1986, 494 contracts signed with China were under the above four categories, involving US$719 m or accounting for 44.8% of all such contracts China signed in that period.[17] Looking at these contracts with reference to individual countries, (see Table 5), West Germany, France and the United Kingdom top the list.

The transfer of technology from foreign countries has played a substantial part in developing China's economy. Of the 3,000 items of

16 *China Economic News*, 2 March 1987, p. 5.
17 *Id*, p. 6.

Table 5: Economic exchanges with West European countries (1983–1986)

Country	**% in terms of no. of contracts**	**% in terms of investment**
West Germany	45.5	29.5
France	9.1	40.1
United Kingdom	16.0	6.4
Sweden	5.5	2.3
Switzerland	8.1	2.5
Austria	3.6	7.6
Italy	7.3	7.4
Others	4.9	4.2
Total	100	100

Source: China Economic News, 2 March 1987, p. 6.

advanced technology imported by China in the 1983–1985 period, 1,800 have been put into production and have upgraded China's level of technology. In the North China port city of Tianjin, over 15% of its increased output value has been generated from technological progress.[18] Moreover, as a result, many products manufactured with imported technology have entered the international markets. In 1986, China's procurement agencies were able to purchase 40 more kinds of manufactured goods for export than they were able to in 1985.[19]

Indeed, China's open policy, together with foreign investment, has introduced many changes to the Chinese economic system and has revitalized the Chinese economy. For instance, in the area of refrigerators, China was a net importer less than a decade ago. With the development of Sino-foreign joint ventures and cooperative ventures, China now is not only able to produce refrigerators for domestic use but also for export. An enterprise group manufactures annually about 400,000 'Wanbao brand' refrigerators, of which 60,000 are for export.[20]

China's economic reforms, which started without much (if any) theoretical or economic preparation, are now more mature. The Chinese government is now more certain about what changes should be made and the extent of the current open policy. The position is well summarized by Mr Xue Muqiao, an outstanding Chinese economist, who has pointed out that since socialism resulted from capitalism and China's socialist system was established when China's capitalism was at its primitive stage, market elements and techniques, technology and methods which have been used and have proved to be useful for production and construction in Western countries must be adopted by China. He stated that adoption by China of all the positive aspects of capitalism was

18 *Id.*
19 *Id*, p. 8.
20 *China Economic News*, 12 January 1987, p. 9.

necessary and in accordance with Marxist theory. According to Xue, since China is a developing country, in order to develop its economy, as 'an indispensable process in building China's socialist economy', private enterprises should be permitted and the central government should delegate its power to local governments which in turn should delegate their power to the enterprises themselves; at the same time, competition among State-owned enterprises, collectively-owned enterprises and private enterprises should be encouraged.[21]

II. Trends and characteristics of Sino-foreign commercial exchanges

Historical perspective

Over the last eight years, Sino-foreign commercial exchanges as well as foreign investment in China went through several changes. In general, foreign investment was slow for the first four years starting from 1979. In 1984 and 1985, however, foreign investment increased dramatically. It slowed down again in 1986. As Table 6 indicates, the number of joint

Table 6: Joint ventures

Year	No of ventures	Change over the previous year/period
1979–82	83	
1983	105	1.3 times more*
1984	741	7 times more
1985	1,371	1.8 times more
1986 Jan.–June	400	42% less
Total	2.700	

* Over the past three years, 1979–82.

Source: China Trade Report, 21 October 1986, p. 16.

venture contracts signed in 1984 was about seven times that of the previous four years. The number of joint venture contracts signed in 1985 almost doubled that of the previous year.

In the first four years after China started its open policy, foreign investors hesitated to conduct commercial transactions with or in China as they lacked knowledge and understanding of China's economic policies. The then underdeveloped Chinese legal systems also impeded the growth of foreign investment. The expansion of foreign trade, the achievements made in domestic economic reforms, the growth of foreign

21 *Da Kung Po*, 6 March 1987, p. 1.

exchange reserves and the adoption of a number of important pieces of legislation in respect of foreign investment led to the influx of foreign capital into China in 1984 and 1985.

The slowdown in foreign investment in 1986 can be analyzed from two aspects. On the one hand, it resulted from the bad publicity concerning China's poor foreign-investment environment, particularly the excessive 'red tape', restraints on management autonomy, high investment costs etc. On the other hand, it was a direct consequence of the Chinese government's shift of foreign investment policy in 1986. In that year, China borrowed US$6.49 b in loans from foreign institutions, including international financial institutions, in the form of buyer's credit, commercial loans, and the issuance of bonds and other commercial paper. China's foreign loans in 1986 represented a 96.6% increase over the previous year's.[22] Foreign-investment contracts signed in 1986 fell 48% from the previous year's level to US$3.31 b. The amount actually invested, however, was up 10% from the previous year's level to US$2.12 b.[23]

Recent developments

The structure of foreign investment in China saw a change in 1986. Between 1979 and 1985, foreign investment projects were concentrated in taxi companies, tourist facilities, hotels, colourphoto development firms and other non-productive sectors. Projects in productive enterprises in that period constituted 45% of the total foreign investment. In 1986, however, 76% of the projects approved by the Chinese authorities were productive enterprises in such fields as industry, agriculture, transportation and telecommunications. In addition, the technology involved in those projects was generally more advanced.[24]

The forms of foreign investment have also been through a process of evolution over the last eight years. Between 1979 to 1983, foreign investment was essentially in the form of joint ventures, cooperative ventures (especially for exploration and exploitation of offshore oil resources) and medium- and small-sized compensation trade. Wholly foreign-owned enterprises were established only in the special economic zones. Thereafter, cooperative ventures in almost all kinds of main industries and sectors were established throughout China, and they have become the most popular form of Sino-foreign economic cooperation. Wholly foreign-owned enterprises have also been established in Beijing, Tianjin, Shanghai, Fujian Province etc. In addition, starting from 1984, several holding companies (sometimes referred to as 'umbrella enterprises' in China) have been set up with special approval from the Chinese

22 *Wen Wei Po*, 12 March 1987, p. BN2.
23 *The Asian Wall Street Journal*, 9 March 1987, p. 5.
24 *Wen Wei Po*, 12 March 1987, p. BN2.

government to engage in funds transfer (especially foreign exchange), productive technology and know-how as well as to impart other business techniques to their subsidiaries. This type of enterprise was confirmed by the Chinese government as a standardized legal form when the Provisions of the State Council on the Question of the Balancing of Foreign Exchange Receipts and Expenditures of Chinese-Foreign Joint Ventures were promulgated in early 1986.[25] Thereafter, the establishment of such holding companies did not require any special approval from the central government.

Another development in foreign investment in China is that most of the newly-established joint ventures, cooperative ventures as well as wholly foreign-owned enterprises are technologically advanced or export-oriented. Many of them do not have foreign exchange problems. This is the result of China's foreign investment policy adopted in 1986 which will be discussed in detail in the following chapters.

An increase in technology imported by China is another feature of Sino-foreign commercial exchanges. In 1986 alone, 744 technology transfer contracts were signed with a total value of US$4.455 b. This may be compared with transactions for the importation of technology in the previous five years: 1981 – 73 contracts, valued at US$107 m; 1982 – 102 contracts, valued at US$363 m; 1983 – 219 contracts, valued at US$558 m; 1984 – 332 contracts, valued at US$951 m; and 1985 – 671 contracts, valued at US$2.96 b.[26] In the period 1981 to 1985, 1,397 technology transfer contracts worth US$4.939 b were signed. The 1986 figure equals 53.2% of the previous five years' total in terms of number of contracts and 90.2% in terms of value.

Consultancy fees in connection with the transfer of technology accounted for 14% of the total contract value of all technology transfer contracts signed in 1986. The proportion of these fees to the contract value of the technology transfer contracts signed by the Ministries of Aviation, Electronics, Petroleum, Light Industry, Textiles and Machinery was 100%, 43.6%, 43%, 40.5%, 31.8% and 26%, respectively, in the same year.[27] Another feature of technology transfer in 1986 was the active role played by local governments and enterprises. Before 1986, most of the technology transfer contracts were approved by the central government. In 1986, however, about 38% of the technology transfer contracts of the entire country were approved by provincial and municipal governments.[28] In addition, technology transfers took place not only in large or coastal cities but also in hinterlands and remote areas such as Innermongolia.

25 Articles 6 and 9 of Provisions of the State Council on the Question of the Balancing of Foreign Exchange Receipts and Expenditures of Chinese-foreign Joint Ventures which were promulgated by the State Council on 15 January 1986.
26 *China Economic News*, 26 January 1987, p. 5.
27 *Id.*
28 *Id.*

In 1986, China adjusted its heavy technology and equipment reliance on Japan and the United States by increasing its technology imports from European countries, including Eastern European countries. The top 11 foreign countries and regions which signed technology transfer contracts with China in 1986 were France, Japan, the United States, the Soviet Union, Britain, Italy, West Germany, East Germany, Canada, Bulgaria and Hong Kong.[29]

Most of the technology and equipment imported by China in 1986 was for renovation and improvement of existing enterprises, whereas the past practice favoured investment in new projects. In 1986, a number of projects with imported technology were put into production. Of the 3,000 items of advanced technology imported in the 1983 – 1985 period, 1,800 have been put into production and have upgraded China's level of technology.[30]

As indicated above, China's current policy is to open itself to all countries rather than to focus its attention on developed countries, which was the case in the early 1980s. For instance, China's bilateral trade with the Soviet Union, which was nominal in 1980, totalled US$2.6 b in 1986.[31] China's trade with Mongolia and other Eastern European countries has also risen sharply.

Economic and commercial cooperation with other developing countries has also been expanded. By the end of 1986, China had signed 144 contracts with 25 developing countries for promoting technical co-operation. Of the 144 cooperative contracts, 98 were technical assistance projects offered by China involving training for acupuncture, methane treatment, and the design and construction of small irrigation systems. The remaining 46 projects were offered by other developing countries to China.[32] China has also concluded construction and labour-services projects with the developing world.

III. Legal framework for foreign investment

Structure of the legal system and interrelationship of legislation

China's legal system comprises laws and regulations enacted by the National People's Congress of China, the State Council, ministries under the State Council, provincial people's congresses, and local governments.

29 *Id*, p. 6.
30 *China Economic News*, 12 January 1987, pp. 8–9.
31 *South China Morning Post*, 9 March 1987, p. BN9.
32 *China Economic News*, 12 January 1987, p.9. According to incomplete statistics, China had established, by March 1987, more than 200 Sino-foreign joint ventures and Chinese State-owned enterprises in over 60 countries and regions. Among the places where Chinese direct investments have been made, Hong Kong and Macau top others on the list with 65 Chinese investment enterprises being located there; 31 in the United States, 16 in Japan and 12 in Thailand. See *China Economic News*, 16 March 1987, p. 5.

As a unitary state, the Constitution of China carries the highest authority. Legislation adopted by the National People's Congress is superior to regulations adopted by other legislative or administrative bodies either at the central government or local government level.

In general, the regulations adopted by the State Council, ministries thereunder and local governments are for the implementation of the Constitution and the laws and policies adopted by the National People's Congress. According to the Organic Law on Local Congress and Local Government of China, local congresses and governments at various levels are permitted to enact laws suitable to local conditions, provided that such laws and regulations do not contravene the Constitution, or the laws or policies adopted by the central government.[33] In other words, local governments may promulgate laws which vary slightly from those enacted by the central government. These local laws are valid and are equal in force to the legislation enacted by the central government so long as they are in conformity with the general principles and policies of the latter. For example, as soon as the State Council passed provisions for the encouragement of foreign investment in October 1986, many provincial governments and local governments promulgated similar regulations to give foreign investors more incentives. These local provisions carry a step further the standards adopted by the central government but are still within the general principle of encouraging foreign investment involving advanced technology or for the production of export goods. They are therefore valid laws to be implemented in their respective localities.

Most of the laws adopted by the National People's Congress are general in nature and are therefore usually supplemented by more detailed rules and regulations promulgated by the State Council or relevant ministries thereunder. Rules and regulations enacted by the State Council or other relevant ministries deal with specific matters, especially economic activities, and are applied nationwide. For instance, China's Joint Venture Law was enacted on 1 July 1979.[34] One year later, the State Council promulgated regulations regarding labour management in Sino-foreign joint ventures, and regulations in respect of the registration of joint ventures in China.[35] Three years after the adoptation of the Joint Venture Law, the State Council adopted regulations for the implementation of the Joint Venture Law which provide more detailed provisions

33 See Article 6 of The Organic Law on Local Congress and Local Government of the People's Republic of China, adopted at the 2nd Session of the 5th National People's Congress on 1 July 1979 and amended at the 5th Session of the 5th National People's Congress on 10 December 1982.

34 The Law of the People's Republic of China on Joint Ventures Using Chinese and Foreign Investment was adopted at the 2nd Session of the 5th National People's Congress on 1 July 1979 and promulgated on 8 July 1979.

35 Both the Regulations of the People's Republic of China on Labour Management in Joint Ventures Using Chinese and Foreign Investment and Regulations of the People's Republic of China on the Registration of Joint Ventures Using Chinese and Foreign Investment were promulgated by the State Council on 26 July 1980.

for the establishment and management of joint ventures using Chinese and foreign investment.[36]

Over the last few years, the State Council's legislative power has been increased. In April 1984, the Standing Committee of the National People's Congress passed a resolution requiring its working committees to cooperate with the State Council and various ministries to research and draft legislation for the implementation of the economic policies of China.[37]

Ministerial provisions are more limited in nature and their application is generally within the sphere of the function of the ministry in question. Very often, the ministerial provisions are intended to supplement and implement regulations adopted by the State Council. Immediately after the State Council promulgated provisions for the encouragement of foreign investment in October 1986, for example, the Ministry of Foreign Economic Relations and Trade (MOFERT), the People's Bank of China, and the Ministry of Finance etc subsequently issued implementing rules covering such areas as examination and confirmation of export-oriented enterprises and technologically-advanced enterprises with foreign investment, import and export licences, loans in Chinese currency and taxation. The Ministry of Labour and Personnel also issued labour and wage rules for the implementation of the State Council's Provisions. These ministerial regulations have a nationwide application and may be supplemented by local legislation which take into account the conditions and circumstances in the local areas.

In short, Chinese legislation can be subdivided into three categories, namely, laws adopted by the National People's Congress, regulations enacted by the State Council and ministries, and local legislation.

The Chinese legislation may also be characterized according to the nature of the laws in question ie general laws and special legislation. The general laws include the Constitution, the General Principles of the Civil Law, the Civil Procedure Law, Criminal Law etc. Special legislation includes legislation dealing with foreign investment, such as the Joint Venture Law, Wholly Foreign-owned Enterprises Law, Foreign Economic Contract Law and legislation governing such matters as registration of business, labour and management, taxation, exchange control, financial matters, customs duties etc. In addition, unlike many Western countries, China has adopted a number of statutes which are applicable exclusively to foreign enterprises, Sino-foreign joint ventures, Sino-foreign cooperative ventures or other forms of Sino-foreign economic cooperation. An obvious example is the contract law. There are currently two contract statutes, one governing contracts between domes-

36 Regulations for the Implementation of the Law of the People's Republic of China on Joint Ventures Using Chinese and Foreign Investment were promulgated by the State Council on 20 December 1983.

37 See the Standing Committee of the National People's Congress Decision adopted on 3 April 1984.

tic enterprises and the other governing contracts between Chinese and foreign enterprises as well as individuals.

The Constitution

The Constitution of China, adopted by the National People's Congress at the 5th Session of the 5th Congress on 4 December 1982,[38] provides the legal basis for the open policy, foreign investment and Sino-foreign economic cooperation. Article 18 of the Constitution stipulates that China permits foreign enterprises, other economic institutions as well as individuals to engage in economic cooperation with Chinese enterprises and other economic institutions in various forms in accordance with the law of China. The legal rights and interests of those foreign enterprises, institutions and individuals are protected by the law of China and the economic activities which they carry out in Chinese territory are governed by Chinese law.[39]

The Joint Venture Law

The Law of the People's Republic of China on Joint Ventures Using Chinese and Foreign Investment (the 'Joint Venture Law'), enacted on 1 July 1979, provides that 'with the view of expanding international economic cooperation and technological exchange, the People's Republic of China permits foreign companies, enterprises, other economic entities or individuals to incorporate themselves, within the territory of the People's Republic of China, into joint ventures with Chinese companies, enterprises or other economic entities on the principle of equality and mutual benefit and subject to authorization by the Chinese Government'.[40] The inclusion of the principle of equality and mutual benefit into the Joint Venture Law is natural and logical, for the principle has been a very important part of China's foreign trade and commercial policy. Pursuant to this general principle, the establishment of Sino-foreign joint ventures must meet certain specific economic requirements and conditions, including the ability to promote the development of China's economy and to raise the level of science and technology for the industrialization of the domestic economy.[41] Joint ventures are per-

38 Since 1949, China has amended its Constitution by adopting an entire new version rather than enacting an amendment to the existing constitution. The first Chinese constitution was adopted in 1954 after the establishment of the People's Republic of China in 1949.

39 The Constitution of the People's Republic of China was adopted by the 5th National People's Congress at its 5th Session on 4 December 1982.

40 Joint Venture Law, Article 1.

41 Regulations for the Implementation of the Law of the People's Republic of China on Joint Ventures Using Chinese and Foreign Investment promulgated by the State Council on 20 December 1983 ('Joint Venture Regulations'), Article 3.

mitted to conduct activities in the industrial, agricultural and service sectors. In fact, a joint venture may invest in almost all the main industries with the exception of national defence, transportation, communications, public media, culture and education.[42]

Sino-foreign joint ventures equipped with internationally-advanced technology are accorded preferential treatment. These ventures may apply 'for reduction of or exemption from income tax for the first two to three profit-making years'.[43] Joint ventures established for the exploration of natural or energy resources as well as transportation systems are also entitled to preferential treatment.[44]

A joint venture company is a limited liability company and each party to the venture is liable to the extent of the capital subscribed by it. A joint venture must apply all of its assets in satisfaction of its debts.[45] As a limited liability company established in accordance with Chinese law, a joint venture is a legal person who is subject to the jurisdiction and protection of China.[46] Although most of the joint ventures are limited liability companies, several of them were established as partnerships.[47] Joint ventures in the form of limited liability companies may be converted into partnerships or vice versa.[48]

Under the Joint Venture Law, foreign parties to a joint venture must contribute no less than 25% of the registered capital.[49] Contributions by both the Chinese and foreign parties to a joint venture may be made in a variety of forms, such as cash, buildings, premises, machinery, equipment, industrial property rights, know-how, etc. In general, the Chinese party contributes the site, existing buildings, machinery or cash (in which case, Renminbi). The foreign party to a joint venture usually contributes cash (foreign exchange), advanced machinery or equipment, industrial property rights and technology in any other form. Nevertheless, the foreign party to a joint venture is not usually permitted to make an investment by providing only non-tangible property or rights, without any tangible contribution.

The total amount of registered capital of a joint venture is the amount contributed by the parties concerned, and registered at the registration and administration office, for the establishment of the joint venture.[50] Joint venture parties, however, may make actual investments of amounts

42 *Id.*
43 Joint Venture Law, Article 7.
44 Provisional Rules on Preferential Treatment to Joint Ventures Using Chinese and Foreign Investment to Build Harbours and Wharves promulgated by the State Council on 30 September 1985.
45 Joint Venture Law, Article 19 and Joint Venture Regulations, Article 106.
46 Joint Venture Regulations, Article 2.
47 Yao Zhuang, 'Some Legal Problems Arising From Joint Ventures Using Chinese and Foreign Investment', paper delivered at *China's Economic Law Seminar* sponsored by the Hong Kong People's Association on 2 August 1986, p. 107.
48 *Id.*
49 Joint Venture Law, Article 4.
50 Joint Venture Regulations, Article 21.

which are larger than the registered capital. In practice, prior to the end of 1986, the ratio of investment amount to registered capital was as follows:[51]

Investment amount	*Ratio of investment amount to registered capital*
US$3 m or less	1:1
US$3–10 m	1/2 or US$3 m whichever is higher
US$10–30 m	1/3 or US$5 m whichever is higher
US$30 m or more	1/4 or US$10 m whichever is higher

The investment amount is defined as 'the total amount of investment (including loans) of a joint venture referring to the sum of capital construction funds and the circulating capital needed for the joint venture's production scale as stipulated in the contract and the articles of association of the joint venture'.[52] In other words, the investment amount is the amount needed for the carrying out of the business of the joint venture which serves as the standard for determining the extent of the exemption from custom duties and Industrial and Commercial Consolidated Tax payable on materials imported by the joint venture.[53] If the actual investment by the parties to a joint venture is less than the investment amount needed by the joint venture, the joint venture may borrow from commercial banks or other financial institutions in its own name.

As a limited liability company, each joint venture must have a board of directors which is the highest authority of the enterprise.[54] The number of directors and the distribution of directorships are determined by agreement of the parties, provided that the number of directors is not less than three. As a general rule, the party making the larger contribution is entitled to nominate more directors.[55]

The board of directors is empowered to discuss matters and take action, in accordance with the provisions of the articles of association of the joint venture, on all major issues such as expansion projects, production and business programmes, the budget, distribution of profits, staffing and pay, the appointment of the general manager and deputy general managers etc. These matters may be decided by a simple majority vote of the board of directors. However, matters such as the amendment of the articles of association, discontinuance and dissolution, increase or assignment of the registered capital, or merger, must be decided by unanimous vote.[56]

51 Yao Zhuang, *op cit*, at pp. 109–110.
52 Joint Venture Regulations, Article 20.
53 *Id*, Article 71.
54 *Id*, Article 33.
55 *Id*, Article 34.
56 *Id*, Article 36.

Wholly foreign-owned enterprises

On 12 April 1986, China enacted the Law of the People's Republic of China on Enterprises Operated Exclusively with Foreign Capital (hereinafter referred to as the 'Wholly Foreign-owned Enterprise Law') to permit foreign firms, other economic entities or individuals to set up enterprises in China exclusively with foreign capital.[57] As in the case of joint ventures, a wholly foreign-owned enterprise must also promote the development of China's national economy and must use advanced technology and equipment or market all or most of its products outside China.[58] At the same time the profits and other lawful rights and interests of foreign investors are protected by Chinese law.

Before the adoption of the Wholly Foreign-owned Enterprise Law, the number of wholly foreign-owned enterprises established in China was very small and most of them were located in the SEZs. The enactment of this law has enabled foreign investors to establish wholly-owned enterprises in other parts of the country. It should be noted that wholly foreign-owned enterprises are encouraged to sell all or most of their products in the international market. This provision reflects China's recognition of the foreign exchange problem suffered by many joint ventures and cooperative ventures. The requirement of advanced technology and equipment represents China's continuing desire to upgrade its economy.

In order to set up a wholly foreign-owned enterprise, foreign investors must apply to the relevant authorities under the State Council.[59] Currently, the MOFERT is in charge of examining and approving the establishment of wholly foreign-owned enterprises. Once an application is approved, investment must be made within the period approved by the Chinese authority. If the foreign investors in question fail to do so, the authorities in charge of the administration of industry and commerce may revoke their business licence.[60]

A wholly foreign-owned enterprise has the right to conduct its business freely so long as the operation and management of the enterprise is in accordance with the approved articles of association. Nevertheless, a wholly foreign-owned enterprise must submit its production and business programmes to the competent authorities in China for record.[61] A wholly foreign-owned enterprise is also entitled to employ Chinese workers and administrative staff at will. In practice, an enterprise has to sign a contract with an employee upon hiring him. An employment contract usually includes provisions relating to employment, dismissal, remuneration, welfare, occupational safety and workers' insurance.

57 Article 1 of the Wholly Foreign-owned Enterprise Law adopted at the 4th Session of the 6th National People's Congress on 12 April 1986.
58 *Id*, Article 3.
59 *Id*, Article 6.
60 *Id*, Article 9.
61 *Id*, Article 11.

A wholly foreign-owned enterprise is permitted, within the scope of its approved operations, to purchase raw and semi-finished materials, fuels, and other materials either in China or from the international markets. It is, however, encouraged to use Chinese sources when both Chinese and foreign items are available.[62]

In connection with the marketing requirements imposed on wholly foreign-owned enterprises, Article 18 of the Wholly Foreign-owned Enterprise Law provides that these enterprises should take care to balance their foreign exchange receipts and payments. It also stipulates that if, with the approval of competent authorities, a wholly foreign-owned enterprise markets its products in China and consequently experiences an imbalance in foreign exchange, the said authorities shall be responsible for helping the enterprise to eliminate the imbalance.[63] Apparently, such assistance from the Chinese authorities will not be provided unless the enterprise manufactures products that China needs badly or has to import from foreign countries.

A wholly foreign-owned enterprise is treated largely on the same basis as a Sino-foreign joint venture in respect of tax and other incentives. It may enjoy preferential treatment in the form of tax reduction or exemption. If the enterprise reinvests a portion of its after-tax profits in China, it may, in accordance with relevant state regulations, apply for a refund of the income tax paid on the reinvested amount.[64]

Cooperative ventures

The law governing Sino-foreign cooperative ventures is still in the process of being drafted. Since there is no company law in China, Sino-foreign cooperative ventures are largely regulated by contracts between the parties in question. Generally, there is no specific form for a cooperative venture and investment may be made by the parties in the form of cash or otherwise. The organization and management of a cooperative venture is flexible. Parties to a venture may decide to form a board of directors, or a joint committee which is responsible for the management and operation of the venture.

A cooperative venture is in fact a contractual arrangement between a foreign investor and a Chinese enterprise. It resembles in many ways a Sino-foreign joint venture. Nevertheless, at least in one major aspect, a cooperative venture is different from a joint venture; a joint venture is a Chinese legal person whereas a cooperative venture is not. This difference in legal status leads to a difference in the tax treatment of these two kinds of venture. A joint venture is taxed before dividends are paid to its shareholders, whereas a cooperative venture is not subject to income

62 *Id*, Article 15.
63 *Id*, Article 18.
64 *Id*, Article 17.

taxation and parties to a cooperative venture are subject to taxation only after they have received profits from the venture.

Taxation

In addition to the Consolidated Industrial and Commercial Tax, the Urban Asset Tax, and the Individual Income Tax, foreign investors may be subject either to the joint venture or foreign enterprise income tax. The Joint Venture Income Tax Law, which was promulgated on 10 September 1980 at the 3rd Session of the 5th National People's Congress, is applicable only to Sino-foreign joint ventures. The total income of a joint venture will be taxed at a flat rate of 30%.[65] In addition, a local income tax of 10% of the assessed income tax is levied, making the total income tax rate 33%.[66] Joint ventures engaging in the exploitation of petroleum, natural gas and other resources are not taxed under the Joint Venture Tax Law.

When a foreign partner to a joint venture remits its share of profits out of China, a tax equal to 10% of the amount remitted is also levied. This provision reflects China's desire for reinvestment by foreign investors.

The kinds of income which are subject to taxation include those derived from production and business operations in industry, mining, transportation, communications, agriculture, forestry, animal husbandry, fishery, commerce, tourism, service, trades, dividends, bonuses, interests, and income derived from leases or transfers of property, patent rights, technology know-how, trademarks and copyrights.[67]

Foreign enterprises, including wholly foreign-owned enterprises and other Sino-foreign commercial arrangements, as well as foreign enterprises which have no establishments in China but which have income derived from sources in China, are subject to taxation under the Foreign Enterprise Income Tax.[68] The Foreign Enterprise Income Tax Law provides for two categories of tax rate, one progressive and the other flat. The progressive tax rates apply to income earned by enterprises having establishments in China, while the flat rate applies to income earned from sources in China by foreign enterprises which have no establishments in China. Under the progressive method, there are five tax rates, the lowest being 20% on income not exceeding RMB250,000 and the highest being a rate of 40% on the amount of any income in excess of RMB1 m. A local tax of 10% is also levied on such income.[69]

65 Joint Venture Income Tax Law, Article 3.

66 *Id.*

67 Detailed Rules and Regulations for the Implementation of the Income Tax Law of the People's Republic of China Concerning Joint Ventures with Chinese and Foreign Investment approved by the State Council on 10 December 1980 and promulgated by the Ministry of Finance on 14 December 1980, Article 2.

68 The Foreign Enterprise Income Tax Law of the People's Republic of China was enacted by the 5th National People's Congress at its 4th Session on 13 December 1981.

69 *Id*, Articles 3–4.

Foreign enterprises which have invested in remote areas in China, in agriculture, forestry, transportation etc are entitled to certain tax reductions and exemptions. Enterprises which use advanced technology and equipment or which are export-oriented also enjoy certain kinds of tax reduction and exemption. This preferential tax treatment is also applicable to joint ventures.

Foreign Economic Contract Law

The Foreign Economic Contract Law of the People's Republic of China (hereinafter referred to as the 'Foreign Economic Contract Law')[70] applies to all economic contracts between Chinese enterprises and foreign businesses or individuals, excluding international transport contracts.[71] It is important to note that the Foreign Economic Contract Law does not apply to contracts between a Chinese individual and a foreign party or to contracts between enterprises with Chinese nationality. The non-applicability of the Foreign Economic Contract Law to the above contracts is apparently due to the fact that currently no individual with Chinese nationality is permitted to conduct foreign trade or other international commercial activities, and that legislation in respect of maritime matters and railway transportation is being drafted separately.

The Foreign Economic Contract Law does not apply to contracts between Sino-foreign joint ventures and Chinese enterprises or between the joint ventures themselves, because these enterprises are Chinese legal persons. Under the General Principles of Civil Law, 'Sino-foreign equity joint venture enterprises, Sino-foreign contractual joint ventures and wholly foreign-owned enterprises established in the territory of the People's Republic of China that meet the requirements for legal persons acquire the status of Chinese legal persons upon approval and registration in accordance with the law by the administrative agencies for industry and commerce'.[72] The conditions which are imposed on a Chinese legal person include:

> (1) it must be established in accordance with law; (2) it must possess the necessary property or funds; (3) it must possess its own name, organization structure and premises; (4) it must be able to assume civil obligations independently.[73]

The first three conditions are factual while the fourth one is granted by law. Article 48 of the General Principles of Civil Law provides:

70 The Foreign Economic Contract Law of the People's Republic of China was adopted at the 10th Session of the Standing Committee of the National People's Congress on 21 March 1985 and became effective on 1 July 1985.

71 *Id*, Article 2.

72 Article 41 of the General Principles of Civil Law of the People's Republic of China adopted at the 4th Session of the 6th National People's Congress on 12 April 1986, effective on 1 January 1987. Citations of the statute in this chapter are from an English translation by Whitmore Gray and Henry R Zheng which appeared in the *American Journal of Comparative Law*, Vol 34, Fall 1986, no. 4.

73 *Id*, Article 37.

> Sino-foreign joint venture enterprise legal persons, Sino-foreign contractual joint venture enterprise legal persons and wholly foreign-owned enterprise legal persons bear civil liability to the extent of the property the enterprise owns, unless the law provides otherwise.

Thus, joint ventures, contractual ventures and wholly foreign-owned enterprises are, by virtue of law, Chinese legal persons. Therefore, contracts between these institutions or contracts between these institutions and other Chinese enterprises are not subject to the Foreign Economic Contract Law. Such contracts are governed by China's Economic Contract Law which applies exclusively to contracts between enterprises with Chinese nationality.[74]

The Foreign Economic Contract Law does not stipulate whether it applies to contracts between a Chinese enterprise and an enterprise from Hong Kong, Macao or Taiwan. Nevertheless, since enterprises from these areas have been regarded as overseas concerns, contracts between them and Chinese enterprises should be governed by the Foreign Economic Contract Law.

Under the Foreign Economic Contract Law, a contract is formed when terms of the contract are agreed upon in writing and signed by the parties.[75] Generally speaking, the conclusion of a contract requires an offer and an acceptance. The Foreign Economic Contract Law does not stipulate this process explicitly. Nevertheless, since the Foreign Economic Contract Law is based on the principles of China's Economic Contract Law and on international practice,[76] the offer and acceptance procedure is necessary for the formation of a contract. In addition, each contract must contain the basic and substantive terms of the transaction.[77]

The parties to a contract subject to the Foreign Economic Contract Law may choose the law applicable to the settlement of disputes arising from the contract. In the absence of such a choice by the parties concerned, the law of the country which has the closest connection with the contract applies.[78] Equity or contractual joint venture contracts, and contracts which are made in China for the cooperative exploration and development of natural resources, are, however, subject to Chinese law.[79] The contracting parties' freedom in respect of choice of law is not unlimited. When the contract in question is signed or to be performed in

74 For a discussion of China's Economic Contract Law and China's Domestic Contracting Practice, see Guiguo Wang, 'A Survey of China's Economic Contract Law', *UCLA Pacific Basin Law Journal*, Spring/Fall, 1985, Vol. 4, nos. 1 and 2, p. 14; for a general discussion of contracting in China, see Preston M. Torbert, 'Contract Law in the People's Republic of China', *Foreign Trade, Investment and the Law in the People's Republic of China* edited by Michael J. Moser, Hong Kong: Oxford University Press, 1984, p. 214.

75 Foreign Economic Contract Law, Article 7.

76 China's Economic Contract Law, Article 55.

77 Foreign Economic Contract Law, Article 12.

78 *Id*, Article 5.

79 *Id*.

China, parties to the contract are encouraged to choose Chinese law. They may also select the laws of other countries but the laws selected must have some connection with the contract, such as the law of the country where the contract in question is signed, is to be performed, or where the goods are located, or where the arbitration tribunal or courts are located.[80]

Following the tradition of resolving disputes through non-judicial means, the Foreign Economic Contract Law stipulates that 'disputes arising over a contract ought to be settled, if possible, through consultations or mediation by a third party'.[81] Nevertheless, parties to a contract may decide to submit their dispute to an arbitration tribunal directly and bypass the consultation or mediation procedure, depending on the provisions of the contract in question. A contractual dispute may be adjudicated by an arbitration tribunal either in China or in another country. Disputing parties may also take their case to a court in China, provided that no arbitration clause is stipulated in the contract.[82] This provision is consistent with Article 192 of the Civil Procedure Law of China which provides that when disputing parties to a contract have agreed in writing to arbitrate, they are not allowed to take the case to a court in China subsequently.[83]

To summarize, since China started its open policy in 1979, the country has made substantial economic progress through its economic and commercial cooperation and exchanges with foreign countries. The influx of foreign capital and technology has contributed greatly to the Chinese economy and is starting to play an important role in China's industrialization programme. The Chinese laws governing foreign commercial activities, which were virtually non-existent a decade ago, have now been established and are improved constantly to keep pace with the growth of Sino-foreign economic relations. These developments have made the general foreign investment environment in China more conducive. According to interviews conducted by A.T. Kearney, a US consulting company, in early 1987, out of 70 US investors in China, 50% of the companies interviewed regarded their operations in China as very good or good; 6% of them viewed their operations as not successful; 90% of them concluded that they would still have invested in China with their present knowledge.[84] Nevertheless, foreign investors in China are still facing certain problems and difficulties and therefore further improvements to the investment environment are needed.

80 Wei Yuming, 'Explanatory Report to the 9th Session of the 6th National People's Congress in connection with the Foreign Economic Contract Law (Draft)', *People's Daily*, 1 February 1985, p. 4.
81 Foreign Economic Contract Law, Article 33.
82 *Id*, Article 38.
83 Civil Procedure Law of the People's Republic of China, adopted by the Standing Committee of the 5th National People's Congress at its 22nd Session on 8 March 1982.
84 *The Asian Wall Street Journal*, 9 March 1987, p. 5.

Chapter two

Foreign investment: experience and lessons

Every foreign investor entering a new market comes across difficulties and problems, the major ones usually being culture shock, unfamiliarity with local economic and legal systems as well as customs of the host country. The foreign investors and the host government usually take different approaches in respect of foreign investment issues. Generally speaking, the host government is more concerned with macro-economic aspects such as the overall industrial development patterns, technology transfer, foreign exchange earnings and effects on employment, whereas foreign investors are business-oriented and profit-driven. The host government is keen to protect its domestic industries from foreign competition on macro-economic considerations, while foreign investors are more interested in the domestic market. These are just a few of the many major foreign-investment issues which arise from investment in developing countries by investors from developed countries.

China is a developing country and its economy is, essentially, a planned one. It therefore experiences many of the difficulties and problems associated with collaboration between developed and developing countries. In addition, since the Chinese economic system is different from that which private foreign investors are familiar with, difficulties in connection with such cooperation are thus unavoidable. This chapter will analyse several of the successful, and unsuccessful, foreign investment projects and point out the essential problems facing both the Chinese government and foreign investors. Sino-foreign joint ventures represent the closest form of cooperation between the parties concerned and the issues they have to deal with are more complicated than those encountered by foreign investors involved in other forms of economic cooperation. This chapter will look at the operation of Sino-foreign joint ventures.

I. Strategic approaches

Experts in international investment and experienced foreign investors are generally in agreement that the success of a joint venture can only be achieved through the mutual trust and respect of the parties involved. It therefore follows that the success of a joint venture to a large extent depends on the long term-view the parties in question take, the preparation, including feasibility studies, prior to the establishment of the joint venture, the mutual understanding of each other's needs, as well as efforts by one party to meet the needs of the other. Several of the successful joint ventures in China demonstrate that when foreign investors treat the venture as a lasting relationship between the parties and plan accordingly, they achieve greater success than others. China Schindler Elevator Company Limited is a good example.

China Schindler was formed in July 1980 between China National Construction Machinery Corporation, Schindler, and the Hong Kong-based Jardines Schindler Company. The joint venture employs a work force of 2,500 in its two plants, one in Beijing and the other in Shanghai. It was the first joint venture to be established after the adoption of China's Joint Venture Law.[1] The term of the joint venture is twenty years. Schindler and Jardines contributed technology and equipment while the Chinese party provided the factory site and labour.

In 1980, China Schindler produced 490 elevators and in 1986 its total output reached 1,180. Over the seven-year period (1980–1986), China Schindler became the largest supplier of elevators in China's domestic market.[2]

Summarizing their experience, the foreign investors in the joint venture believed that their policy in treating the venture as a long-term investment was crucial to their success.[3] They also attributed their success to their attitude of mutual respect and mutual benefit in the management of the venture. Both Jardines and Schindler have kept their management team as unchanged as possible for the sake of continuity. They have also tried to understand, and to adopt, Chinese ways of handling matters. This has certainly won the trust and understanding of the Chinese party.

Shangri-La International Hotel Management Ltd took a similar approach to that of Schindler and Jardines, when making an investment in the Hangzhou Hotel in early 1985. The hotel, which is managed by Shangri-La's Wolf Dieter Flecker, as general manager, and his largely Hong Kong management team, has undergone a major renovation, the total cost of which was about US$20 m.[4] When the renovation was half done and with only 40% of the hotel rooms available for guests, the hotel had already started to make profits.

Explaining their own experience, Flecker stated that Shangri-La's top management had considered the Hangzhou Hotel project an excellent preparation for the company's two much larger joint ventures in China ie the China World Trade Centre, a US$280 m hotel and marketing

1 *Wen Wei Po*, 10 September 1986, p. BN10.
2 *Id.*
3 *South China Morning Post*, 12 August 1986, p. BN5.
4 *South China Morning Post*, 14 August 1986, p. BN5.

complex which is due to open in 1988, and the Shangri-La Hotel Beijing which is expected to open in 1987.[5]

Beijing Air Catering also represents a successful joint venture based on mutual trust and understanding. The venture is owned by the Civil Aviation Administration of China (the 'CAAC') (with 51% ownership), and three foreign partners, Maxims, Dairy Farm and Bank of East Asia (with a total ownership of 49%). In a short period of three years, the venture recouped its capital investment of RMB5.88 m.[6] Prior to the establishment of the joint venture, international airlines which had business in China were reluctant to use the Chinese food service because it was not up to world standards. When the CAAC showed an interest in upgrading its food service in cooperation with foreign enterprises, several foreign companies wanted to participate. Most of them, however, failed because they did not take into consideration the CAAC's needs. For instance, a Japanese company which wanted to form a joint venture with the CAAC preferred to build a new kitchen block, while the CAAC wanted to keep its old one in order to reduce costs. Maxims however agreed that the existing building could be used after renovation. Maxims' decision was interpreted by the Chinese party as a sincere wish to help China and the joint venture was established in April 1980. The good start to the joint venture and mutual sincerity paved the way for the success of the venture. In mid-1987, the parties to the venture decided to extend the cooperation agreement for another 12 years upon the expiration of the existing eight-year agreement on 30 April 1988.[7]

It is essential for every venture with foreign participation to adopt a business strategy which accords with the economic development plans of the host government. When China started its open policy in 1979, it expected a stable and rapid flow of high technology and capital-intensive investment to help modernize its economy. Although China acknowledges the profit-seeking desire of foreign investors, government officials often view foreign investment in China as providing support for the country's modernization programme. The government also regards investment by Hong Kong and overseas Chinese as patriotic acts.

Many foreign companies, however, do not make investments in the areas in which China really needs investments. They have invested in areas of quick returns, such as property, services and light industries. According to an analysis of 841 joint ventures formed between 1979 and 1984, more than half of them involved a maximum investment of US$1 m and were due to run for only a maximum ten-year lifespan. Less than 30% of these ventures are long-term or high-technology investments in such crucial areas as mining, heavy industry and animal husbandry.[8]

5 *Id.*
6 *South China Morning Post*, 12 August 1986, p. BN5.
7 *China Economic News*, 29 June 1987 p. 3.
8 *South China Morning Post*, 11 August 1986, p.BN4.

In addition, although a good number of foreign enterprises have invested in hotels or other property businesses, many of them do not have sufficient expertise in operating hotels. Many foreign participants are actually traders in disguise who are interested only in making a profit out of selling the building materials and engineering services of the joint venture and not in running a successful hotel in China. There are also other fly-by-night traders who use their connections in China to secure hotel contracts and make profits through reselling their ownership in the joint ventures to be established. This situation led to the adoption of stricter rules for hotel development and more thorough scrutinization of hotel projects by the Chinese government in 1986.

When a joint venture adopts an economic philosophy compatible with that of China's, it comes across fewer difficulties. For instance, the Guangzhou-British Textile Factory which was established by Tootal, one of the world's largest sewing thread suppliers, and the Standard Chartered Bank, as foreign participants, is a case in point. In this venture, the Chinese partner holds 50% of the ownership and the foreign partners hold the other 50%. The total foreign investment amounted to US$12 m. When Tootal first proposed the factory in Guangzhou it wanted to export two-thirds of the products and sell one-third of the products domestically. After Tootal acquired Standard-Cosa-Thatcher, a US company, in November 1985, however, it decided to export all the products of the Guangzhou-British Textile Factory through Tootal's distribution system. This decision was greatly appreciated by the Chinese party and the Chinese authorities in charge. It also led to the renovation of the textile factory into a modern one which is comparable to similar factories in developed countries. The factory now employs 290 employees and its total annual output is two million kilograms of sewing thread.[9] It appears that the Guangzhou-British Textile Factory has benefited from its export-oriented strategy because the Chinese government gives such enterprises priority in the supply of raw materials, energy, water etc and grants them preferential tax treatment. These measures help in the reduction of operating costs.

The Fujian Hitachi TV Company Limited, a Sino-Japanese joint venture, represents a case of failure due mainly to its approach. When the joint venture was established in 1981, the intention of the Japanese investors was questioned by the Chinese authorities who viewed the venture as a mere bridge-head for the entry of Japanese products into the Chinese market, in view of the heavy reliance on spare parts from Japan.[10] According to the joint venture contract, the plant would export more than 50% of its products and procure at least 50% of its components from local sources by 1983. Nevertheless, by mid-1986 the joint venture had exported only about 6% of its products and local components made

9 *Wen Wei Po*, 10 March 1987, p. BN2.
10 *South China Morning Post*, 13 August 1986, p. BN5.

up only 40% of the total components used. The joint venture thus remained essentially an assembly factory.

Due to its concentration on the domestic market and heavy reliance on imported components, the joint venture suffered a serious shortage of foreign exchange which in turn resulted in a reduction in both production and the number of employees. Thus, this joint venture's experience illustrates the importance of business planning in accordance with the local conditions and needs of the host country. It is true that Hitachi may not have run into such difficulties had it invested in a developed country such as the United States. As the Chinese currency, Renminbi, is not freely convertible and China's export capacity is limited, foreign investors entering the China market must be fully aware of the situation and plan in advance.

An important part of the preparation for foreign investment is the feasibility study. In this respect, foreign investors usually play an essential role, particularly in the case of export-oriented high-technology or technology-intensive projects. Having been isolated from the rest of the world for more than three decades and left behind in the technology race, Chinese partners in general do not have the ability to assess international market situations or the appropriateness of technology to be imported. The Pine Hill Duck Farm in Guangdong is a case where the joint venture failed because of poor feasibility studies.

The Pine Hill Duck Farm joint venture was established in 1981 with a paid-up capital equivalent to HK$6 m split equally between the two parties. The chosen site was 1,000 acres of remote hillside in Dongkuan County in southern Guangdong. Five years later, the joint venture suffered big losses and, by early 1986, its operations could no longer continue. After thorough investigations by some senior Chinese officials, it was concluded that, among other things, the failure of the venture resulted from a flawed feasibility study which had overlooked such crucial factors as depreciation of equipment and buildings, the absence of roads, water supplies and power lines to the site and the need for back-up power generators.[11] The initial investment of HK$6 m, for example, was barely enough to pay for imported feed, the acquisition of duck species from the United Kingdom's Valley Farm, the installation of rearing equipment and the construction of workers' accommodation and shelters for the ducks. Without a subsequent injection of HK$6 m raised by a loan, the venture could not even have begun operations in 1981.[12]

Another major error in the feasibility study was that calculations of the handling fees charged by wholesalers in Hong Kong, the venture's only export market, were omitted. This amounted to between 8% and 9% of the ducks' selling price. As a result, even selling at cost, the venture resulted in losses. The Chinese party blamed the Hong Kong investors,

11 *Id.*
12 *Id.*

who claimed to have management skills, for not foreseeing the need to include wholesalers' fees in production costs and for the inadequacy of the feasibility study.[13]

It is difficult to determine to what extent each party to the joint venture was responsible for the failure. Nevertheless, it is clear that a sufficient and adequate feasibility study would have identified or even resolved some of the problems in advance. It should be noted, however, that many foreign investors as well as Chinese enterprises participating in joint ventures (or cooperative ventures) very often fail to do an objective feasibility study and regard the feasibility study simply as a document to win the approval of the Chinese authorities rather than an appraisal of the business venture.[14] Unless this practice stops immediately, failures of joint ventures and other types of cooperation will be inevitable.

The mutual understanding of the Chinese and foreign parties to a joint venture is vital to the success of the venture. As one China consultant commented: 'The best thing is to win your Chinese partners to your side. They can get you through the bureaucracy and help you source raw materials.'[15] At the moment, there does not seem to be great difficulty in gaining support from the Chinese parties to Sino-foreign ventures, although in certain cases Chinese partners may be more interested in protecting the State interest. However, there are many investment issues on which the Chinese and foreign partners hold similar positions. According to a study of 93 enterprises with foreign participation conducted by the Foreign Exchange Administrative Bureau of Fujian Province, 50% of the general managers and deputy managers appointed by the Chinese parties thought the tax system and foreign exchange policies should be improved for the benefit of their ventures.[16] Forty-four percent of them were interested in short-term investments, 21% in medium-term (five to eight years) investments, and 31% in long-term (more than ten years) investments.[17] This statistic coincides with the current trend of foreign investment in China.

II. Management of labour

The labour issues relating to foreign investment comprise the labour cost, the freedom of the management in hiring and dismissing employees, and the efficiency of the labour force. Many foreign investors have been attracted by the cheap labour force in China. Nevertheless, as soon as they enter the Chinese market they realize that the actual labour cost per employee is higher than the average salary paid to a Chinese employee by

13 *Id.*
14 This conclusion is based on the author's various discussions with the Chinese officials in charge of foreign investment.
15 *South China Morning Post*, 12 August 1986, p. BN5.
16 *Wen Wei Po*, 13 December 1986, p. BN4.
17 *Id.*

a State-owned enterprise in China. Foreign investors are required to pay, in addition to the direct salaries of their employees, indirect salaries in the form of pensions and allowances for medical services, housing and education. According to the Regulations of the People's Republic of China on Labour Management of Joint Ventures Using Chinese and Foreign Investment, the wages of employees working in enterprises with foreign participation should be 120% to 150% that of employees working in similar State-owned enterprises.[18] A joint venture is also required to pay its employees an indirect wage[19] which is in practice equivalent to 123% of the direct wage. Generally speaking, 65% of the indirect salary is for the housing allowance, and the other 35% is for food, edible oil, foodstuffs etc. Although first-time foreign investors may be puzzled by the Chinese wage structure, the Chinese authorities argue that since housing, the basic daily necessities, medical care etc are highly subsidized by the government, foreign investors should pay the subsidized portion to the State government. In addition, the Chinese government thinks it is justifiable for employees in a joint venture to receive salaries 20% to 50% higher than those of their counterparts in State-owned enterprises because greater productivity is expected of joint venture employees.

In general, the actual labour cost in China is lower than that of other nearby countries or regions. Foreign investors treat the low labour cost as a major attraction and many of them have benefited from it. China Schindler Elevator Company, while refusing to give details of its operating costs, commented that the joint venture had achieved 15% cost savings compared with its European factories. The foreign partner in that joint venture attributed the company's efficiency to the goodwill and hard work of the employees.[20]

Applied Electronics which invested in two Chinese factories to manufacture lower-end electronic toys has saved more than HK$2 m per month in labour costs since its plants started operation in Guangdong in early 1986.[21] Applied Electronics' investment involves two assembly plants employing a total of 1,550 employees. According to the company, the unskilled workers employed in these two plants need, on average, two weeks' training before they can do the work themselves. The productivity of the Chinese employees has been estimated at about 70% that of Hong Kong workers. The chairman and managing director of Applied Electronics, Raymond Hung, said that a 90% level could be achieved after further training.[22] In 1986, Applied Electronics paid a total of HK$570,000 per month for its 1,550 Chinese workers, HK$2.3 m less

18 Regulations of the People's Republic of China on Labour Management of Joint Ventures Using Chinese and Foreign Investment promulgated by the State Council on 26 July 1980, Article 8.
19 *Id*, Article 11.
20 *South China Morning Post*, 12 August 1986, p. BN5.
21 *South China Morning Post*, 15 August 1986, p. BN4.
22 *Id.*

than it would have had to pay the same number of Hong Kong workers.[23]

On average, Applied Electronics pays HK$300 (about RMB120) to each of its workers. Of this amount, HK$60, equivalent to 20% of the worker's salary, is paid to the district authorities as a housing allowance. It also pays 2% of each worker's salary to the local government as tax.[24]

An important aspect of labour cost is labour efficiency. Several of the successful ventures show that training and education of employees is crucial to the venture. When Shangri-La first invested in Hangzhou Hotel in 1985, the employees of the hotel, including those who began working there 30 years ago, had trouble adjusting to the more efficient and less-forgiving management.[25]

The foreign partner in the Tianjin Winery Joint Venture also laboured in teaching and persuading its Chinese employees to adopt new methods and technology in respect of grape growing. 'It took a long time to persuade them not to water the plants on certain days so that the sugar content of the grapes would grow. For many years, the workers followed the same method to grow grapes, and with some achievements. They were worried that our method would not work,' recalled Remy Martin, the representative of the foreign party to the joint venture.[26]

The most important part of labour management is in fact the management's freedom in hiring and dismissing employees. This right is affected by three factors ie Chinese traditions and customs, bureaucratic intervention and the lack of a labour market. The lack of a labour market hinders enterprises involving foreign participation from hiring qualified employees from areas other than those where the enterprises are located. Bureaucratic intervention takes many forms. It includes a case where government officials favour those who have special relationships with them and do not give due regard to the actual qualifications of the employees. On other occasions, qualified employees including senior managers of ventures may be 'dismissed' by administrative organs of the local government. To challenge the Chinese tradition of forgiving rather than dismissing or punishing those who make mistakes is also a painstaking process.

According to five joint venture managers who have been successful in China, in order to run a venture efficiently and effectively, the management must have the right to hire and dismiss staff and to reward good workers. In addition, a bonus system and training programme should be established.[27] Applied Electronics also believes that 'retaining control of personnel management is imperative to [their] success'.[28] Applied Electronics' system of labour management has been backed by the

23 *Id.*
24 *Id.*
25 *South China Morning Post*, 14 August 1986, p. BN5.
26 *South China Morning Post*, 12 August 1986, p. BN5.
27 *The Asian Wall Street Journal*, 1 December 1986, p. 1.
28 *South China Morning Post*, 15 August 1986, p. BN4.

Chinese authorities especially in connection with the dismissal of problem staff members. Shortly after the company's Guangdong plants started operations, it dismissed several workers who had failed to perform their duties, including one who 'was linked to [a] senior official of the district'.[29]

The Beijing Air Catering Joint Venture and Tianjin Winery Joint Venture have taken a different approach. The foreign partners in these two ventures have left, to a large extent, the management of labour to their Chinese partners. Asked why his venture had been so successful, Mr Yan Yongqin, General Manager of Beijing Air Catering said that both sides had been determined to do their best. Regarding labour management, Mr Yan pointed out that firing workers was a long and laborious process. The Chinese way of handling the matter 'was to give many chances to the workers in question to rectify their mistakes. Those who failed to improve would be demoted or have their salary reduced, but they would not be fired right away.'[30]

One factor regarded by foreign investors as critical to the success of a joint venture is the provision by the foreign partner of a well-qualified management team.[31] The Hangzhou Hotel venture is one such example. As soon as the venture was established, Shangri-La Hotel appointed one of its senior members as the general manager of the Hangzhou Hotel who, together with his nineteen-strong team, introduced Western-style management to the hotel. Of the original 800 staff in Hangzhou Hotel, 80 were transferred to other hotels in Hangzhou and 21 were dismissed because they could not perform their duties efficiently.[32] The general manager has used various methods to make the staff more responsive to the needs of their guests. The management has also adopted a strict set of house rules which include, among others, punctuality, clean uniforms, no smoking on the job and a cheerful attitude. Employees who break the rules are subject to censure and fines (including large ones). English language lessons at the hotel, which all employees are required to attend at least three times a week, have proved to be beneficial as well.[33]

The Hangzhou Hotel's general manager believes that the jump in wages of the hotel's employees has been a factor in the smooth running of the hotel. The Hotel pays its staff an average of RMB153 a month while the average local salary remains around RMB70 a month.[34]

The Fuwan Toy Co Ltd, a Sino-Japanese joint venture established in Fuzhou of Fujian Province, is another case of successful investment where foreign management skills were introduced. The joint venture started operations in 1985 and had received orders totalling

29 *Id.*
30 *South China Morning Post*, 12 August 1986, p. BN5.
31 *The Asian Wall Street Journal*, 1 December 1986, p. 1.
32 *South China Morning Post*, 14 August 1986, p. BN5.
33 *Id.*
34 *Id.*

RMB14.61 m (equivalent to US$3.9 m) by the end of 1986. This figure compares favourably with its initial investment of US$2.2 m.[35]

Two fundamental changes have contributed to the success of Fuwan Toy factory. The joint venture imported not only advanced production facilities from Japan but also its vertical management system. Apart from the full authority invested in the general manager who is accountable to the board of directors, management power is delegated to the departmental and sectorial levels. Members of the board of directors are concurrently heads of the production departments. In each department or section, a system of one-person leadership is enforced. According to the joint venture, this vertical system has raised the efficiency of the management group as well as the productivity of the company.[36]

The joint venture has also paid special attention to the training of its personnel. It has invited five technical experts from Japan and Hong Kong to assist the management team and to train the staff members. In addition, it has sent 24 technicians to Japan for on-the-job training. A system of upgrading the technical skills of workers before assigning them to new posts has also been established.[37]

In short, all the success stories illustrate that the right of the management to hire and dismiss employees is absolutely essential to every venture. This right can be used jointly by the parties to the venture, or chiefly by the Chinese or foreign partner. A strong management team sent by a foreign partner has also proved to be effective in running an enterprise with foreign participation.

III. Administrative interference

China's open policy in respect of foreign investment may be enhanced or weakened by the actions and attitudes of government officials at all levels. Both foreign investors and Chinese government officials complain about the bureaucracy in China and regard it as one of the major problems foreign investors have to encounter. Very often, when a foreign investor makes a transaction, he has to go through several complicated and identical procedures. Even if the project in question is to be located in the capital city of a province, the foreign investor concerned must first seek approval from the city government and then the provincial government, and sometimes back and forth.[38] State Councillor Gu Mu once commented that 'there are many departments responsible for the enterprises [with foreign participation] but no one can solve their problems'.[39] Mr Gu said that in some places officials either do not follow

35 *China Economic Review*, 16 March 1987, p. 1.
36 *Id.*
37 *Id*, p. 2.
38 *Wen Wei Po*, 27 January 1987, p. BN2.
39 *The Asian Wall Street Journal*, 20 January 1987, p. 11.

the law or simply regard their own word as law. He added that 'Many people have no sense of urgency and do not realize that China has a good opportunity to attract foreign investment.' These problems have arisen because government officials do not know enough about international economic relations, foreign investment and the attitudes of foreign businessmen.[40]

In fact, in some places, government officials understand neither international business transactions nor China's open policy. They may interrupt the normal business operations of enterprises involving foreign participation and, in particular, look disapprovingly on successful ventures. As a result, even those who are satisfied with China's investment climate are afraid of telling the true story, because by doing so they may fall prey to the jealousies of local authorities, provoke allegations of profiteering, or encourage appeals for 'donations' or suffer price rises by suppliers.[41] Parker-Hubei Seals Co Ltd, a Sino-US joint venture in Wuhan City of Hubei Province, is a case in point.

The joint venture was established in late 1983. The Chinese party is Hubei Province Auto Industry Corporation. In the first two years, the operations of the joint venture were very satisfactory and it was among the best enterprises in the auto industry in terms of per worker output and profit.[42] As the joint venture continued operating very smoothly, the Machinery Bureau of Hubei Province, through the Hubei Auto Industry Corporation which is its subordinate entity, arbitrarily and unilaterally removed the general manager and deputy general manager, Mr Chen Weijen and Mr Cai Guoning. The reasons for the removal were as follows: officials from the Machinery Bureau felt the joint venture had not heeded the Bureau's directives and had therefore operated as a 'colonial enterprise'. Mr Chen and Mr Cai, however, believed that the joint venture should represent the interests of both China and the US investors and that these two interests were the same, and that the protection of these interests would be beneficial to the expansion of Sino-foreign economic cooperation. The chief officers from the Machinery Bureau accused Mr Chen and Mr Cai of 'speaking for foreigners' and of 'wearing the same pair of trousers with foreigners'.[43]

Mr Chen did not admit to any of the accusations made by the officials from the Machinery Bureau. Instead, he discussed this matter with his former teacher, Professor Liu in Wuhan University, who is a member of the Hubei Provincial People's Congress. Professor Liu criticized the behaviour of the Machinery Bureau at the following Hubei Provincial People's Congress meeting and this provoked the officials of the Machinery Bureau to dismiss Mr Chen and Mr Cai immediately. When

40 *Id.*
41 *South China Morning Post*, 12 August 1986, p. BN5.
42 *Wen Wei Po*, 13 March 1987, p. 7.
43 *Id.* 'Wearing same pair of trousers with someone' is a Chinese expression which refers to actions by more than one person in collusion with each other.

others voiced views that the decision to dismiss should have been made by the board of directors of the joint venture, which included representatives of the US party, the Machinery Bureau officials retorted by saying that the removal was an internal Chinese matter which foreigners were not permitted to interfere with.[44]

The requests and suggestions of the US partner, Parker-Hannifin, in this matter were totally ignored by the Machinery Bureau. The latter even prevented the US investors from paying a visit to Mr Chen and Mr Cai. This matter was not brought to the attention of the higher authorities until the US party threatened to stop support for the joint venture. Eventually, thanks to the intervention by the Ministry of Foreign Economic Relations and Trade and one of the vice chairmen of the National People's Congress, Mr Chen and Mr Cai were reappointed as the general manager and deputy general manager of the joint venture.

The Parker-Hubei joint venture case demonstrates the extent to which enterprises with foreign participation may be subjected to interference by various administrative authorities. On other occasions, foreign investors have complained about the excessive involvement of government departments in the daily operations of joint ventures. 'Often we don't know what their functions are,' commented a foreign investor.[45]

There are places where joint ventures are treated better. A good example is Tianjin City. The Tianjin government has paid close attention to the development of Sino-foreign economic cooperation and has appointed a vice mayor to be specifically in charge of foreign investment matters. As a result, most of the joint ventures in Tianjin are well-operated and profitable. The Tianjin government has also managed to ensure that joint ventures in the city balance their foreign exchange accounts. In general, joint ventures in Tianjin do not have foreign-exchange balancing difficulties which ventures in other areas face. Vice mayor Li Fengqing, who is in charge of foreign investment in Tianjin, said that he believed in educating and training promising senior and junior officials in the foreign trade and investment fields and then to entrust them with power and authority. Tianjin has also excluded, from the government departments responsible for foreign investment, 'leftists' and those who oppose the making of profits by foreigners.[46]

Corruption is another problem. As early as November 1980, the State Council issued legislation which specifically prohibited presentation or acceptance of gifts in the course of foreign trade or other economic relations. The prohibition extended to all kinds of gifts except articles of educational value, such as books and scientific data, commercial samples and non-consumer-type souvenirs exchanged during friendly activities. Nevertheless, economic crimes are still committed by government

44 *Id.*
45 *The Asian Wall Street Journal*, 27 January 1987, p. 7.
46 *Wen Wei Po*, 4 October 1986, p. BN12.

officials involved in foreign economic activities and this is detrimental to foreign investment in China.

Some Chinese officials involved in foreign investment favour a foreign partner who sponsors overseas trips, frequently under the guise of 'study' or 'training' tours. Some of them even solicit bribes from foreign counterparts. For example, a sales representative for a European vehicle manufacturer revealed that when inspecting a display of vehicles, one potential Chinese buyer asked where the photocopier was kept. Upon hearing that such an item was not available, the potential buyer simply asked 'how about a mini-computer?'[47] This type of behaviour by government officials as well as managerial staff members is harmful to the improvement and development of Sino-foreign economic relations and increases the general feeling of uncertainty and the expenses which foreign investors have to bear. They are not strictly part of the bureaucratic or administrative interference in foreign investment but they are bureaucracy-related and destructive to foreign investment.

IV. Balancing of foreign exchange

China has adopted a foreign exchange system under Article 14 of the Articles of Agreement of the International Monetary Fund (the transitional arrangement) and its currency is therefore not freely convertible. In view of this system and China's restricted foreign exchange reserves, enterprises involving foreign participation, particularly those which import materials and components from foreign countries, may have difficulties relating to foreign exchange shortages. The Chinese government provides foreign exchange quotas mainly to technologically-advanced enterprises and enterprises which produce import-substituting products. Other foreign-investment enterprises are required to earn enough foreign exchange for importation of materials and equipment and repatriation of profits. Enterprises which do not have adequate foreign exchange can swap their Renminbi earnings with other enterprises which have foreign exchange surpluses. The exchange rate for this kind of transaction is higher than the official rate and enterprises in need of foreign exchange may not be able to acquire a sufficient amount, as a number of foreign-investment enterprises may have the same problem. Foreign exchange shortages may also result from the exchange rates between Renminbi and foreign currencies. Each Chinese enterprise involved in foreign trade or investment is allowed a certain amount of foreign exchange expenditure valued in Renminbi. If Renminbi is devalued, the amount of foreign exchange assigned to the enterprise in question will be reduced. If a Chinese enterprise had signed a contract for importation of foreign products or components prior to the devaluation

47 *China Trade Report*, 11 March 1987, p. 16.

of Renminbi, it may not be able to honour the contract after devaluation of the local currency.

Any one of the above situations may affect the operations of an enterprise with foreign participation. The most publicized case involving the balancing of foreign exchange is the Beijing Jeep Corporation, a joint venture between a Chinese company and American Motors Corporation ('AMC'). The joint venture was established on the assumption that the plant would first import components for assembling the Cherokee jeep and then increase the use of local components. According to the plan, the joint venture would be able to earn foreign exchange through exports only a few years after starting operations and the plant would use 80% local components by 1988 and export a total of 10,000 vehicles in 1990. Since December 1985, after the joint venture started operations, many end-users proved unwilling or unable to buy, with foreign exchange, the vehicles manufactured by the Beijing Jeep Corporation, chiefly because foreign exchange allocations to those enterprises had been slashed and also because a 60% duty on imported parts made the Cherokee jeep price in Beijing higher than the price in the North America.

During the first part of 1986, the local authorities were unwilling to renew foreign exchange allocations or loans to the venture because its expected foreign exchange earnings were not forthcoming. The worsened foreign exchange shortage problem disrupted the operations of the joint venture for about two to three months. Eventually, the Chinese government decided to guarantee additional foreign exchange to the venture so as to enable it to import components. In addition, the Chinese government advanced a US$2 m loan for the jeeps already assembled.[48] Thus, the crisis afflicting the venture was over. With the joint efforts by both the Chinese and US partners, the venture managed to export 21 Cherokee jeeps in 1986. It plans to export more than 10,000 jeeps and 8,000 engines during the five-year period starting from 1987.[49]

According to a source, the original joint venture contract called for the Chinese and US sides to jointly design a new jeep using only Chinese components. However, 'after several months of work by Chinese and American engineers ... it was found that the vehicle designed was defective in such areas as its exhaust system, noise, visibility, and speed, none of which could match international standards. ... AMC suggested that the idea of joint design be postponed .... The Chinese, however, took AMC's suggestions as a symbol of the Americans' unwillingness to cooperate on a jointly-designed vehicle and ... of AMC's desire to control China's market'.[50] Thus, the cooperation started in suspicion which foreshadowed the more serious troubles that arose later. At the same time, a number of foreign observers pointed out that AMC's initial

48 *China Business Review*, July–August 1986, p. 34.
49 *The Asian Wall Street Journal*, 6 November 1986, p. 3.
50 *China Business Review*, July–August 1986, p. 34.

cash contribution of US$8 m was very small in relation to its goal of building an export-quality jeep in China.[51]

The Guangzhou Peugeot Automobile Ltd, a Sino-French joint venture, once suffered from a change in foreign exchange rates. The automobile joint venture was established with an understanding that it would first import components from France and subsequently increase the use of local components. As a result of the appreciation of the Franc (about 110% against the Renminbi) in mid-1985, automobiles assembled by the joint venture could not find end-users in the domestic Chinese market. This situation was worsened by the competition from imported Japanese cars.[52] The Guangzhou government allocated foreign exchange to a company responsible for the wholesale of Peugeot products in China and urged local banks to sell foreign exchange to the car-trading concern at official exchange rates, because it regarded the joint venture as possessing advanced technology and therefore entitled to foreign exchange allocations. Nevertheless, due to the increase in costs, which resulted from a change in exchange rates, the market for Peugeot products was very limited. Eventually, the joint venture had to revise its plan so as to produce 15,000 light trucks with 34% local components, of which one-third would be exported to countries in Africa and Middle East.[53] It also planned to use 98.5% local components for the production of 30,000 automobiles by 1991.[54] Obviously, these measures were intended to assist the venture to balance its foreign exchange accounts.

There are also success stories which demonstrate how the problem of balancing of foreign exchange can be resolved. For instance, the China Schindler Elevator Company sells most of its elevators in the domestic market but it has been able to balance its foreign exchange accounts because only a quarter of the parts used are imported.[55] Although the joint venture has not achieved its target of exporting 25% of its products as originally planned, it has been able to earn enough foreign exchange for its foreign exchange expenditure.

A joint production venture established by Shanghai Aviation Industry Corporation and US-based McDonnell, Douglas Corporation, for the assembly of 25 Md-82 air planes from 1986 to 1990, has balanced its foreign exchange by compensation trade. According to the cooperation agreement, 30% of the foreign exchange expenditure on the cooperative programme would be paid with cash substitutes, half of which would be aviation products. By early December of 1986, the compensation trade volume had already reached more than US$6 m.[56]

The Shanghai-Yichu Motor Cycle Ltd Co, a joint venture between a Hong Kong-registered company owned by a Thai corporation and

51 *Id.*
52 *The Asian Wall Street Journal*, 27 January 1987, p. 1.
53 *Wen Wei Po*, 28 January 1987, p. BN4.
54 *Id.*
55 *South China Morning Post*, 12 August 1986, p. BN5.
56 *China Economic News*, 5 January 1987, p. 2.

Shanghai Tractor and Automobile Corporation, has been very successful in balancing its foreign exchange. Since the joint venture started operations, in January 1985, it has posted profits every half year and the foreign partner has therefore been able to repatriate its share of the profits. According to the general manager of the joint venture, its success is based on the policy of developing new products through improvement of the existing products. 'That way not only normal production and a cash flow are maintained, better returns on the investment are ensured,' Mr Chen Jingfu, the General Manager nominated by the foreign partner, pointed out.[57] Mr Chen believes that his company's policy of developing products in accordance with China's particular circumstances has contributed to the venture's rapid growth. 'According to China's situation, one way to expand joint venture operations is to improve old products to raise money to support the development of new products. Joint ventures generally require injections of funds to import advanced technology and equipment. So it is impossible to modernize a motor cycle factory without enough time, and enough money to pay for the imports of equipment,' concluded Chen.[58]

Fuwan Toy joint venture's foreign exchange account has been balanced with the aid of equipment leasing. When the venture was established, both the Chinese and Japanese partners realized and agreed that they had to do their best to achieve a balance of foreign exchange income and expenditure. Accordingly, the joint venture leased a major portion of production equipment and facilities instead of purchasing them. As a result, there was a reduction of US$500,000 in foreign exchange expenditure.[59] The joint venture's success in balancing foreign exchange was also attributable to the increased use of domestic parts and materials.

V. Operating costs

Foreign investors are in favour of stable operating costs as this would enable them to predict and calculate investment returns correctly. Owing to the lack of experience and the backward communications and information systems in China, foreign-investment costs charged by Chinese governments at various levels are sometimes criticized by foreign investors. Currently, China's tax rules are relatively predictable and tax planning is possible. This makes other factors affecting business budgeting, such as expenditure for water, electricity etc, the more important issues when it comes to calculating the profits of enterprises with foreign participation.

Some of the most frequently criticized operating costs include administrative costs in setting up offices, uneven charges of land use fees

57 *China Economic News*, 15 September 1986, p. 3.
58 *Id.*
59 *China Economic News*, 16 March 1987, p. 2.

by authorities in different areas and cities, frequent adjustments of fees, and invisible costs. Foreign investors complain about the high costs of setting up representative offices in China and the high basic living expenses of foreign businessmen eg for accommodation, transportation and housing. They also complain about having to pay high rates for train and plane tickets.

Prior to the adoption of the Provisions of the State Council for the Encouragement of Foreign Investment in October 1986, there was no national law or regulation governing rent and other land use fees. As a result, each city or province set its own standards. This practice resulted in uneven charges of land use fees and complaints from foreign investors, because the local authorities were left with too much discretion, and thus it was impossible for foreign investors to plan in advance.

Frequent adjustments in fees, which led to wide fluctuations in production costs, have also been severely criticized by foreign investors who are used to slow adjustments in response to market situations. An example of an obvious case of fee adjustment would be the raising of rates by hotels without warning. For instance, room rates at the Beijing Hotel increased by 40% in 1986. Shenzhen's car-hire rate was raised from RMB1.4 to RMB2.4 per km within months, an increase of 70%.[60] These increases meant that foreign investors were scarcely able to plan their budgets. Big fluctuations in expenditure and income have put pressure on foreign businesses which are unable to make reasonably accurate forecasts about the cost of their operations in China. Even price reductions sometimes may make foreign investors panic. For instance, in contrast to the price rises in Beijing in 1986, Shekou industrial zone announced fee reductions averaging 40% (and as high as 95% in some cases) for 50 items.[61] The zones' administrative committee decided to reduce the fees after an investigation which determined that some 200 items had unreasonably high prices. Although reductions are generally welcomed by foreign investors, they also cause budget-planning problems.

In addition to the usual operating costs associated with foreign investment, foreign enterprises sometimes have to pay invisible costs. Since China's infrastructure is relatively poor, foreign investors may sometimes need to make additional expenses to improve existing working conditions. For instance, when a foreign enterprise invested in a South China electronic factory it was guaranteed the supply of electricity. However, the supply was a mile away and the factory itself had to pay for the cost of cable. In addition, as a result of frequent power-cuts, the venture had to build its own back-up generator.[62]

Studies conducted indicate that, prior to the end of 1986, China's cost efficiency was lower than that of many developed as well as developing

60 *China Trade Report*, 13 February 1987, p. 8.
61 *Id.*
62 *South China Morning Post*, 13 August 1986, p. BN5.

countries and regions, chiefly as a result of invisible costs including slow administrative decision-making. According to a World Bank report, the average Chinese wage was much lower than that in the United States, Japan or Hong Kong but the rate of cost-saving hardly existed. It estimated that if the production efficiency (expenditure/net income ratio) in the United States was regarded as 100%, the production efficiency in Japan would be 70%, Singapore 60%, Taiwan 35%, Hong

Table 1: Investment costs in Shenzhen

Anticipated cost	**Unanticipated cost**
Wages, bonuses, subsidies, and higher salaries for administrative personnel	Buying and renting houses to accommodate workers as required by Chinese authorities, paying fees for renovation, maintenance and housing-management services. Home-leave, temporary residence fees, fees for administrative staff, similar to Hongkong's labour-insurance fee and medi-care.
Water and electricity	Electricity is more expensive than in Hongkong. Maintenance and spare parts are expensive, and take a long time to secure. Reserve electricity for sudden blackouts needs to be installed.
Factory rent and management fees	0.5–1% of annual sales turnover of foreign-owned factories is exacted for public amenities and their maintenance, and is much like another form of taxation.
Prices of materials	Handling fees of raw materials.
Traffic fees, gas, licences, maintenance	Maintenance fees are twice those of Hongkong's.
Communications — telephone, telex, fax installation fee, line charges	Subcharges on telecommunications installation, registration fees, maintenance of licence fees and maintenance training examination fees.
Transportation	No port outlets to the European market; goods have to be taken to Kwai Chung in Hong Kong for export.
Customs and customs duty	Subcharges for duty (for example on cars); expensive and non-standardized custom-reporting fees at the discretion of government units (maximum: 1% of import value).

Source: *China Trade Report*, 13 February 1987, p. 8.

Kong 33%, South Korea 22%, Shanghai 28% and Shenzhen 18%.[63] As Table 1 indicates, investment fees in Shenzhen, including invisible fees, were generally higher than those in Hong Kong.

In conclusion, the above difficulties and problems facing foreign investors slowed down the inflow of foreign capital in the first part of 1986 which had been increasing rapidly for the previous seven years. Starting from late spring of 1986, foreign investors in China raised strong complaints about the general environment in which they had to operate. These events forced the Chinese government to give careful and serious thought to the situation and to decide to improve the investment climate throughout the country for foreign investors.

63 *Wen Wei Po*, 27 January 1987, p. BN2.

Chapter three

New provisions promulgated by the central government

The examination by the Chinese Government of the foreign investment environment in mid-1986 resulted in the enactment of new legislation by the State Council and various ministries to improve conditions for foreign enterprises operating in China. This chapter will examine the characteristics of the new provisions adopted by the State Council and the supplementary regulations promulgated by the relevant ministries and their impact on the crucial issues such as the freedom of enterprises to hire and dismiss employees, balancing of foreign exchange, land use fees, taxation, import and export rules and measures to restrict administrative interference with the business operations of enterprises with foreign participation, and to increase the efficiency of the bureaucracy.

I. Characteristics of the new laws

In response to the complaints of foreign investors and 'in order to improve the investment environment, facilitate the absorption of foreign investment, introduce advanced technology, improve product quality, expand exports in order to generate foreign exchange income and develop the national economy', the State Council of China promulgated Provisions for the Encouragement of Foreign Investment on 11 October 1986 (the 'Provisions').[1] The Provisions were designed to encourage foreign companies, enterprises and other economic entities or individuals to establish Sino-foreign equity joint ventures, Sino-foreign co-operative ventures and wholly foreign-owned enterprises in China.[2]

According to the Provisions, preferential treatment will be granted to two kinds of enterprises ie productive enterprises whose products are mainly for export (the 'Export Enterprises') and enterprises possessing advanced technology (the 'Technologically Advanced Enterprises'). In order to qualify as an Export Enterprise, the company must have a foreign exchange surplus after deducting from its total annual foreign exchange revenue, the annual foreign exchange expenditures incurred in

1 Article 1 of the Provisions of the State Council of the People's Republic of China for the Encouragement of Foreign Investment promulgated on 11 October 1986.
2 *Id*, Article 2.

the production and operation of the enterprise in question and the foreign exchange needed for the remittance of profits.[3] Technologically Advanced Enterprises are those which are engaged in developing new products or improving the quality of domestic products, in order to increase foreign exchange earnings from exports, or those engaged in producing import-substitutes.[4]

Both Export Enterprises and Technologically Advanced Enterprises are entitled to a number of preferential treatments including the following – deductions in and exemptions from tax payments, reductions in the minimum amount of salary contributions payable to the State, reductions in land use fees etc. In addition, they are given priority in the supply of water, electricity, transport services and telecommunications facilities.[5] Fees to be paid by these enterprises must be computed and charged in accordance with the standards for local State-owned enterprises.[6]

It is important to note that the Provisions represent a formal departure from China's previous policy in respect of foreign investment. Prior to the enactment of this legislation, the Chinese government had provided preferential treatment to foreign-investment enterprises operating in remote areas or in agriculture, animal husbandry, forestry and other low-profit sectors of the economy. In order to attract more foreign capital to those sectors, the Chinese Joint Venture Income Tax Law and the Foreign Enterprise Income Tax Law provide that enterprises which are to operate for a period of ten years or more in those sectors will, upon approval of the tax authorities, be granted an exemption from income tax in the first profit-making year and be allowed a 50% reduction in the second and third years. At the same time, the Chinese Ministry of Finance may allow a further 15 to 30% reduction in income tax for a period of ten years following the expiration of the above tax exemptions and reductions.[7] Neither of the above-mentioned tax laws provides for preferential treatment to be granted to export-oriented or technologically-advanced enterprises. This reflects China's belief, when it first opened itself to the outside world, that advanced foreign technology and capital would flood in. It did not foresee the potential foreign exchange problems. In addition, the non-provision of preferential treatment for export and hi-tech ventures had apparently resulted from the Chinese government's heavy reliance on the requirements under other legislation such as the Joint Venture Law which requires foreign investors to provide advanced technology or equipment.[8] Since joint ventures and other ventures or economic arrangements need to be approved by the Chinese government,

3 *Id.*
4 *Id.*
5 *Id*, Article 5.
6 *Id.*
7 Article 5 of the Chinese Joint Venture Income Tax Law and the Foreign Enterprise Income Tax Law.
8 Joint Venture Law, Article 5.

the drafters of the law seemingly believed that enterprises with less advanced technology or which were oriented towards the local market might be denied approval automatically. Experience has proved this assumption to be wrong.

Nevertheless, the provision of preferential treatment for Export Enterprises and Technologically Advanced Enterprises in the Provisions is not entirely new. The Provisions are a codification of China's previous practice over the last several years. The significance of the enactment of these Provisions is that the Chinese government has become more experienced in attracting foreign investment and has recognized the urgent need to give differential treatment to different kinds of foreign-investment enterprises. The enactment of the Provisions demonstrates that the Chinese government has turned to rely more on incentives than on mandates, more on formal legislation than on administrative measures or discretions. The elevation of the previous policy to law enables foreign investors to enjoy preferential treatment as their lawful right rather than as a discretionary grant by the administrative bodies.

In order to qualify for the preferential treatment stipulated in the Provisions, an enterprise must apply to and be examined and confirmed by the relevant Chinese authorities as satisfying the necessary requirements. An Export Enterprise with foreign investment must meet the following requirements: (1) It must manufacture products for export; (2) The products in question must be mainly for export with an annual export value of more than 50% of the total annual value; (3) The enterprise must be able to balance its annual operating foreign exchange revenue and expenditure or have a foreign exchange surplus.[9]

These three prerequisites mentioned above are in fact interrelated. First, unless an enterprise is producing merchandise mainly for export, it should not be regarded as export-oriented. Secondly, so long as an enterprise is manufacturing products for export, say exporting more than 50% of its products, it will be able to balance its foreign exchange accounts. The purpose of this Article is to provide clear and specific guidelines for local authorities to follow. This Article also distinguishes enterprises which are able to balance their foreign exchange accounts but are nonetheless not export-oriented (such as hotels) from export-oriented productive ventures. This distinction reflects China's policy of not encouraging foreign investors to develop non-productive sectors.

Under Article 2 of the Rules for Defining Two Categories of Enterprises, when calculating whether an enterprise's products are mainly for export or not, the products exported directly by the enterprise, by entrusted foreign trade corporations and through other channels are all

9 Implementing Rules of the Ministry of Foreign Economic Relations and Trade for Examination and Confirmation of Export Enterprises and Technologically Advanced Enterprises with Foreign Investment promulgated on 27 January 1987 (hereinafter referred to as 'Rules for Defining Two Categories of Enterprises'), Article 2.

regarded as products exported by the enterprise concerned. To calculate the foreign exchange surplus of an enterprise, the following formula must be used: surplus of foreign exchange revenue and expenditure at the end of the current year ('Surplus') = carry-over surplus from the previous year + the operating foreign exchange revenue of the current year − the operating foreign exchange expenditure of the current year.[10] Needless to say, using the above formula, an Export Enterprise's surplus must be a positive one, at least zero.

The requirement that an Export Enterprise export 50% of its annual output is in fact the minimum requirement. An Export Enterprise which exports more than 70% of its total output is entitled to a further 50% tax deduction under the Provisions.[11]

The foreign partner in the venture must provide the technology or equipment which a Technologically Advanced Enterprise will require. The technology or equipment must also meet the following requirements: the technique, production technology and key equipment used by the enterprise must be items that pertain to projects which the State Government publicly and officially encourages foreign investors to invest in; it must be appropriate and advanced in nature; in short supply in China; or the products so manufactured are up-to-date, and conducive to the upgrading of similar local products, or are capable of being import-substitutes or expanding exports.[12] These requirements will help to ensure that the advanced technology is absorbed locally and that the products are able to compete in the international markets. Clearly, this is the most detailed regulation in respect of technology transfer. This regulation contrasts sharply with the Joint Venture Law and the Wholly Foreign-owned Enterprise Law which only require foreign investors to supply advanced technology in general terms.

A foreign-investment enterprise which believes that it has met the requirements for either an Export Enterprise or a Technologically Advanced Enterprise or both, must apply to the foreign economic relations and trade department in the province, autonomous region, municipality or city under the direct leadership of the State government[13] where it is located, for examination and confirmation. The application documents to be submitted include application forms for Export Enterprises or Technologically Advanced Enterprises, a copy of the contract, a feasibility study of the project in question and other approval documents provided by the relevant Chinese authorities.[14]

In order to maintain its status as an approved Export Enterprise, an enterprise is required to work out independently its annual export plans

10 *Id.*
11 State Council Provisions, Article 8.
12 Rules for Defining Two Categories of Enterprises, Article 4.
13 Under the current system, only a few large cities are subject to the direct jurisdiction of the central government. Other cities are only under the direct leadership of the relevant provincial government which is accountable to the central government.
14 Rules for Defining Two Categories of Enterprises, Article 6.

and report its export operations periodically to the relevant authorities.[15] By the end of each year, if the records show that an Export Enterprise has not exported more than 50% of its products, it will have to refund the tax reductions or exemptions previously granted to it.[16] Although this provision is equally applicable to Technologically Advanced Enterprises, it is difficult to determine whether a given item of technology or equipment has lost its superiority. Nevertheless, this provision encourages and in fact requires foreign investors to apply the latest innovations to the technology which was originally provided for their projects in China. In other words, a foreign investor is expected to provide advanced technology on a continuing basis, otherwise once the technology or equipment employed by the venture in China is out-of-date when compared with similar technology from other sources or from the same investor, the venture will lose its status as a Technologically Advanced Enterprise.

The examining and confirming authorities for Export Enterprises and Technologically Advanced Enterprises are required to complete their tasks and make a decision in respect of the application within 30 days from the date of receipt of the application documents. They are also required to cooperate with other departments in determining whether a certain enterprise should be regarded as a Technologically Advanced Enterprise.[17] This provision is necessary and important because the right of examination and confirmation is generally vested in foreign economic relations and trade departments at provincial or city levels and these departments may not be familiar with the nature and level of the technology involved.

After the authorities have given their decision, they must verify each year the actual output of the Export Enterprises and Technologically Advanced Enterprises under their authority and determine whether the enterprises in question should continue to enjoy preferential treatment in the following year. The verification procedure should have regard to each enterprise's approved contract, annual export plan, actual export result for the year, technical indices, and reports on the quality of the products produced and the percentage of local materials used in production.[18] It is clear that Technologically Advanced Enterprises are encouraged, if not required, to use local components for their products. Nevertheless, none of the statutes has stipulated the percentage which local components should make up. As a result, the extent to which local components are used in production should be determined by the relevant contracts or other documents approved by the relevant Chinese authorities. If an enterprise in question fails by the end of the year to achieve such a requirement stipulated in these documents, it may lose its status as a

15 *Id*, Article 9.
16 *Id*, Article 11.
17 *Id*, Article 7.
18 *Id*, Article 10.

Technologically Advanced Enterprise despite the fact that the technology and equipment provided are advanced.

In order to guarantee foreign investors preferential treatment, the examining and confirming authorities at provincial or city level are required to issue confirmation certificates to enterprises which qualify and to file the application documents and confirmation certificates with the Ministry of Foreign Economic Relations and Trade (MOFERT) and the State Economic Commission.[19] This provision is again a ratification of previous practice. Before the promulgation of the Rules for Defining Two Categories of Enterprises, the Beijing Municipal Foreign Economic Relations and Trade Commission had published two lists, giving the names of Export Enterprises and Technologically Advanced Enterprises which would be eligible to enjoy the preferential treatment stipulated in the Provisions issued by the State Council and in the relevant rules adopted by the Beijing Municipal Government. The first list was published as early as 12 October 1986.[20]

The statutory requirement of the issuance of confirmation certificates is an improvement on the previous practice. It enables foreign investors to present such certificates to relevant or government departments for appropriate action. Foreign investors therefore do not have to rely on the internal communications, over which they have no control, between various government departments. As such, this requirement may lead to greater administrative efficiency.

II. Labour regulations

The right of foreign-investment enterprises to make independent decisions, particularly with respect to hiring and dismissing employees, is another feature of the new legislation. Generally speaking, as discussed in the previous chapter, the most difficult labour problems facing foreign investors include scarcity of skilled workers and the lack of mobility of these workers. Apart from the dearth of workers trained to international standards, foreign employers have often been frustrated in their attempts to lure skilled employees away from their work units despite the desire of these prospective employees to leave. Often, the only option was to bring in outside personnel – a time-consuming process that is mired in red tape. Other employment issues resulting from China's continuing reforms include the shortage of qualified technicians, scientists and managerial staff outside urban cities as well as the paucity of channels available for urban collective enterprises to recruit highly-skilled workers in other cities. Despite some success stories where the individual triumphs over the bureaucracy, the current practice in China makes

19 *Id*, Article 8.
20 *China Economic News*, 23 February 1987, p. 7.

recruitment and transfer of non-local personnel an exercise in futility.

The Provisions of the State Council provide that foreign-investment enterprises may, in accordance with their production and operational requirements, independently determine their organizational structure and personnel system, employ and dismiss senior management personnel, and recruit and dismiss staff and workers.[21] These enterprises may recruit and employ technical and managerial personnel and workers in their locality. The units to which these persons belong must give their support and permit the transfers.[22] A foreign-investment enterprise also has the right to dismiss any employee who breaks the rules and regulations and thereby causes certain adverse consequences. When an enterprise exercises its right to hire and dismiss employees, it must file a report with the local labour and personnel department for purposes of record.[23]

A foreign-investment enterprise, in determining its organizational structure and personnel system, should take into consideration its production and operational requirements. With the assistance of the labour and personnel department in its locality, the enterprise may recruit and employ staff and workers on its own through an examination and selection process.[24] This provision is in sharp contrast to the previous practice whereby prospective employees were recommended by the local labour and personnel departments. As a result, foreign-investment enterprises could not hire directly the workers they needed because they did not have full power to make decisions. Under the new legislation, local labour and personnel departments are not permitted to intervene with the hiring process of foreign-investment enterprises and are required to assist these enterprises.

In the event that engineering and technical personnel or operations and management personnel needed by a foreign-investment enterprise are not available in the locality, the enterprise may request the labour and personnel department in its locality to consult with and seek the consent of the labour and personnel departments in other provinces, autonomous regions or municipalities where prospective employees may reside.[25] The establishment of this formal channel for recruiting staff and workers from other cities or provinces can resolve to some extent the employment problems resulting from the lack of a labour market in China.

The corporations or working units in which the prospective employees are employed must actively 'give their support and permit the trans-

21 State Council Provisions, Article 15.
22 *Id.*
23 *Id.*
24 Provisions of the Ministry of Labour and Personnel of the People's Republic of China on the Right of Autonomy of Enterprises with Foreign Investment in Hiring Personnel and on Wages, Insurance and Welfare Expenses of Staff and Workers promulgated on 28 November 1986 (hereinafter referred to as the 'Labour Provisions'), Article 1.
25 *Id.*

fers'.[26] In a case where the current employer of a prospective employee does not allow the transfer or some other dispute arises, the foreign-investment enterprise in question may submit the dispute or disagreement to the labour and personnel department in the prospective employee's locality. This department has the right to adjudicate on the matter. This formal system of appeal may mitigate the problems involved in staffing managerial, service and blue-collar positions. Until the end of 1986, the majority of foreign-investment enterprises had no choice but to employ high-school graduates.[27] The major problem with hiring graduates is, firstly, that the enterprises must invest in an in-house training programme and, secondly, that these employees occasionally leave the enterprise for supervisory positions in collective enterprises. According to a Chinese trading company, the setting up of a formal channel for tapping the labour pool 'is an important and new resource which will lower the cost of operating in China'.[28]

Foreign-investment enterprises have the power to remove senior management personnel. Under the new labour provisions, senior management personnel designated by the Chinese party should be persons who are well versed in existing policies, technically competent, have managerial ability, are ready to accept new challenges and are able to cooperate and work together with foreign investors.[29] Any transfer of senior managers must have the consent of the board of directors of the enterprise in question. This provision will encourage continued foreign investment in China. In fact, unless senior managers working in these enterprises are open-minded, understand China's open policy, and possess managerial ability, they cannot and will not be able to cooperate well with foreign investors. In addition, this labour provision is intended to further strengthen the Joint Venture Law and other relevant statutes which provide full autonomy for the board of directors. The power of the board in respect of the transfer of senior management officials will prevent other Chinese companies, institutions or organs from enticing successful managers away from the enterprises which they work in.

The board of directors of a foreign-investment enterprise is vested with full powers to determine the wages of its staff and workers. The minimum wage is 120% of the average wage of the staff and workers of State-owned enterprises which are of the same trade and in the same locality. In addition, the wages of the staff and workers of a foreign-investment enterprise must be adjusted in accordance with the economic performance of the enterprise. Enterprises which have performed well should give bigger wage raises, while those which have performed poorly may give smaller raises or none at all.[30]

26 *Id.*
27 *Far Eastern Economic Review*, 25 September 1986, p. 49.
28 *Id.*
29 Labour Provisions, Article 1(C).
30 *Id*, Article 2(A).

Apart from the direct wage, a foreign-investment enterprise must make payments to the retirement and pension fund and the unemployment insurance fund, in accordance with the stipulations of the local government, for the benefit of the staff and workers from the Chinese party. The insurance and welfare benefits of the staff and workers during their employment must be made in accordance with the relevant legislation of the Chinese government concerning State-owned enterprises.[31] Foreign-investment enterprises must also contribute to the housing subsidy fund in accordance with the stipulations of the local government. The Chinese party to the enterprise is required to use this fund to subsidize the cost of building and purchasing housing for the staff and workers.[32]

These indirect wages are the minimum payments to be made by foreign investors. While Export Enterprises and Technologically Advanced Enterprises are exempted from paying subsidies to their staff and workers, except for labour insurance, welfare costs and housing subsidies for Chinese staff and workers,[33] other ventures involving foreign investment must continue to pay all the subsidies, including foodstuff and edible oil subsidies, transportation allowances etc.

A consequence of this minimum indirect wage payment requirement is that it gives local governments more discretion in setting up wage levels for employees in foreign-investment enterprises. Local governments may decide to give all foreign investors this favourable treatment. The purpose of this provision is obviously to reduce labour costs for foreign investors and to set a ceiling on the amount of indirect wages (subsidies) that a local government may require Export Enterprises and Technologically Advanced Enterprises to pay. According to the Beijing Jeep Joint Venture, this new labour regulation will save the joint venture 'RMB3.36m (about US$900,000) a year'.[34]

III. Methods of balancing foreign exchange

A shortage of foreign exchange is one of the most serious issues facing foreign investors in China. To tackle the problem, a number of measures have been adopted by the Chinese government over the last few years. For instance, the Chinese government has encouraged domestic end-users, when making purchases, to give priority to products manufactured by enterprises with foreign participation, if the products are up to international standards in respect of quality, and the terms of the purchase contracts are similar to those which would have been applicable if the products had been purchased from abroad. Such enterprises which produce import-substitutes may charge purchasers foreign exchange

31 *Id*, Article 2(B).
32 *Id*, Article 2(C).
33 State Council Provisions, Article 3.
34 *The Asian Wall Street Journal*, 23 December 1986, p. 6.

upon the approval of the relevant foreign exchange administration authorities. In addition, several foreign exchange centres have been established in large cities to enable foreign-investment enterprises to swap their foreign exchange with Renminbi or vice versa. Enterprises with foreign participation may also conduct swap transactions directly with each other. For instance, the Great Wall Sheraton Hotel in Beijing, a joint venture which has a foreign exchange surplus, often purchases Renminbi from other Sino-foreign ventures with its hard currency.

Direct lending by Chinese banks

Having realized that import-substitutions and swaps would not be able to solve the foreign exchange problem, the Chinese government introduced some new measures with the adoption, by the State Council, of the Provisions. Currently, Export Enterprises and Technologically Advanced Enterprises are given priority in receiving loans (in both Renminbi and foreign currencies) for production and distribution, after the Bank of China has examined and determined their needs and requirements.[35] The Chinese banks and financial institutions are authorized to provide foreign-investment enterprises with fixed-assets loans, working-capital loans, foreign exchange mortgage loans, and stand-by letters of credit.[36]

A fixed-assets loan is used to finance the costs of capital construction projects and technological upgrading projects, to purchase technology and equipment as well as to meet installation expenses. It takes the following forms:

(1) medium- and short-term loan;
(2) buyer's credit;
(3) syndicated loan; and
(4) project financing loan.[37]

A working-capital loan is used to provide funds for production, marketing of products and normal operations. It takes the following forms:

(1) production reserves and production loans;
(2) temporary credit; and
(3) overdraft on current account.[38]

35 State Council Provisions, Article 6.

36 Chu Baotai and Dong Weiyuan, 'Improve Foreign Investment Structure and Increase Foreign Investment Returns', *Wen Wei Po*, 27 February 1987, p. BN2. Mr. Chu Baotai is deputy director of the department in charge of foreign investment under the Ministry of Foreign Economic Relations and Trade.

37 Regulations of the Bank of China on Providing Loans to Foreign-investment Enterprises approved by the State Council on 7 April 1987 and promulgated by the Bank of China on 24 April 1987, Article 5.

38 *Id.*

Every foreign-investment enterprise which meets the following conditions will be entitled to apply to the Bank of China for a loan:

(1) It has obtained a business licence issued by the Chinese Administration for Industry and Commerce and has opened an account with the Bank of China;
(2) It has fully paid up its registered capital at the specified time;
(3) It has passed the requisite board resolutions, as well as a power attorney, in respect of the borrowing by the enterprise;
(4) Its capital construction projects have been approved by the planning authorities; and
(5) It has the ability to repay the loan and can provide reliable security for repayment/payment of the principal and interest.[39]

In general, the term of a fixed-assets loan is seven years or less, while the term of a working-capital loan does not exceed 12 months.[40] The interest rate for Renminbi loans is set by the People's Bank of China ('PBOC') and this rate also applies to China's State-owned enterprises.[41] For foreign currency loans, the interest rate may be either the consolidated interest rate set by the Bank of China or the rate agreed upon between the creditor and borrower in the light of international market conditions.[42]

The provision by the Bank of China of loans in foreign currencies will help to reduce the problems which foreign-investment enterprises may have in respect of foreign exchange shortages. It will thus directly assist the enterprises in balancing their foreign exchange accounts. The local currency loans have an indirect effect on the balancing of foreign exchange, as in the case of Renminbi mortgage loan transactions to be discussed later.

In addition, the Provisions have confirmed the practice of direct foreign exchange swaps by Sino-foreign ventures or wholly foreign-owned enterprises. These enterprises are permitted to mutually adjust their foreign exchange surpluses and deficiencies among each other as per their respective needs, under the supervision of the foreign exchange control departments.[43] Under the swap programme, enterprises which need to sell or purchase foreign exchange must report to the local foreign exchange administration offices or foreign exchange adjustment centres. They must seek the approval of the foreign exchange administration department before conducting any foreign exchange transactions. Once approval is secured, the enterprises in question may negotiate the exchange rates themselves. The local governments are not allowed to intervene. As a matter of principle, foreign-investment enterprises must

39 *Id*, Article 7.
40 *Id*, Articles 9 and 10.
41 *Id*, Article 11.
42 *Id*.
43 State Council Provisions, Article 14.

not purchase foreign exchange for purposes other than for their own use. They must not sell any foreign exchange other than that which is generated from their own businesses. In other words, no enterprise is allowed to conduct pure foreign exchange transactions ie act as brokers.

Mortgage loans

Very often, foreign enterprises make investments in China by contributing cash in the form of freely convertible currencies. At the same time, as soon as a foreign investment project is set up, the foreign investors in question will incur expenses in Renminbi. Since these foreign investors do not have cash in Renminbi (Chinese partners often contribute the factory site or existing equipment), they have to convert their foreign exchange contributions into Renminbi to pay for local costs. If they can put aside momentarily whatever foreign exchange they contribute and obtain enough Renminbi to cover local expenses, they can use the foreign exchange to import materials or parts as well as to repatriate investment profits later on. In order to help foreign investors to resolve their foreign exchange problems, the PBOC promulgated the Regulations Governing the Application of Renminbi Loans Mortgaged by Foreign Exchange on 12 December 1986 (hereinafter referred to as the 'Mortgage Loan Regulations').

Under the Mortgage Loan Regulations, Sino-foreign joint venture enterprises, Sino-foreign cooperative enterprises and wholly foreign-owned enterprises are eligible to apply for Renminbi loans which are to be secured by foreign exchange either generated from their businesses or borrowed from abroad.[44] The PBOC branches in various provinces, autonomous regions, municipalities directly under the jurisdiction of the central government, and Shenzhen Special Economic Zone have the right to examine and approve loan applications. They are required to prepare Renminbi mortgage loan plans annually and are restricted from granting such loans for amounts above the limits fixed by the PBOC head office.[45] Branch offices of the State Administration of Exchange Control are in charge of the examination of the sources and the amounts of foreign exchange to be mortgaged. Applicants are required to report the source of their foreign exchange to the offices of the State Administration of Foreign Exchange Control. If the foreign currency is borrowed from a foreign institution, the applicant must submit the original loan contract and the debt repayment plan along with the application.[46] The PBOC branches are to coordinate operations with the offices of the State Administration of Foreign Exchange Control at government level regarding such loans. In addition to the provincial PBOC branches, lower-level

44 Mortgage Loan Regulations, Article 1.
45 *Id*, Article 7.
46 *Id*, Article 6.

PBOC branches and designated banks can also approve Renminbi mortgage loan applications within the approved limits.[47]

In areas outside the Special Economic Zones, a mortgage loan agreement must be negotiated and signed between the applicant and the Bank of China or other financial institution authorized by the PBOC, while the Renminbi funds for mortgage loans will be provided by the PBOC.[48] In other words, the Bank of China branches and other authorized financial institutions act as agents for the PBOC in extending Renminbi loans and keeping the foreign exchange collateral. The loan agreement is to be in triplicate: one for the bank which extends the loan, another for the branch of the State Administration of Exchange Control for purposes of record and the last for the borrower. All loan contracts must include the provisions of the sample contract attached to the Mortgage Loan Regulations.

Renminbi mortgage loans can be either short-term or medium-term facilities. The maturity dates of short-term loans are three months, six months or one year. The medium-term loans are for periods of one year to five years.[49] Foreign currencies that can be used as collateral are limited to the US Dollar, Japanese Yen, Hong Kong Dollar, Deutsche Mark and Pound Sterling.[50]

The maximum amount of a Renminbi mortgage loan must not exceed the equivalent amount of the foreign exchange to be mortgaged, calculated according to the exchange rate as announced by the State Administration of Exchange Control on the day the loan is made.[51] By implication and at least in theory, designated banks are permitted to demand an amount as security collateral which is larger than that calculated under the applicable exchange rate. No interest would be credited on either the Renminbi funds or the mortgaged foreign exchange by either side.[52]

The Mortgage Loan Regulations provide for very strict terms in respect of maturity and exchange rates. A borrower is required to repay the same amount of Renminbi funds which were borrowed in exchange for the return of the mortgaged amount of foreign exchange.[53] In other words, the repayment amount will not be affected by changes in exchange rates. If the borrower does not redeem the mortgaged amount of foreign exchange upon maturity, the foreign exchange will become the property of the PBOC.[54] This provision which obviously reflects China's foreign exchange reserve situation may give foreign investors an advantage in that they can make use of changes in foreign exchange rates. For instance, when a foreign investor invests in an export-oriented project and

47 *Id*, Article 7.
48 *Id*, Article 5.
49 *Id*, Article 3.
50 *Id*, Article 4.
51 *Id*, Article 10.
52 *Id*, Article 11.
53 *Id*, Article 9.
54 *Id*.

mortgages its foreign exchange (cash contribution) with a bank, it may decide not to redeem the mortgaged amount of foreign exchange upon maturity if Renminbi appreciates, provided that it has a foreign exchange surplus. On the other hand, if Renminbi depreciates, the borrower is likely to redeem the mortgaged amount of foreign exchange in order to benefit from the change in the Renminbi exchange rate.

If the foreign exchange (mortgage collateral) is borrowed from abroad, the borrower must continue to be liable to the creditor for the repayment of the principal and interest of the foreign exchange so borrowed. This provision must be included in the Renminbi mortgage loan contract.[55]

Renminbi funds borrowed under mortgage loans may be used by the borrower for working capital needs or for investment in fixed assets. Funds to be used for investment in fixed assets must be brought in line with the state's or region's investment plans for fixed assets.[56] In this regard, so long as a Sino-foreign venture is approved by the relevant Chinese authorities, the investment in capital construction of the project should be regarded as being in accordance with the state or local plans.

Compensation trade

Another method of resolving the foreign exchange shortage problem which has been approved by the Chinese government is to permit foreign-investment enterprises to purchase and export Chinese products upon the approval of the relevant Chinese authorities. Such approvals will be given only to those productive enterprises, as defined in Chinese law, that have run into temporary difficulties in balancing their foreign exchange accounts.[57] The limited number of eligible enterprises and the relatively short duration of the approval demonstrate that on the one hand, the Chinese government is keen to resolve foreign exchange problems facing foreign investors, while on the other hand it is attempting to prevent foreign-investment enterprises from carrying on a purely import-export business in China. By limiting the authorized enterprises to productive ventures, China is assured that its relatively small foreign trade business will be essentially restricted to Chinese enterprises.

Enterprises which qualify as productive enterprises under Chinese law and need to purchase and export domestic products to balance their foreign exchange accounts should apply to the local provincial departments dealing with foreign economic relations and trade for

55 The Sample Contract for Mortgage Renminbi Loans Attached to the Mortgage Loan Regulations.
56 Mortgage Loan Regulations, Article 2.
57 Provisions on the Purchase and Export of Domestic Products by Foreign Investment Enterprises to Balance Foreign Exchange Accounts issued by the Ministry of Foreign Economic Relations and Trade on 20 January 1987, Articles 1 and 2.

authorization. The application should state the amount of foreign exchange and the corresponding amount of Renminbi needed in the current year for the purchase of domestic products.[58] No enterprise is allowed to purchase a quantity of domestic products for export which is larger than that needed to cover the shortfall of foreign exchange resulting from production and operations, profit repatriation or termination and liquidation. In addition, each authorized enterprise should as far as possible purchase Chinese domestic products in the province, autonomous region or municipality where it is located. If it is necessary for a given enterprise to purchase Chinese products from other provinces, the approval of the relevant province, autonomous region or municipality where the products are manufactured should be secured in advance.[59]

The products so purchased must be exported out of China either by the enterprise in question or by China's foreign trade corporations acting as its agents.[60] Where the commodities to be purchased by authorized enterprises require state export licences or are subject to export quotas, approval should be obtained from the Ministry of Foreign Economic Relations and Trade (MOFERT). Provincial-level departments dealing with foreign economic relations and trade are authorized to approve the export of products which do not require export licences.[61]

Under the current Chinese system, local governments are allowed to retain a certain portion of the foreign exchange resulting from exports. They are encouraged to use such retained foreign exchange to balance the foreign exchange accounts of foreign-investment enterprises.[62]

IV. Financial guarantees

Very often, foreign enterprises make investments in China by borrowing loans from overseas. This practice is particularly favourable to project financing. In order to ensure repayment of the loans, foreign creditors often demand a guarantee from Chinese institutions, such as the Bank of China, when advancing facilities. From the Chinese government's point of view, this arrangement is acceptable as it will help to ease China's foreign exchange shortage and may provide investors with incentives to export their products. In the past, there was no clearly-worded piece of legislation on this point and foreign creditors as well as borrowers were not certain as to which institution was qualified to provide such guarantees. In order to remedy this shortcoming, the PBOC enacted the Provisional Regulations on Providing Foreign Exchange Guarantees by

58 *Id*, Article 3.
59 *Id*, Article 5.
60 *Id*, Articles 6 and 7.
61 *Id*, Article 9.
62 *Id*, Article 8.

Institutions Inside China on 20 February 1987 (hereinafter referred to as the 'Foreign Exchange Guarantee Regulations').[63]

Under the Foreign Exchange Guarantee Regulations, both financial institutions and non-financial institutions with foreign exchange income in China are permitted to act as loan guarantors.[64] Foreign exchange guarantees may be provided to enterprises which have Chinese nationality and operate inside China. However, Chinese enterprises which have their principal places of business outside China, China-based foreign institutions, or wholly foreign-owned enterprises, generally do not qualify for such guarantees.[65]

Nevertheless, China-based foreign institutions or wholly foreign-owned enterprises in China may be granted guarantees by Chinese institutions if they can provide foreign exchange assets, equal in value to the guaranteed amount, as security.[66] According to an official from the State Administration of Exchange Control, foreign exchange assets include negotiable securities in foreign currency such as cash, foreign exchange bills, foreign currency bonds and debentures, foreign currency stock and shares as well as other assets that can be immediately converted into foreign exchange in cash.[67]

When providing guarantees, guarantors are required to examine:

(1) the feasibility study of the project to be guaranteed;
(2) the financial situation of the debtor; and
(3) the necessity for anti-guarantee measures.[68]

The total amount of the foreign exchange guarantee and foreign debt that a financial institution can provide must be less than 21 times the amount of its own foreign exchange reserve. The maximum amount of foreign exchange guarantee that a non-financial institution may provide must not exceed the amount of its own foreign exchange reserve.[69]

Three issues require further clarification. First, as regards a financial institution (guarantor) what constitutes 'its own foreign exchange reserve'? Secondly, through what procedure can a foreign creditor determine a given guarantor's foreign exchange position? Thirdly, does this guarantee ceiling apply to foreign financial institutions in China as well?

It is understood that, for financial institutions, the term 'its own foreign exchange reserve' refers primarily to the capital in foreign exchange or foreign currencies which the guarantor possesses and has the

63 The Chinese version of the text and an English translation of the Provisional Regulations of the People's Bank of China on Providing Foreign Exchange Guarantees by Institutions Inside China can be found in *China Economic News*, 9 March 1987, p. 16 and 4–5, respectively.
64 Foreign Exchange Guarantee Regulations, Article 4.
65 *Id*, Article 5.
66 *Id*.
67 *China Economic News*, 18 May 1987, p. 2.
68 Foreign Exchange Guarantee Regulations, Article 6.
69 *Id*, Article 4.

right to use. In the case of a non-financial institution guarantor, the term refers to the foreign exchange funds which have been allocated to it by its superior department and which it is authorized to use. This foreign exchange allocation includes the portion of foreign exchange earnings which the enterprise is allowed to retain.[70]

Based on the interpretation by the State Administration of Exchange Control, the ceiling provided for in Article 4 of the Foreign Exchange Guarantee Regulations does not apply to foreign financial institutions in China.[71] As to how a lender can verify whether a Chinese guarantor has exceeded its authorized amount, procedures which are universally applied in foreign countries have been adopted in China. For instance, a foreign lender, with the consent of the guarantor, can check the guarantor's financial situation with its bank or the foreign exchange control administration.[72]

The creditor, debtor and guarantor in a loan transaction are required to conclude written contracts to state explicitly the rights, interests and obligations of each party. As soon as a guarantee goes into effect, any amendment to the loan agreement or other document secured by the guarantee must be consented to by the guarantor. Otherwise, such revisions will become null and void automatically and the guarantor will be released from its original obligations.[73] This right, however, is restricted to revisions of the main clauses of a given contract such as changes to the currency involved, amount of the facility, interest rate, term of the loan etc.[74]

Another important provision of the Foreign Exchange Guarantee Regulations is that in a case where the creditor fails to perform its obligations as set forth in the relevant contract, the obligations of the guarantor automatically become null and void.[75] The guarantor is entitled to compensation for losses arising from the non-performance of the creditor.[76] At the same time, if the creditor has already performed part of its obligations prior to its breach of contract, the guarantor is bound by the provisions of the contract in so far as the fulfilled portion of the contract is concerned.[77]

The Foreign Exchange Guarantee Regulations were adopted in the light of complaints from foreign bankers regarding their difficulties in obtaining guarantees from Chinese institutions. The purpose of these provisions is to tighten control on guarantees by Chinese institutions and at the same time to increase the number of authorized guarantors and to provide clear guidelines for the operation of loan guarantees. These

70 *China Economic News*, 18 May 1987, p. 2.
71 *Id.*
72 *Id.*
73 Foreign Exchange Guarantee Regulations, Article 9.
74 *China Economic News*, 18 May 1987, p. 2.
75 Foreign Exchange Guarantee Regulations, Article 11.
76 *Id.*
77 *China Economic News*, 18 May 1987, p. 2.

provisions have been welcomed by the foreign bankers who believe they have clarified many of the gray areas surrounding loan guarantees.[78]

V. Land use fees

Under Chinese law, all land in China is owned by the State. Enterprises and individuals are therefore not permitted to own any land, although they can acquire the right to use land upon the approval of the relevant government authorities. When foreign investors or enterprises are in need of land, they must apply to the local land authorities which are above the county level. Applicants are required to submit applications together with design and construction plans and other legal documents. They will be issued land use certificates upon the approval of the relevant Chinese authorities. The land use certificates are categorized into temporary and long-term permits. Temporary permits are valid for not more than two years. Such certificate holders are not allowed to build any permanent projects on the land. The long-term land use certificates should be issued in accordance with the business contracts of the enterprise in question. The terms of both the certificates and contracts should match each other. Upon termination of the certificate, the enterprise in question is required to return the land to the government. In addition, for the duration of the land use permit, an authorized enterprise is not allowed to transfer, mortgage or charge the land, or exploit resources underneath the land. Such land use permission may be extended pursuant to a reapplication six months prior to the termination date of the permit.

There is currently no national law regulating land use fees. Such fees are therefore determined by the governments at provincial, autonomous region or city levels, in accordance with the conditions of their respective localities. Generally speaking, enterprises with foreign participation which are engaged in scientific research, eduation, public health, environment protection or other public interest activities are exempted from land use fees for a certain period of time. In addition, foreign-investment enterprises which have acquired land through reclamation, by flattening mountains or through improvement of unusable land may be exempted from land use fees for a certain period or allowed a reduction in land use fees upon the approval of the relevant local government.[79]

Local regulations regarding land use fees sometimes cause problems for foreign investors. This is because local governments and authorities sometimes adjust land use fees and rentals unreasonably, thus seriously affecting the budgeting plans of foreign investors. In late 1986, for instance, China-Outsuka Seiyaku Co Ltd, a Sino-Japanese joint venture,

78 *South China Morning Post*, 25 February 1987, p. BN1.
79 Chu Baotai and Dong Weiyuan, *op cit*, n 36 above.

ran into a dispute with the Niutou Village in the suburb of Tianjin in connection with land rental. The Niutou Village increased the rental in breach of the contract terms, citing the joint venture's increased revenue and profits as reasons. The disputing parties eventually had to bring the case to a court in Tianjin City which decided in favour of the joint venture. On appeal, the high court of Tianjin upheld the lower court's ruling and decided that the increase was void.[80]

Such publicized land use fee disputes are not many but land use fee adjustments are frequent. In order to guarantee Export Enterprises and Technologically Advanced Enterprises stable and reasonable land use costs, the State Council Provisions have laid down specific standards. According to Article 4 of the Provisions, except for land located in the busy urban sectors of large cities, land use fees payable by the abovementioned two kinds of enterprises should be computed and charged according to the following criteria:

(1) At RMB5 to RMB20 per sq m per year in areas where the development fee and the land use fee are computed and charged together;
(2) At not more than RMB3 per sq m per year in areas where the development fee is computed and charged on a one-time basis, or in areas which are developed by the enterprises themselves.

In addition, the Provisions provide that local governments are permitted to exempt foreign-investment enterprises from paying land use fees for certain periods of time.[81] Thus, Export Enterprises and Technologically Advanced Enterprises are entitled not to pay any land use fees in excess of the statutory standard. At the same time, local governments may further reduce such fees so as to promote foreign investment.

VI. Tax reductions

Export Enterprises and Technologically Advanced Enterprises are granted special tax treatment. The foreign partners of such enterprises are exempted from income taxation when remitting abroad profits distributed to them.[82] This provision is applicable to the remittance of profits by foreign investors in the fiscal year 1986 and the following fiscal years. The exempted income tax is 10% of the amount remitted. In a case where the foreign investor in question had paid the income tax upon remittance of profits, prior to the promulgation of the Provisions, the amount of paid income tax will be refunded to the investor. Any

80 *China Economic News*, 5 January 1987, p. 7.
81 State Council Provisions, Article 4.
82 State Council Provisions, Article 7.

remittance tax paid prior to the fiscal year 1986, however, will not be refunded.[83]

Both Export Enterprises and Technologically Advanced Enterprises currently enjoy certain tax reductions or exemptions either under the relevant Chinese laws or under contracts approved by the Chinese authorities. An Export Enterprise which exports 70% or more of its products is entitled to a 50% tax deduction after the expiration of the above-mentioned period allowed for reduction or exemption of income tax. This provision also applies to Export Enterprises which have not been granted exemptions from or reductions in enterprise income tax under the relevant Chinese laws or contracts.[84] Nevertheless, an Export Enterprise must pay a minimum enterprise income tax at a rate of 10%, regardless of where it is located.[85] In addition, except for crude oil, refined oil and other products which are subject to special State provisions, the export products of foreign-investment enterprises are exempted from the Consolidated Industrial and Commercial Tax.[86]

A Technologically Advanced Enterprise is also entitled to a 50% tax deduction after expiration of the period of its tax reduction or exemption in accordance with Chinese laws and regulations. The 50% tax reduction should be allowed for the following three years. If such enterprise has not enjoyed any such tax reduction or exemption prior to the promulgation of the State Council Provisions, it will be granted a 50% tax reduction for three years beginning from the year it is confirmed as being technologically advanced.[87] The minimum 10% tax rate is also applicable to Technologically Advanced Enterprises.

Article 10 of the State Council Provisions provides: 'Foreign investors who reinvest the profits distributed to them by their enterprises in order to establish or expand an Export Enterprise or a Technologically Advanced Enterprise for an operational period of not less than five years, after application to and approval by the tax authorities, shall be refunded the total amount of the enterprise income tax already paid on the reinvested portion.' This tax refund provision applies only to the profits distributed and reinvested in 1986 and thereafter.[88] If the reinvestment is withdrawn prior to the end of the above-mentioned five-year operational period, the amount of refunded income tax must be repaid by the foreign investor in question.[89]

83 Article 1 of the Rules for the Implementation of Relevant Articles Concerning Preferential Tax Terms Stipulated in the Provisions of the State Council for the Encouragement of Foreign Investment promulgated by the Finance Ministry on January 30, 1987 (hereinafter referred to as the 'Tax Implementation Rules').

84 *Id*, Article 2.

85 *Id*, and State Council Provisions, Article 8.

86 State Council Provisions, Article 11.

87 Article 3 of the Tax Implementation Rules and Article 9 of the State Council Provisions.

88 Tax Implementation Rules, Article 4.

89 State Council Provisions, Article 10.

An enterprise with foreign participaton, which qualifies as either a Technologically Advanced Enterprise or an Export Enterprise, may choose one of the two categories and enjoy the preferential tax terms accordingly. Due to the special nature of the exploration and development of natural resources such as oil and precious metals, these preferential tax terms do not apply to Sino-foreign enterprises engaged in such activities.

VII. Import and export rules

As part of the efforts by the Chinese government to improve China's investment climate and to attract more foreign investments, important measures were taken towards the end of 1986 to simplify procedures for the import and export goods by foreign investors. Under the current system, foreign investors who contribute equipment and other materials in a Sino-foreign venture must apply to the relevant Chinese authorities for import licences. Such import licences are issued in accordance with the list of imported equipment and materials approved by the Chinese authorities for the enterprise in question.

The importation of goods which do not require import licences is examined by the Chinese Customs.[90] Enterprises with foreign participation may import, without import licences, machinery and other equipment (including those requiring import licences), vehicles to be used in production, raw materials, fuel, spare parts, accessories and components for use in production, if such importation is for the purpose of carrying out export contracts between the enterprise and a foreign party.[91] The imported materials and items must be for the exclusive use of the enterprise in question and are not to be resold in the domestic market. The Customs authority will inspect and release such import items on the strength of the enterprise's contracts and other legal documents.[92]

Enterprises with foreign participation, which manufacture products for sale in China's domestic market, should apply, within the scope of their approved business operations, for import licences every six months. Such import licences may cover equipment and vehicles for use in production, raw materials, fuel, spare parts, accessories and components which are needed for the production process.[93] Nevertheless, materials and parts imported by enterprises which manufacture import-substitutes

90 Rules for Foreign-investment Enterprises Applying for Import and Export Licences promulgated by the Ministry of Foreign Economic Relations and Trade on 24 January 1987 (hereinafter referred to as 'Rules for Application of Import and Export Licences'), Article 2.

91 *Id*, Article 3, and State Council Provisions, Article 13.

92 Procedures of the Customs of the People's Republic of China for the Administration of Materials and Parts That Enterprises with Foreign Investment Need to Import in Order to Perform Product Export Contracts issued by the General Administration of Customs on 24 November 1986 and effective on 1 December 1986, Articles 2 and 3.

93 Rules for Application of Import and Export Licences, Article 4.

may be treated as bonded warehouse goods over which the Customs authorities exercise supervision and control.[94] These enterprises are therefore permitted to postpone paying the import duties and Consolidated Industrial and Commercial Tax leviable on the imported materials and parts. They are required to complete the import procedures retroactively once they have sold their products to domestic users.[95] If domestic users are entitled to enjoy preferential tax reductions or exemptions when importing similar products, these foreign-investment enterprises should also be entitled to similar preferential tax treatment.[96]

Import licences are issued by the Ministry of Foreign Economic Relations and Trade (MOFERT). Import licences for products which are needed for an enterprise's own use may be issued by the provincial-level departments in charge of foreign trade and economic relations.[97] The quantity of the products which can be imported is nonetheless restricted and should not be beyond the reasonable use of the enterprise in question. The purpose of this provision is to prevent the importation of large quantities of goods under the guise of law to evade import restrictions.

The customs procedures pertaining to 'processing enterprises' with foreign investment which import materials and parts and export finished products have also been simplified. Every processing enterprise can register with the Customs authority in its locality and request a Registration Manual.[98] When such an enterprise imports materials and parts and exports finished products after processing, it should make declarations to the Customs at the place of entry and exit by submitting the Registration Manual together with the customs declaration forms for the imported and exported goods, the invoice for the goods, packing lists and other relevant lists and certificates. The Customs then makes its comments in, and affixes a seal on, the Registration Manual which is then kept by the enterprise for purposes of verification.[99] Usually, except with special approval from the Customs, processing enterprises must complete processing and export the finished products within one year from the date of importation of the tax-exempted materials and parts.[100] If two or more processing enterprises manufacture on a joint basis (such as where one produces semi-finished products and passes such products to the another for completion), the enterprises involved must complete the

94 Procedures of the Customs, Article 5.
95 *Id.*
96 *Id.*
97 Rules for Application of Import and Export Licences, Article 5.
98 The full name of the Registration Manual is Manual of the Customs of the People's Republic of China for the Registration of Materials and Parts Needed to be Imported for Processing and Re-export by Enterprises with Foreign Investment in Order to Perform Product Export Contracts. Such registration manuals are issued only after the Customs have received and examined the applicant's export contracts and other valid documents.
99 Procedures of the Customs, Article 8.
100 *Id*, Article 10.

Customs procedures with regard to transfer, verification and cancellation. They are required to submit to the Customs relevant purchase and sales contracts, production and processing contracts between the parties and other relevant documents.[101]

Processing enterprises are not supposed to sell their products domestically. However, on special occasions, such processing enterprises may, upon the approval of the relevant Chinese authorities, be permitted to sell their finished products in a Chinese market. In such cases, the enterprises must, within one month of the date of approval, pay retroactively to the Customs the customs duties and Consolidated Industrial and Commercial Tax on the imported materials and parts that were originally exempted from tax.[102] Every processing enterprise with foreign investment is required, as regards imported materials or parts, to keep separate records concerning their importation, storage and care, and allocation for further processing. As regards finished products, it must keep separate records of the storage, exportation, and domestic sales of these products. In addition, it must submit quarterly statements on the above items to the Customs for examination.[103]

These measures are designed to facilitate the import and export activities of processing and export-oriented enterprises. If the business of a processing enterprise is on a large-scale and its export business is very active, the Customs may station its officials at the company's factories to supervise and facilitate its import and export activities.[104]

The simplified Customs procedures and the procedures for obtaining import and export licences will undoubtedly increase the efficiency of foreign-investment enterprises. These procedures will considerably reduce the operating costs of such enterprises. In addition to the simplification of import-export procedures, the Chinese government has set up several tariff-free trading centres to supply imported products, such as vehicles and other equipment, to enterprises with foreign participation.[105] Such enterprises which qualify for duty-free items can purchase them from these centres.

VIII. Measures for dealing with the bureaucracy

In almost every country, bureaucratic interference is a major obstacle to foreign investors. Since China is essentially a planned economy country, its bureaucracy plays a very important part in attracting foreign investment and carrying out economic cooperation with foreign enterprises. The excessive interference of the bureaucracy in the business

101 *Id*, Article 11.
102 *Id*, Article 9.
103 *Id*, Article 8.
104 *Id*, Article 13.
105 *Wen Wei Po*, 7 February 1987, p. BN4.

operations of enterprises with foreign participation and the inefficiency of the bureaucracy have been much criticized by both foreign investors and the Chinese people. In order to tackle this serious problem, the Provisions of the State Council specifically stipulate that the governments at all levels and the relevant departments in charge must guarantee the right of autonomy of these foreign-investment enterprises and must encourage them to introduce internationally-advanced or scientific management methods.[106] This provision clearly demonstrates that the Chinese government has recognized the gravity of the bureaucratic problem which has been hindering foreign investment in China. The government has now given foreign investors a statutory right to challenge Chinese officials who interfere with the autonomous and independent operation of the enterprises. As an American investor commented, the Provisions 'gave [him] a big clap to hit those guys on the head'.[107] In addition, foreign investors who encounter unreasonable charges may refuse to pay them and may also appeal to the local economic commissions right up to the State Economic Commission.[108]

The Provisions of the State Council require the governments at all levels and the relevant departments in charge of foreign investment to strengthen the coordination of their work, improve efficiency in handling matters and examine and approve promptly matters reported by foreign-investment enterprises as requiring prompt action.[109] All agreements, contracts and articles of association of Sino-foreign ventures must be examined and approved by the relevant departments under the State Council. The examining and approving authority is required to make a decision within three months from the date of receipt of all the requisite documents.[110]

It is important to set deadlines for the departments in charge of foreign investment and economic activities. Currently, the management systems of these departments are rife with malpractices. Foreign investors have to go through dozens of procedures and an equal number of 'chops' (signatures) have to be affixed before a project can be approved and launched. Worse still, a large number of authorities stand in the way but none of them is willing or ready to take the necessary action.

Having realized the extreme difficulties arising from the bureaucratic system and the impossibility of resolving such problems in a short time or by legislation, the Chinese government has established special leadership groups at various levels to handle foreign investment matters. The special office set up in the central government under the State Council is headed by State Councillor Gu Mu, with representatives from the State Planning Commission, State Economic Commission, Ministry of Foreign

106 State Council Provisions, Article 15.
107 *The Asian Wall Street Journal*, 23 December 1986, p. 6.
108 State Council Provisions, Article 16.
109 State Council Provisions, Article 17.
110 *Id.*

Economic Relations and Trade (MOFERT), People's Bank of China, Bank of China, Ministry of Labour and Personnel, Ministry of Urban and Rural Construction and Environmental Protection, General Administration of Customs, State Foreign Exchange Administration and State Administration of Industry and Commerce. The function of this office is to make proposals to the State Council, coordinate and supervise efforts by the departments concerned and mediate in commercial disputes arising from foreign economic activities. In other words, this office has been established to improve the investment climate in China and to promote foreign investment.

Internal directives which are enforced as law by regional authorities are also major irritants to foreign investors who have no access to the contents of these directives but have frequently faced pressure from the relevant authorities to comply with the provisions set out in the directives. At the beginning of 1987, the MOFERT announced that it would drop the practice of issuing such internal circulars relating to foreign investment.[111] The first step taken by the Chinese government was the issuance on 1 March 1987 of the Provisional Regulations of the State Administration for Industry and Commerce Concerning the Proportion of Registered Capital to Total Investment of Sino-foreign Joint Ventures (the 'Registered Capital Ratio Regulations'). Prior to the adoption of this legislation, the registered capital/investment ratio was regulated by internal guidelines which were criticized by many foreign investors.[112] The adoption of these regulations shows that the Chinese government may eventually eliminate all existing internal directives.

In summary, the new efforts made by the Chinese government and the adoption of new legislation, will, in the words of an American business-

111 *South China Morning Post*, 13 January 1987, p. BN12.

112 Under the Registered Capital Ratio Regulations, investors who are partners of joint ventures and cooperative ventures or are owners of wholly foreign-owned enterprises are required to put up a certain percentage of the project costs in registered capital and the remainder can be raised by bank loans in accordance with the following formula:

Equity Ratio

Project cost (US$ million)	*Minimum registered capital(%)*
4 or less	70
3–10	50
10–30	40
30 or more	33.3

The required percentage of registered capital may be revised upon a joint approval of the Ministry of Foreign Economic Relations and Trade and the State Administration for Indusry and Commerce. One of the characteristics of this new legislation is reduction of the equity requirement for small projects under US$3m. Prior to the adoption of this statute, such enterprises had to invest 100% equity in the project. They are now allowed to put up 30% of the project cost by raising loans. On the other hand, this new law has increased the equity requirement for projects worth more than US$10m. See Registered Capital Ratio Regulations, Articles 3 and 4.

man, 'be conducive to solving a good number of existing problems encountered by foreign investors'.[113] Nevertheless, these new pieces of legislation will not resolve overnight the foreign investment problems and difficulties which are inherent in the Chinese system, culture and history but they are a step in the right direction. Indeed, the local authorities have been quick to enact supplementary measures for the implementation of the national statutes.

113 *China Economic News*, 5 January 1987, p. 6.

Chapter four

Regional measures

China is a large country and its conditions for foreign investment are not uniform. The implementation of the laws enacted by the central government therefore depends to a large extent on the willingness and readiness of local governments at various levels. Provincial governments as well as city governments are authorized to adopt their own legislation in accordance with the principles, general guidelines and framework of the national law. Since the central government of China promulgated the Provisions for the Encouragement of Foreign Investment in early October 1986, a number of provincial as well as city governments have adopted their own measures to enforce the national statute. The open coastal cities and ports and SEZs are especially active in this regard. This chapter will examine the foreign-investment legislation of some leading cities and provinces, such as Shanghai City, Fujian Province and Fuzhou City, Beijing, Guangzhou, Dalian, and provisions of the non-coastal provinces of Yunnan and Guizhou.

I. Shanghai's investment environment

Shanghai is one of the leaders in attracting foreign investment and in carrying out economic cooperation with foreign enterprises. It was reported that by the end of 1986, Shanghai had approved 222 Sino-foreign ventures.[1] Of these, 120 involve capital from Hong Kong, 37 from the United States, 30 from Japan and others from Europe and Asia-Pacific countries. So far, the United States is the largest investor in terms of investment value, followed by Hong Kong. Most of the US investment projects have been made in the manufacturing industry, while the majority of the Hong Kong funds have been used to finance projects in service industries such as hotels and office complexes.[2]

Sino-foreign enterprises are playing an increasingly important role in Shanghai's economy. According to the Shanghai-based World Economic Herald Newspaper, 22 foreign-owned or jointly-owned industrial enterprises produced a total output value of RMB508 m in 1986, up 61% over

1 *Wen Wei Po*, 6 March 1987, p. BN4.
2 *Id.*

1985. Total net income from these enterprises amounted to RMB75 m, 140% up from the previous year. The value of exports of these enterprises in 1986 doubled that of 1985, reaching RMB27.5 m.[3] The majority of Sino-foreign joint ventures have operated very satisfactorily. For instance, a Sino-Hong Kong textile joint venture which was established in 1981 managed to make an average after-tax profit of 34.7%. Its output in 1986 increased by 38% from that of 1985.[4]

Procedures for establishment of Sino-foreign ventures

The successful operation of Sino-foreign ventures in Shanghai has been attributed to the untiring efforts of the Shanghai municipal government in encouraging foreign investment. As early as June 1986, the Standing Committee of the People's Congress of Shanghai enacted legislation in respect of applications and approvals for the establishment of Sino-foreign joint ventures, cooperative ventures and wholly foreign-owned enterprises.[5] This statute which provides the procedural basis for the establishment of such ventures is aimed at raising administrative efficiency. Under the statute, applications for the establishment of foreign-investment enterprises will be examined and approved exclusively by the Foreign Economic Relations and Trade Department of Shanghai (hereinafter referred to as the 'Approval Authority of Shanghai'), except those which require the approval of the State Council of China.[6]

Foreign investors who are interested in forming joint ventures or cooperative ventures are required to negotiate with their Chinese partner(s) directly and work out letters of intent. Thereafter, both the Chinese and foreign partners should conduct an initial feasibility study of the project.[7] The Chinese partner is required to draft a project proposal and submit it to the authorities at district or county level who will then forward the proposal to the Approval Authority of Shanghai. Prior to the approval of the Approval Authority of Shanghai, neither party is permitted to conclude any valid agreement. In a case where more than two Chinese parties participate in the same project, one of them should be designated by the Approval Authority of Shanghai to be in charge of drafting proposals and seeking approval of the project on behalf of the other parties.[8]

3 *China Daily*, 5 March 1987, p. 1.
4 *Wen Wei Po*, 6 March 1987, p. BN4.
5 Regulations of Shanghai Municipality on Application and Approval for the Establishment of Sino-foreign Joint Ventures, Sino-foreign Cooperative Ventures and Wholly Foreign-owned Enterprises adopted at the 22nd Session of the Standing Committee of the 8th People's Congress of Shanghai on 20 June 1986 (hereinafter referred to as the 'Shanghai Application and Approval Regulations').
6 Shanghai Application and Approval Regulations, Article 3.
7 *Id*, Articles 4 and 5.
8 *Id*, Article 7.

Once the project is approved, the parties concerned are required, within one year, or in extraordinary cases, a year and half, to complete a detailed feasibility study of the project, covering finance, factory sites, equipment, raw materials, distribution, labour and wages, balancing of foreign exchange, and infrastructure needed for the project. Such a feasibility study will also require the confirmation of other relevant institutions or authorities which specialize in technical matters.[9]

After the feasibility study is concluded, the Chinese and foreign parties in question should submit to the Approval Authority of Shanghai all the relevant legal documents, including the feasibility study, contracts between the parties and articles of association, for final approval of the project.[10]

Foreign investors who are intending to establish wholly foreign-owned enterprises in Shanghai should follow the same procedures applicable to joint ventures and cooperative ventures, except that they must appoint a Chinese institution as their agent to handle procedural matters.[11]

The Approval Authority of Shanghai is required to complete the examination and make a decision within 30 days from the date it receives the initial feasibility study or detailed feasibility study, contracts and articles of association.[12] In addition, the Approval Authority of Shanghai is required to issue licence certificates within 10 days from the date of receipt of the following documents: (1) the certificates of the Chinese and foreign parties showing their corporate status; (2) approved project proposal; (3) approval feasibility study, contracts and articles of association; and (4) list of the board of directors and senior managerial personnel.[13]

Foreign representative offices

Procedures for the establishment of foreign representative offices in Shanghai are similar to those for the establishment of foreign-investment enterprises.[14] Nevertheless, the term of the resident representative office is limited to three years. Upon expiration of the authorized period, the enterprise in question may request for further extensions each of which is no more than three years.[15] In general, a representative office should be established with an introduction by a local corporation or institution that deals with foreign businesses. The latter acts as agent for the foreign

9 *Id*, Article 9.
10 *Id*, Article 10.
11 *Id*, Articles 14–16.
12 *Id*, Articles 5 and 10.
13 *Id*, Articles 11 and 12.
14 The establishment of foreign representative offices in Shanghai is governed by the Regulations of Shanghai Municipality Concerning the Control of Resident Representative Offices of Foreign Enterprises effective as of 1 September 1986 (hereinafter referred to as 'Shanghai's Regulations on Foreign Representative Offices').
15 Shanghai's Regulations on Foreign Representative Offices, Article 17.

enterprise in question. In addition, the foreign enterprise is required to submit the following documents:

(1) An application form signed by the chairman of the board of directors or the general manager of the foreign enterprise;

(2) A legal document, issued by the authorities of the country or region in which the enterprise operates, authorizing the operation of the enterprise;

(3) 'Creditworthiness' documentation provided by banking institutions which have business contacts with the enterprise;

(4) The credentials and brief biographies of the members of the resident representative office appointed by the chairman of the board of directors or the general manager of the enterprise.[16]

Supplementary regulations

For the implementation of the Provisions of the State Council, the Shanghai municipality enacted its own regulations for the encouragement of foreign investment on 1 November 1986. Essentially, these regulations provide for further reductions in tax and other operating costs for foreign-investment enterprises, particularly the Export Enterprises and Technologically Advanced Enterprises, as defined in the State Council Provisions. All Export Enterprises and Technologically Advanced Enterprises are exempted from local income tax, during the period of exemption from enterprise income tax, in accordance with the laws of the State. Upon the expiration of the above period, such enterprises will be exempted from local income tax for another three years and will thereafter be entitled to a 50% tax reduction for an additional three years.[17] After the expiration of the period for local income tax exemption provided above, Export Enterprises which export more than 70% of their products are entitled to enjoy continued local income tax exemptions.[18] Obviously, the effect of these provisions is to reduce or eliminate the local tax expenditure of these two kinds of enterprises. These reductions in and exemptions from local enterprise income tax are similar to those set forth in the Provisions of the State Council. Nevertheless, these local preferential tax terms are more liberal than those provided by the central government.

The priority of Export Enterprises and Technologically Advanced Enterprises to the supply of water, electricity, gas, transportation services and communications facilities is also confirmed by the local statute.[19] These enterprises are exempted from land use fees for three years after their establishment. Beginning from the fourth year, they are entitled to a

16 *Id*, Article 4.
17 Provisions of the Shanghai Municipality for the Encouragement of Foreign Investment promulgated on 1 November 1986, Article 2.
18 *Id*, Article 3.
19 *Id*, Article 7

50% reduction in such fees as are prescribed in the relevant regulations. In any event, such enterprises must not be charged with land use fees higher than RMB2.5 per sq m per year.[20]

Although Export Enterprises and Technologically Advanced Enterprises are entitled to special treatment in some circumstances, they are encouraged and required to meet the conditions for such enterprises. According to an official from Shanghai municipality, in determining whether a foreign-investment enterprise qualifies as an Export Enterprise, the Shanghai government essentially relies on the annual export report and export record issued by the Customs for the enterprise. The qualifying standard for Technologically Advanced Enterprises is set up in accordance with the development level of the technology concerned and will be adjusted from time to time.[21] Thus, an Export Enterprise or a Technologically Advanced Enterprise may lose its status and will not be entitled to preferential treatment if the level of its exports is reduced or the technology in question is out of date. This provision is apparently designed to provide foreign investors with both incentives and punishments in order to attract foreign capital to the export-oriented and technology-intensive sectors.

Except for the special provisions relating to Export Enterprises and Technologically Advanced Enterprises, the Provisions of the Shanghai Municipality for the Encouragement of Foreign Investment authorize foreign-investment enterprises to employ and recruit technical personnel, managerial personnel and workers, within the area under Shanghai's jurisdiction, through methods of public recruitment such as advertising in newspapers.[22] Under the guidelines of the Labour and Personnel Department of Shanghai, enterprises with foreign participation are permitted to employ staff and workers from other provinces and cities, provided that such employees return to their original abodes once they complete their employment or are dismissed by their employer.[23] These measures reflect Shanghai's liberal attitude towards the employment issues of foreign-investment enterprises.

As for the housing allowances of employees, enterprises with foreign participation operating in Shanghai are exempted from paying such subsidies to the government. They are, however, required to retain the money to improve the housing conditions of their Chinese staff and workers.[24] This provision is very important taking into consideration the serious housing problems in Shanghai. Since these enterprises are allowed to use the money directly for the benefit of their employees, higher labour efficiency can be expected in return. These enterprises may

20 *Id*, Article 4.
21 *Wen Wei Po*, 27 October 1986, p. BN9.
22 Provisions of the Shanghai Municipality for the Encouragement of Foreign Investment, Article 6.
23 *Id*.
24 *Id*, Article 5.

also be able to hire more qualified individuals who cannot have their housing problems resolved elsewhere. In order to facilitate the supply of raw materials for enterprises with foreign participation, the Shanghai statute provides for the establishment of an agency to supply materials.[25]

This local legislation also authorizes the setting up of a municipal level foreign-investment office to provide administrative services to foreign investors.[26] The functions of this office, which started operations on 1 January 1987, are as follows:

> Providing timely and clear feedback to foreign investors on the basis of the municipal government's investment strategy and programme for the utilization of foreign investment;
>
> Assisting foreign investors to find the right Chinese partners as well as consultants, agents and notaries public (institutions) provided their investment projects are acceptable;
>
> Providing foreign investors with information concerning the investment environment, preferential terms, laws and regulations in Shanghai and answering any question on such matters from foreign investors;
>
> Acting on behalf of foreign investors in going through the necessary formalities in the examination and approval process of investment projects; and
>
> Handling correspondence with foreign investors, and meeting with them.[27]

The office is headed by a vice mayor of Shanghai. Other members include principal officials from several key departments in charge of foreign investment in the city. With such a consolidated office, a number of foreign-investment issues can be decided within the office rather than by various departments under the city government. The enforcement of such decisions is less problematic, for the representatives from the departments concerned participate in decision-making and are aware of the situations in their own departments.

Significance of local reforms

Foreign investment in Shanghai is also assisted by local reforms, in particular, the restructuring of the financial system, which has rebuilt a sense of market values and competitiveness in the public. This in turn has enhanced the sense of responsibility of employees in foreign-investment enterprises. Shanghai was a financial centre in the Far East in the 1920's, and it has carried out various financial reforms since 1985. Both a money market and a capital market took shape in 1986. The money market or currency market (also called 'short-term fund market' in China) thus far covers inter-bank lending, bill discounting (including transferrable discount and rediscount), and short-term bill circulation.

Shanghai's inter-bank lending started in the second quarter of 1986,

25 *Id*, Article 11.
26 *Id*, Article 9.
27 *China Economic News*, 19 January 1987, p. 7

involving all the city's specialized banks and most non-banking financial institutions. In fact, the local inter-bank lending operations are not confined to the city of Shanghai alone. They have spread to the neighbouring cities and provinces that make up the Shanghai Economic Zone and then northward to Beijing and Tianjin. In August 1986, a short-term fund market was formally established in Shanghai and in the following six weeks inter-bank loans transacted were valued at RMB960 m, and this amount had reached more than RMB3 b by the end of November 1986.[28]

Meanwhile, the Shanghai Industrial and Commercial Bank resumed the business of bill discounting in April 1986. Other specialized banks and credit cooperatives also followed suit. By the end of 1986, the total volume of discount transactions was over RMB1 b, including RMB130 m in inter-departmental discounts and RMB6 m in transferrable discounts.[29] The key player in the revival of the short-term bills market in Shanghai is the Bank of Communications. It had issued transferrable deposit certificates totalling about RMB30 m by the end of 1986.

The re-establishment of financial markets in Shanghai has greatly reduced the pressure on financial institutions. Previously, financial institutions could only use funds allocated by the central government. As a result, some of the institutions had surpluses which they could not invest, while others were inconvenienced by a lack of funds. Under the current system, financial institutions and banks can obtain loans from each other and lend to each other. With this flexibility in the supply of money to domestic institutions, foreign investors will face less pressure when negotiating commercial transactions and in operating existing ventures with their Chinese partners. This situation will enable financial institutions to provide facilities to Sino-foreign ventures and enable wholly foreign-owned enterprises to cover their Renminbi expenditures. Most importantly, the market element (interest differential) of funds will equip managers of Chinese enterprises with the standard of expertise and knowledge which most foreign investors are used to.

Another phenomenon of the financial reforms in Shanghai is the emergence of capital and stock markets. In 1986, the Shanghai Industrial and Commercial Bank and the Shanghai Construction Bank, for the first time since 1949, raised money by issuing transferrable bonds to finance manufacturing projects. At present, a number of State-owned and collectively-owned enterprises are trying out the issue of stocks and shares. The emergence of a primary securities market has laid a foundation for the circulation of securities. The Shanghai Trust and Investment Co, a subsidiary of the Shanghai Industrial and Commercial Bank, now acts as a mini-stock exchange. By the end of 1986, more than

28 *China Economic News*, 9 February 1987, p. 2
29 *Id*, p.3.

6,000 shares had been transacted.[30] The price of shares is decided each day in accordance with market movements. Nevertheless, the stock market in Shanghai is still at an underdeveloped stage and its development into a full-fledged market will take some time. The significance of this progress, however, is that it will create a more favourable climate for foreign investment in the locality and that it has paved the way for enterprises with foreign participation to issue stocks in future.

II. Fuzhou's foreign-investment regulations

Under the current system, China is subdivided into provinces and municipalities under the direct jurisdiction of the central government. Within each province there are cities and they come under the direct jurisdiction of the province. Each city government is responsible not only for urban areas but also for rural areas surrounding the city. Almost all the 14 open coastal cities and ports have established economic and technical development zones (the 'ETDZ') and have identified old urban areas as priority locations for foreign investment. To a very large extent, foreign investors in old urban areas enjoy privileges and terms which are similar to those provided in the ETDZ. It is therefore fair to say that in each open coastal city there is a three-tier legal system for the implementation of the State Council Provisions ie provincial law, city legislation and statutes specifically governing the ETDZ. This section will examine provisions adopted by Fujian Province and Fuzhou city (the capital of Fujian Province) for the encouragement of foreign investment and the implementation of the State Council Provisions.

Over the last few years, Fujian Province has emerged as one of the forerunners in establishing economic cooperation with foreign enterprises. By the end of 1986, Fujian Province had concluded 990 projects with foreign enterprises, amounting to a total foreign investment of US$980 million, of which US$510 million has been actually invested.[31] Currently, Fujian Province is the fourth largest host for foreign investment, following Guangdong Province, Shanghai City and Beijing City. The regime for foreign investment established by Fujian Province and Fuzhou City can therefore illustrate the operation of the three-tier system applicable to other coastal cities and ports.

Administration of the ETDZ

Following Fuzhou's designation by the State Council as one of the 14 open coastal cities, the Fuzhou ETDZ was officially established in January 1985. Adjacent to Mawei Port, the zone is located in Qingzhou

30 *China Economic News*, 9 February 1987, p. 3.
31 *Wen Wei Po*, 6 April 1987, p.3.

of Mawei, on the north bank of the lower reaches of Min River and 23 km from the city of Fuzhou. Covering an area of 4.4 sq km, the ETDZ is further subdivided into two districts: Qingzhou district which covers an area of 2.7 sq km and Luoxing district which has an area of 1.7 sq km. After extensive development of the infrastructure over two years, the Fujian Provincial People's Congress enacted laws governing the development of the Fuzhou ETDZ at the end of 1986.

Under the Provisions of Fuzhou Economic and Technological Development Zone,[32] the establishment of the Fuzhou ETDZ is for the introduction of advanced technology and scientific management skills and for the establishment of industrial enterprises that are technology- or knowledge-intensive, manufacturing-specific, and/or export-oriented. Foreign individuals and enterprises are encouraged to invest in the ETDZ by setting up export-oriented and/or technologically-advanced manufacturing enterprises and scientific research institutes.[33] The forms of foreign investment include Sino-foreign joint equity ventures, non-equity cooperation ventures, wholly foreign-owned enterprises or other arrangements permitted under Chinese law.[34] Clearly, the specific purposes of the designated zone are for the development of technology, expansion of export trade and raising of the level of general scientific research in the city. Chinese institutions and foreign counterparts are encouraged to conclude various arrangements for scientific research and development.[35]

The governing body of the ETDZ is the Fuzhou ETDZ Administrative Commission which has been set up by and represents the Fuzhou Municipal People's Government.[36] Major functions and powers of the Administrative Commission include the following:

(1) To draw up the development programme and annual plans of the ETDZ;
(2) To formulate provisions for the administration of the ETDZ;
(3) To undertake overall planning of the investment projects in the ETDZ, and to examine and approve them in accordance with the relevant provisions;
(4) To undertake the management, approval and allocation of land in the ETDZ;
(5) To manage the infrastructural facilities in the ETDZ and to determine the level of fees to be charged for their use;
(6) To manage and supervise the enterprises and institutes in the ETDZ;
(7) To manage the revenue and expenditure accounts of the ETDZ;
(8) To inspect and supervise the activities of the subordinate establishments of the municipality in the ETDZ;
(9) To coordinate the activities of the establishments in the ETDZ that are not subordinates of the municipality;

32 The Provisions of Fuzhou Economic and Technical Development Zone were adopted at the 22nd Session of the 6th Standing Committee of Fujian Provincial People's Congress on 12 December 1986 (the 'Fuzhou ETDZ Provisions').
33 *Id*, Articles 4 and 5.
34 *Id*, Article 5.
35 *Id*, Article 6.
36 *Id*, Article 3.

(10) To supervise the management of labour in the enterprises in the ETDZ so as to protect the lawful rights and interests of the workers and staff;
(11) To administer the provisions on environmental protection and prevent pollution in the ETDZ;
(12) To develop non-profit undertakings of public interests in the ETDZ;
(13) To manage the import and export trade of the ETDZ;
(14) To handle ordinary foreign economic affairs of the ETDZ;
(15) To provide consulting services and other services to foreign investors;
(16) To exercise other functions and powers authorized by the Fuzhou Municipal People's Government.[37]

Except for the general administrative functions mentioned above, all other affairs concerning foreign investment, such as taxation, finance, foreign exchange, industrial and commercial administration, customs, commodity inspection and environmental protection, are under the responsibility of and supervised by the various departments in charge and their subordinate offices.[38]

Provincial and city provisions

Various pieces of Fujian Province and Fuzhou City legislation concerning foreign investment have established a very comprehensive legal framework with heavy reliance on preferential tax terms as an incentive for the absorption of foreign investment. Under Fujian's Supplementary Rules for the Encouragement of Foreign Investment,[39] co-managed productive enterprises involving foreign investment and wholly foreign-owned enterprises set up in impoverished areas for a period of more than ten years are exempted from income tax in the first two years beginning from the first profit-making year, and are entitled to a 50% reduction in income tax in the following three years. In addition, dividends, interest, rental income, royalties and other incomes earned by foreign investors are entitled to a 50% reduction on the prevailing 20% withholding tax rate except for those incomes that have already been exempted from income tax based on the existing regulations.[40] This provision is similar to the early Chinese policy on attracting foreign investment. The emphasis on the development of remote areas clearly reflects the current economic situation, namely, that the province has a vast and generally underdeveloped countryside. Thus, the need to raise the level of development in the rural areas is a very urgent one.

Regulations adopted by the Fuzhou municipality further stipulate that foreign-investment enterprises which engage in manufacturing in the old

37 *Id*, Article 10.
38 *Id*, Article 12.
39 The main contents of the supplementary provisions of Fujian Province which implemented the State Council Provisions were published in *China Economic News*, 17 November 1986, p. 2–3.
40 *Id*.

urban areas of Fuzhou City are taxed at a 50% rate if they are technology- or knowledge-intensive projects or projects with foreign investment exceeding US$30 m or with a long recovery period of investment, or if they are projects to develop energy, communications or ports.[41] Foreign-investment enterprises which engage in the machine building and electronics industries, metallurgical, chemicals and building materials industries, light industrial, textile and packaging industries, medical apparatus industry, agriculture, forestry, animal husbandry, processing of agricultural products industry and building industry are granted a 20% tax reduction, if they do not qualify as technology- or knowledge-intensive projects or do not bring in a large amount of investment.[42]

The Measures of Fuzhou Municipality are particularly in favour of Sino-foreign equity joint ventures. Such enterprises are granted a tax exemption for the first and second years beginning from the first profit-making year, and are allowed a 50% tax reduction in the third to the fifth years, if they are scheduled to operate for a period of ten years or more. Further tax reductions are allowed if these enterprises engage in agriculture, forestry or other low profit-making industries. On the other hand, Sino-foreign contractual ventures and wholly foreign-owned enterprises are not given any tax breaks even if they plan to operate for a long period, although they are encouraged, with tax reductions, to invest in low-profit sectors.[43]

The emphasis on the development of agriculture and forestry etc is in conformity with the Supplementary Rules of Fujian Province which stipulate that, in addition to projects involving advanced technology and which are export-oriented, foreign investors are welcome to invest in such domestic projects as industrial and agricultural development, energy, transportation, port construction and other infrastructure construction projects.[44] These provisions apparently are designed to improve the generally backward economy of the province as a whole and the poor infrastructure for foreign investment in particular. They are in contrast to the newly-adopted provisions of other cities and provinces which attach great importance to export-oriented projects and the transfer of advanced technology.

The Measures of Fuzhou Municipality offer investors from Hong Kong, Macau and Taiwan and other overseas Chinese investors special preferential tax terms.[45] This has been the practice of China for several years. Foreign investors from other areas and countries are very critical of this differential treatment. The most recent legislation enacted by

41 The Preferential Measures of Fuzhou Municipality on Enterprises with Foreign Investment enacted at the 22nd Session of the 6th Standing Committee of Fujian Provincial People's Congress on 12 December 1986 (the 'Measures of Fuzhou Municipality'), Article A(1).
42 *Id.*
43 *Id*, Article A(2–4).
44 *China Economic News*, 17 November 1986, p.2.
45 Article A(5) of the Measures of Fuzhou Municipality.

other provinces and cities generally tend to give overseas investors equal treatment based on the nature of the project and technology involved.

The preferential tax treatment for Export Enterprises and Technologically Advanced Enterprises provided for by the State Council Provisions is restated in the Measures of Fuzhou Municipality. At the same time the Measures of Fuzhou Municipality further provide that losses incurred by enterprises in a tax year may be carried forward to subsequent (but no more than five) years.[46] This provision may provide additional assistance to enterprises which do not operate successfully in the initial years and encourage them to perform better in subsequent years.

Although all kinds of foreign investment are encouraged in Fujian Province as a whole, in the Fuzhou ETDZ, only foreign investments in manufacturing industries are given preferential tax treatment. The income tax rate for such enterprises is set at 15%. At the same time, enterprises whose value of export products in a year accounts for 70% or more of the total value of product manufactured in the same year are taxed at a 10% rate.[47] Foreign-investment enterprises which are scheduled to operate for a period of ten years or more or which possess advanced technology are also entitled to certain tax reductions and exemptions.[48] Foreign-investment enterprises in the manufacturing sector are exempted from local taxes and remittance tax.

In order to reduce the operating costs of foreign-investment enterprises, the Supplementary Rules of Fujian Province stipulate that raw materials and parts which are needed by Sino-foreign ventures are to be supplied by the various materials supply departments under the same conditions as those which apply to State-owned enterprises, provided that such materials or parts have been approved to be listed in the construction plans of such Sino-foreign ventures. Required materials which are not listed in the plans may be purchased by the enterprises themselves.[49] Foreign investors need only pay fees and charges which have been approved and promulgated by the Fujian Foreign Investment Administration.[50] This measure represents a full implementation of the State Council Provisions which invest foreign investors with the right to reject unreasonable charges.[51]

For the purpose of balancing foreign exchange, foreign-investment enterprises in Fuzhou City are allowed to sell their products to the SEZs, ETDZs or other foreign-investment enterprises. Such transactions may

46 *Id*, Article A(10).

47 See Preferential Measures of Fuzhou Economic and Technical Development Zone on Enterprises with Foreign Investment enacted at the 22nd Session of the 6th Standing Committee of Fujian Provincial People's Congress on 12 December 1986 (hereinafter referred to as the 'Measures of Fuzhou ETDZ'), Article I(1).

48 *Id*, Article I(2).

49 *China Economic News*, 17 November 1986, p. 2.

50 *Id*.

51 State Council Provisions, Article 16.

be settled in foreign currencies.[52] Products sold to regions or enterprises other than those mentioned above, with the approval of the exchange control authorities, may also be settled in foreign currencies.[53] Foreign investors are also permitted to reinvest their Renminbi profits in other enterprises, which are able to generate foreign exchange earnings, for the purpose of covering their original foreign exchange deficiencies.[54]

Foreign-investment enterprises in the Fuzhou ETDZ are permitted to sell a certain amount of their products in the domestic market, provided that such enterprises are confirmed to possess advanced techniques, or advanced production technology and equipment.[55] The prices of such products are to be determined independently by the board of directors of each enterprise, and governmental authorities are prohibited from interfering with such decisions.[56] Nevertheless, this provision does not apply to products whose prices are determined by the central government under the unified price system. The policy in respect of domestic selling by foreign-investment enterprises is in fact universally applicable in Fujian Province under the Supplementary Rules for the Encouragement of Foreign Investment.[57]

Another provision which is exclusively applicable to foreign investors in the Fuzhou ETDZ is that overseas Chinese and investors from Hong Kong, Macau and Taiwan are permitted to employ their relatives living in the countryside to work in enterprises and institutions established by such investors in the ETDZ.[58] Such relatives are permitted to transfer their permanent residence from the countryside to the ETDZ.[59] This method of encouraging overseas investment has proved to be effective in Guangzhou and other cities in Guangdong Province. Its adoption by Fuzhou City is therefore not surprising, taking into consideration the large number of overseas Chinese from Hong Kong, Macau, Taiwan and other countries and areas, who have their ancestral origins in Fujian province.

Taking the provisions of Fujian Province and Fuzhou City as a whole, the legal framework represents an even-handed policy for the absorption of foreign investment. For instance, Fujian not only encourages export-oriented and technologically-advanced investments, but also places great emphasis on the development of agriculture, animal husbandry, energy, communications and other industries. The legislation to implement the above is more comprehensive than that adopted by other provinces and cities. At the same time, there are still some grey areas which need further clarification. The most obvious example is the term 'direct foreign

52 Measures of Fuzhou Municipality, Article III(C).
53 *Id.*
54 *Id*, Article III(D).
55 Measures of Fuzhou ETDZ, Article IV.
56 *Id.*
57 *China Economic News*, 17 November 1986, p. 2.
58 Fuzhou ETDZ Provisions, Article 24.
59 *Id.*

investment enterprise'. All the three pieces of legislation governing the operation of the Fuzhou ETDZ and foreign investment in Fuzhou City fail to define the term, although the concepts of Sino-foreign equity joint ventures, Sino-foreign contractual ventures and wholly foreign-owned enterprises have all been introduced into the statutes and differential treatment has been provided in that regard. In addition, the effectiveness of heavy reliance on tax reduction and exemption as the main incentive to foreign investors, and the feasibility and appropriateness of the differential treatment granted to foreign investors and investors from Hong Kong, Macau and Taiwan as well as other overseas Chinese, are also quite doubtful.

III. Provisions of Beijing, Dalian and Guangzhou

Beijing, Dalian and Guangzhou are forerunners in attracting foreign investment. Right after the State Council promulgated its Provisions, each of these three cities enacted its own implementing regulations, but with different features.

Measures adopted by Beijing

The provisions enacted by the Beijing Municipality closely resemble the State Council Provisions, with particular emphasis on increasing administrative efficiency.[60] In order to simplify the procedure for examining and approving projects, the Planning Commission of Beijing Municipality has been designated as the sole organ responsible for reviewing and confirming foreign-investment projects and for coordinating the work of various departments within the Municipality regarding foreign-investment matters.[61] In addition, projects with a total investment of less than US$1 m are to be handled by the relevant district or county level governments or bureaus under the Municipality.[62] Every department of the city government is required to make a decision within one month on any application or request concerning foreign investment.[63]

The Beijing Stipulations provide for the establishment of a new company to supply materials and equipment needed by foreign-investment enterprises at the same prices levels applicable to State-owned enterprises. The company also acts as agent for foreign-investment

60 The government of Beijing Municipality issued its supplementary rules entitled 'Stipulations for Improving the Investment Environment and Encouraging Foreign Investment' in Beijing on 12 October 1986 (the 'Beijing Stipulations').
61 Beijing Stipulations, Article 1.
62 *Id.*
63 *Id*, Article 2

enterprises in importing equipment, raw materials, parts and fittings.[64]

As regards the balancing of foreign exchange, foreign-investment enterprises which produce import-substitutes are permitted to sell their products domestically for foreign exchange upon approval of the State Administration of Exchange Control, Beijing Branch.[65] Although these enterprises can sell their products for foreign exchange, when purchasing goods, raw materials, labour or services from Chinese institutions, they will not be required to pay in hard currencies.[66] This double-benefit provision has given foreign investors substantial flexibility in domestic selling and procurement. Together with other measures, it will gradually help to resolve the foreign exchange difficulties of foreign investors.

The Beijing Stipulations have adopted standards in connection with land use fees and tax exemptions and reductions which are similar to those provided for in the State Council Provisions. Nevertheless, the Beijing Tax Department and Beijing Municipal Real Estate Administration are authorized to grant further reductions in land use fees and taxation respectively, upon the recommendation of the Beijing Municipal Foreign Economic Relations and Trade Commission.[67]

This concise statute enacted by the Beijing Municipality has been received warmly by foreign investors. It has substantially reduced the operating costs of foreign-investment enterprises and has increased the efficiency of the administrative bodies. According to the president of Beijing Jeep Corporation, appointed by the American partner to the joint venture, these measures announced by the Beijing government would substantially cut the joint venture's land use and water fees, extend the preferential tax terms for three years and the period in which the joint venture would be entitled to a 50% reduction in income tax and the foreign partner would be exempted from tax on the remittance of profits.[68] In addition, in the second part of 1986, the Foreign Exchange Bureau of Beijing Municipality assisted the joint venture in concluding an agreement with Sheraton Great Wall Hotel to exchange Renminbi for US dollars amounting to US$2.5 m.[69]

Dalian

Dalian is a latecomer in attracting foreign investment. After being designated as an open coastal city in late 1984, Dalian established its own ETDZ covering an area of 20 sq km for the purpose of attracting foreign

64 *Id*, Article 6
65 *Id*, Article 4
66 *Id.*
67 *Id*, Articles 7 and 8.
68 *The Asian Wall Street Journal*, 21–22 November 1986, p. 3. For the effect of the State Council Provisions on labour cost reductions for the Beijing jeep joint venture, see Chapter 3, p. 52.
69 *The Asian Wall Street Journal*, 21–22 November 1986, p. 3.

investment. In the following two years, however, only five companies were established in the zone, two of which were joint ventures.[70] The slow entry of foreign investment was attributed to the poor infrastructure of the city and other common problems facing foreign investors in China, despite the fact that the city had spent RMB250 m on developing the basic facilities of the ETDZ. Having realized the problems that foreign investors were faced with, the city government came up with several measures which were later confirmed and ratified in the State Council Provisions. These were as follows.

First, a foreign-investment office headed by a vice mayor of the city was established in late 1986 to handle matters concerning foreign companies.

Secondly, as early as August 1986, Dalian announced reductions in labour and land costs for foreign investors and decided to give overseas companies greater authority in managing joint ventures and hiring and dismissing employees.

Thirdly, foreign partners of a joint venture or a contractual venture with a great deal of Chinese currency and little foreign exchange were permitted to buy Chinese products for their parent companies outside China. Thereafter, these foreign investors were allowed to swap surplus Renminbi for hard currency, because the parent companies' purchase of Chinese goods contributed foreign exchange to China. Foreign investors were also allowed to act as distributors for the overseas sales of products from other Chinese entities. Such foreign investors could then trade their extra Renminbi for hard currency proceeds from such sales.

Fourthly, Dalian City allowed foreign investors to sell their products domestically for hard currency if such products could not be made by Chinese enterprises or were imported by China. All the above measures have proved to be effective means of resolving foreign-investment issues and have been adopted by the State Council and a number of provinces and cities.

After the State Council issued its Provisions, Dalian also enacted its own regulations. In summary, these regulations are aimed at reducing the investment costs of foreign investors and encouraging export-oriented and technologically-advanced foreign-investment projects. Foreign-investment enterprises are universally exempted from the local surtax for seven years starting from their first profit-making year. Enterprises with an operational period of more than ten years and which have been determined by the municipal government as technologically advanced, are entitled to enjoy a 50% reduction in enterprise income tax for another three years.[71] Foreign investors who reinvest the profits distributed to them by their enterprises, which are export-oriented or technologically-advanced enterprises, with operational periods of three to five years, are

70 *The Asian Wall Street Journal*, 18 September 1986, p. 1.
71 *China Economic New*, 29 December 1986, p. 4 and 5.

to be refunded 40% of the total amount of enterprise income tax already paid on the reinvested portion.

For the better operation of foreign-investment enterprises, the provisions enacted by Dalian City stipulate that water, electricity, gas, fuel, transportation and communications facilities for the production and operation of such enterprises must be charged at the same levels as for State-owned enterprises. Enterprises which have shown good economic results in the past will qualify for preferential treatment in loan applications. Loan application procedures have since been simplified. Special funds are allocated for enterprises whose working capitals have dropped below the 30% level, provided that these enterprises have drawn up contingency plans to boost their working capital and have set out explicit measures to carry out these plans.[72]

Technologically Advanced Enterprises and Export Enterprises, as defined in the Provisions, are entitled to even better treatment. For instance, they are required to allocate RMB25 per month for each Chinese member of staff or worker as a housing allowance, which will be kept by the enterprises for improving the housing conditions of their employees, instead of being turned over to the State, which was the practice in China previously. In contrast, enterprises that do not belong to the above two categories must pay the labour subsidy allowance at a rate of RMB50 per month. They can keep only 30% to 40% of such funds for improving the housing conditions of their employees.[73]

Technologically Advanced Enterprises and Export Enterprises are required to pay their annual land use fees only if they do not need to increase their supply of water, electricity, gas or to construct transportation and communications facilities. The annual rate of the maximum land use fee is set at RMB3 per sq m. Technologically Advanced Enterprises which export more than 70% of their products each year are exempted from land use fees for a period of three to five years.[74]

The regulations adopted by Dalian are quite clear-cut in nature and give foreign investors specific directions as to where the money should be put. These precise and specific provisions will make their implementation by local administrative organs much easier.

Guangzhou – the key player

Located in the southernmost part of China, adjacent to Hong Kong and Macau, Guangdong Province has made considerable progress in attracting foreign investment. In the period of China's 6th Five-year Plan (1980–1985), the province signed 57,900 contracts with overseas companies from more than 20 countries and regions, utilized US$4.26

72 *Id*, p. 5.
73 *Id.*
74 *Id.*

billion in foreign funds, 70% of which was direct foreign investment, and set up over 4,000 foreign-funded enterprises, 60% of the total number in the country.[75] Fifty percent of the enterprises are industrial projects which have introduced over 700 production lines, worth US$1.22 b.[76] The influx of a large amount of foreign funds to Guangdong Province resulted not only from its geographical location but also from the liberal policy adopted by the provincial government.

As the capital of Guangdong Province, Guangzhou's foreign-investment laws are better defined and are more mature than those of other provinces and cities. As the leader in establishing foreign economic cooperation, Guangzhou's Measures for the Implementation of the State Council Provisions adopted on 30 October 1986 have some special features.

The essential feature of Guangzhou's Measures is that enterprises with foreign participation and State-owned enterprises are placed on a similar footing. Labour insurance funds and welfare funds set aside by foreign-investment enterprises for their Chinese workers and staff should follow the same standards set for State-owned enterprises, namely, where the current rate does not exceed 28% of the total wage and salary package.[77] In addition, the level and form of wages and the system of rewards and subsidies for employees in foreign-investment enterprises are subjects for exclusive determination by the board of directors of the enterprises. No report to or approval of local authorities is necessary.[78] Foreign-investment enterprises also enjoy freedom in deciding on the housing needs of their workers and staff. They are required to have these items specifically stipulated in their employment contracts with their employees and to set aside a certain percentage of the employees' total wage or salary for such purposes.[79] Thus, enterprises with foreign participation may operate entirely on their own as far as labour management is concerned. This measure will give foreign investors, especially those who enter the China market for the first time, much comfort, for they can manage their enterprises in a way which is familiar to them.

Foreign-investment enterprises in Guangzhou are not only permitted to borrow Renminbi loans from banks but are also allowed to issue stocks and bonds in China for the purpose of raising capital for production or construction.[80] Such fund-raising is not confined to equity joint ventures or manufacturing enterprises. All kinds of Sino-foreign cooperative arrangements in whatever economic sector may issue stocks or bonds.

75 *China Daily*, 8 April 1987, Supplement p. 1.
76 *Id.*
77 Measures for the Implementation of the Provisions of the State Council adopted by Guangzhou Municipality on 30 October 1986, Article 5.
78 *Id.*
79 *Id.*
80 *Id*, Article 14.

The laws of Guangzhou also provide preferential terms for Export Enterprises and Technologically Advanced Enterprises. Such enterprises are exempted from the urban construction fee, while other foreign-investment enterprises are required to pay the fee at 5% of the total construction expenditure.[81] In addition, land use fees for the two types of enterprises must not exceed RMB2.5 per sq m per year, unless they are located in the busy districts of the city.[82] Although foreign-investment enterprises and State-owned enterprises enjoy equal treatment regarding loans for working capital, Export Enterprises and Technologically Advanced Enterprises are entitled to be granted priority by Chinese financial institutions as regards short-term facilities to meet their cash-flow needs in production and distribution.[83] This principle equally applies to the extension of other credits by banks.

As regards administrative efficiency, local government authorities in charge of foreign investment are required to complete their examination and approval of documents for the establishment of foreign-investment enterprises within two months from the date of receipt of application materials.[84]

In short, the regulations enacted by Guangzhou are encouraging. The equal treatment granted to foreign-investment enterprises and State-owned companies is most inspiring and should be welcomed by foreign investors. The authorization of foreign-investment enterprises to issue shares and other securities is also practical and encouraging. It will meet the local currency needs of enterprises and help in domestic financial reforms.

IV. Rules enacted by Yunnan and Guizhou

The provinces of Yunnan and Guizhou share many things in common. In addition to a common border, both are without any coastal lines, and are economically backward and interested in attracting foreign investment despite their poor infrastructure. An examination of measures adopted by such provinces in attracting foreign investment is therefore necessary for a deeper understanding of China's open policy.

Incentives enacted by Yunnan

Although Yunnan Province is a remote province which is far away from international ports and coastal cities, it had signed 50 cooperative agreements, worth a total of US$100 m, with foreign businesses by the end of May 1987.[85] Of these foreign-investment projects, 23 are joint

81 *Id*, Article 17.
82 *Id.*
83 *Id*, Article 18.
84 *Id*, Article 21.
85 *South China Morning Post*, 29 May 1987, p. BN1.

ventures and cooperative ventures in various fields such as textiles, electronics and hotels. In implementing the State Council Provisions, the Yunnan provincial government issued 12 preferential terms as supplements. As with the State Council Provisions, the regulations adopted by Yunnan Province give Export Enterprises and Technologically Advanced Enterprises preferential treatment. Except for those located in the business hubs, such enterprises which have their development fees charged in a lump sum are granted a five-year exemption on the site use fee beginning from the first day of their business. Thereafter, they will pay a site use fee at a rate not exceeding RMB1.5 per sq m per year.[86] This provision is equally applicable to enterprises that have developed the site themselves.

Such Export Enterprises and Technologically Advanced Enterprises are also exempted from payment to the State of subsidies to Chinese employees.[87] Other foreign-investment enterprises which are not under these two categories must pay to the relevant financial department the allowance to Chinese employees for consumption of grain and edible oil, non-staple food items and fuel. The payment will be charged at a rate of RMB20 per employee per month and no other subsidy is allowed.[88]

All foreign-investment enterprises are exempted from local income tax for the period in which exemption from national enterprise income tax may be granted by the State. Export Enterprises and Technologically Advanced Enterprises are given exemptions from local income tax for an additional period of five years after the expiration of the above-mentioned tax holidays.[89] Enterprises which export more than 70% of their total output value are granted further tax breaks.[90]

As regards administrative efficiency and interference with foreign-investment enterprises, the Yunnan regulations stipulate that except for those departments authorized by the State, no institution or individual in China has the right to intervene in the operations of foreign-investment enterprises. Local authorities in charge of reviewing foreign-investment projects are required to complete their decision-making process in connection with project proposals and feasibility study reports within 40 days of receipt of such application documents if the projects in question are within thc approval limit of the province. The time limit for the examination and approval of the agreement, contract and articles of association is 20 days, while a period of 10 days is provided for the issuance of approval certificates for foreign-investment enterprises.[91] Local authorities are also required to provide prompt assistance to foreign

86 Provisions of Yunnan Province of the People's Republic of China for the Encouragement of Foreign Investment promulgated on 30 December 1986, Article 2.
87 *Id*, Article 3.
88 *Id*.
89 *Id*, Article 4.
90 *Id*.
91 *Id*, Article 8.

investors in resolving problems concerning either the application formalities or the operation of such enterprises.

Obviously, the Yunnan regulations offer more investment cost reductions than those provided by most coastal and open cities and provinces. Both the land use fee and labour expense levels are much lower. The statutory prohibition on interference by local authorities in the operations of foreign-investment enterprises may serve as a guarantee of the success of such ventures.

Provisions adopted by Guizhou

The provisions adopted by Guizhou Province are similar to those of Yunnan Province. Export Enterprises and Technologically Advanced Enterprises pay a land use fee and development fee at a rate of RMB3 to RMB10 per sq m, while the rate set for other foreign-investment enterprises is RMB10 to RMB15 per sq m. Foreign investors who have invested in remote areas and have undertaken to develop the land may enjoy a five-year exemption from the land use fee. These enterprises may also pay their labour service fee at a rate lower than that charged in China's coastal areas.[92]

Foreign-investment enterprises which undertake orders to manufacture products which are not produced by Chinese enterprises and are imported by Guizhou Province, are allowed, in part or in whole, to settle their accounts with their domestic buyers in foreign exchange, provided approval of the Guizhou branch of the State Administration of Exchange Control is secured in advance. This means of easing the foreign exchange shortage of foreign investors is supplemented by the requirement that the relevant departments of Guizhou Province should consider providing assistance to enterprises which have good economic returns and possess potential to generate foreign exchange earnings, if they have temporary foreign exchange circulation problems.[93] The enforcement of this provision is feasible since Guizhou is a considerable exporter of domestic products while the number of foreign-investment projects in the province is relatively small. By May 1987, Guizhou Province had approved 19 Sino-foreign ventures, several of which were export-oriented companies.[94]

The subsidy to be paid by foreign-investment enterprises to their Chinese staff and workers is set at RMB40 per month per person. However, this universal rule does not apply to Export or Technologically Advanced Enterprises which are exempted totally from paying any subsidies. Foreign-investment enterprises are also authorized by the Provisions of Guizhou Province not to pay any unreasonable charges.[95]

92 *China Economic News*, 24 November 1986, p. 5.
93 *Id.*
94 *Wen Wei Po*, 16 May 1987, p. BN24.
95 *Id.*

Conclusion

In conclusion, the supplementary provisions which have been adopted by various provinces and cities reflect the respective local conditions and are in general more relaxed than those provided for in the State Council Provisions. Most of the provincial and city level legislation offer greater reductions for foreign investors in land use costs and labour expenditure. Another common feature of local legislation is the encouragement of export-oriented and hi-tech foreign-investment projects. As regards administrative efficiency, provincial and city laws have set different standards. In some provinces, the approval process can be one to two months, while other provinces such as Yunnan have established more specific time limits for each level of decision-making. The general trend of provincial provisions (including statutes enacted by the central government) is to treat foreign-investment according to the standards applicable to State-owned enterprises. An obvious example is the fee to be charged for water, electricity and other operating facilities. This development, which is assisted by domestic economic reforms, will improve the conditions under which foreign-investment enterprises operate.

Chapter five

The relaxed rules of the SEZs

The Special Economic Zones are fore-runners in the implementation of China's open policy and domestic reforms. Over the last few years, the SEZs have been playing an increasingly significant part in boosting foreign investment and expanding Sino-foreign economic cooperation. Any full evaluation of the SEZs would therefore have to include their impact on China's industrial and agricultural growth, employment, foreign investment and export earnings, and their importance as laboratories for the economic reforms currently taking place in China. Due to the scope of this study, however, this chapter will only survey briefly the economic development of the SEZs (with emphasis on the Shenzhen SEZ), the basic legal framework for foreign investment in the SEZs, and the newly-adopted measures for implementing the Provisions of the State Council.[1] Discussions on corporate legal matters and foreign banking will be conducted in the following two chapters, respectively.

I. Evolution of the SEZs

Establishment

There are currently four Special Economic Zones in China. They are Shenzhen, Zhuhai, Shantou and Xiamen, of which the first three are located in Guangdong Province and the other in Fujian Province. The term 'SEZ' instead of the more conventional designation 'export processing zone' was chosen to convey the broader functions of the SEZs which include not only such standard export processing zone goals as generating foreign exchange, creating employment, attracting foreign investment and facilitating technology transfer, but also serving as laboratories for local economic reforms.[2] Taking into consideration the functions of the SEZs, the Guangdong and Fujian Provinces were natural candidates for

1 For a general discussion of the evolution of the SEZs, see Y C Jao and C K Leung, ed, *China's Special Economic Zones — Policies, Problems and Prospects,* Hong Kong: Oxford University Press, 1986; for a discussion of the Shenzhen SEZ's history and management, see Li Ying, ed, *The Establishment and Business Management of Local Enterprises of The Shenzhen SEZ*, Beijing China: Machinery Industry Press, 1986

2 Xu Dixin, 'China's SEZs', *Beijing Review*, vol. 24, no. 12, 23 March 1984, pp. 14–22.

the establishment of the SEZs by virtue of their physical location, access to funds, expertise and markets, previous experience with foreign business and their close ties with overseas Chinese investors.

Shenzhen is 174 km from Guangzhou City and 32 km from Kowloon (in Hong Kong) which is bordered by the Pearl River. In 1979, when it was designated as an SEZ, Shenzhen was still a sleepy township of 23,000 in largely rural Baoan county and was economically underdeveloped and infrastucturally weak.[3] The Shenzhen SEZ covers an area of 327.5 sq km, stretching 78.4 km along the border of Hong Kong's New Territories, incorporating fully one-third of the area of the Shenzhen municipality. The current population of Shenzhen SEZ is 469,800.[4] To be sure, Shenzhen has, since its establishment, developed from a small rural fishing township into a medium-sized and relatively modern city.

Zhuhai is situated on the western bank of the mouth of the Pearl River and was far less well-developed when it was nominated as an SEZ. The initial size of the Zhuhai SEZ was 6.7 sq km which was subdivided into four separate areas with 45% of the land to be devoted to industrial enterprises. In June 1983, the State Council, in response to local requests, enlarged the size of the SEZ to 15.16 sq km, of which 10.8 were designated for industrial development. With a population of 20,000 and facing Hong Kong across the sea toward the east and bordering on Macau in the south, the Zhuhai SEZ has been developing successfully into an industrial city. Its industry has already become a predominant force with a total output value making up 72% of the city's total industrial and agricultural output value, as against only 39% in 1978.[5]

Unlike Shenzhen or Zhuhai, Shantou in 1980 was already a medium-sized city. With a modest old port area, Shantou had been involved in international trade for over 100 years and about 120 of its 352 factories and enterprises were engaged in production for export in 1983. In 1980, the State Council designated 1.6 sq km as the Shantou SEZ.[6] With such a moderate scheme, it was clear that Shantou would not be built into a comprehensive SEZ and its main goal was to develop a processing industry to support its agricultural industry. In November 1984, however, the State Council decided to expand the Shantou SEZ into a larger area covering 52.6 sq km. The enlarged zone is divided into two areas: Longhu and Guang'ao. Initially, the Longhu area, which covers 22.6 sq km, concentrated on light industry and processing projects, packing and preservation of food and vegetables, and poultry, eggs and aquatic products. However, at present the area has developed into a multi-purpose industrial district. The Guang'ao area, covering 30 sq km,

3 *Business China*, 29 September 1982, pp. 39–40.
4 China International Economic Consultants, Inc, *The China Investment Guide*, 3rd edn, Hong Kong: Longman Group Ltd, 1986, p. 93.
5 *People's Republic of China Yearbook 1986*, Beijing: Xinhua Publishing House, 1986, p. 459.
6 *Id*, p. 460.

concentrates mainly on developing the petrochemical industry and support services for offshore oil exploration and development.[7]

The Xiamen SEZ has undergone a development process similar to that of Shantou SEZ. The State Council of China first designated 2.5 sq km in the Huli area as a special zone in October 1980. Four years later, the SEZ was expanded to include the entire Xiamen Island (including Gulangyu Islet), covering an area of 131 sq km, and with a population of 349,165.[8] Xiamen was an old trading port, with a good natural harbour, rail links to the interior and a modest light industrial base consisting of 770 factories and an industrial workforce of 100,000. Its solid educational and technical foundation and its location in a productive agricultural region have provided strong support for an export-development effort as well as a market for the products of the enterprises in the SEZ.[9] Having developed at a fast pace, the Xiamen SEZ was able to achieve an industrial output value totalling RMB2.141 b in 1985, representing a 45% increase over that of the previous year. Its industrial output value in 1986 recorded a 10% increase over that of 1985.[10]

The development process of Shenzhen SEZ

Over the last eight years, all the SEZs in China have undergone several developmental changes which resulted from changes in domestic economic policies and increases in foreign investment in, and foreign trade with, China. By far, the Shenzhen SEZ is the most successful and fastest-growing among the four. Its success, particularly in converting the local economy from a domestic-market-oriented one to an export- and high-technology-oriented one, exemplifies the overall growth process of the SEZs in China.

In general, the Shenzhen SEZ has been through a four-stage development. In the first stage (1980 to the first quarter of 1982), plans for its economic development were drafted and the preparations for the capital construction of the city were undertaken. In the second period (from the second quarter of 1982 to the end of 1983), the Shenzhen SEZ concentrated on overall capital construction in accordance with a master plan which involved a method of developing one district after another. In the third period (1984), large amounts of foreign investment were made in the Shenzhen SEZ for the development of advanced industry and the expansion of economic cooperation with foreign countries as well as Chinese enterprises in other areas. As a result, many enterprises were established and they became the major force of the local economy. In the fourth period (from 1985 to the present) the Shenzhen SEZ has been

7 *Id.*
8 *Id*, p. 458.
9 *Beijing Review*, no. 50, 14 December 1981.
10 *Economic Reporter*, 7 March 1987, p. 29.

trying to build a strong local manufacturing industry and to reshape the local economy into an export-oriented one.[11]

In fact, all four SEZs face the question of how to convert the local economy from one which is domestic-market-oriented to one which is foreign-market-oriented. In the first five years since their establishment, the SEZs absorbed a considerable amount of foreign investment and established a number of Sino-foreign ventures and wholly foreign-owned enterprises. Unfortunately, and naturally, most of these enterprises were designed for the local and domestic markets. When the foreign exchange issue, which was partially attributable to the nature of foreign investment in China, emerged in late 1984, the central government began from 1985 to expand its role in relation to foreign investment with the purpose of attracting more foreign investment in the manufacturing sector as well as in export-oriented projects. This policy has had a direct impact on the development plans of the SEZs which are now encouraged to curb the rapid pace of capital construction and concentrate on developing manufacturing industries and exporting products manufactured in the SEZs.

Over the last seven years, the Shenzhen SEZ has carried out dramatic domestic economic reforms. First, the planned administrative system was modified, as regards management of the domestic economy, to take market elements into account. In accordance with the overall aims of the central government, the local government has attached great importance to the use of such economic indicators as price, taxation, interest rate etc, to coordinate activities in the various economic sectors, and has also reduced substantially the use of administrative measures.

Secondly, as a result of the policy of the State Council which permits banks in the SEZs to use their deposits to obtain domestic loans on flexible terms, the Shenzhen SEZ has made good use of bank credit. Loans for capital construction were allowed for the first time in history since 1949. At the same time, other financial methods such as the granting of mortgage loans, the issuance of stocks and bonds, the discounting of bills and the variation of interest rates were again permitted. These measures have not only increased the circulation of funds but have also contributed substantially to China's domestic financial reforms.

Thirdly, competition between different industries, different enterprises, including enterprises engaging in foreign trade which is tightly controlled by the Central Government, has been encouraged in the Shenzhen SEZ. The traditional rigid wholesale and retail system is no longer in existence. As for the price structure, there are currently government-fixed prices, government-controlled floating prices and producer- or seller-determined market prices.

Fourthly, all the staff and workers in Shenzhen enterprises are employed under employment contracts and are not guaranteed permanent employment. This policy has substantially increased the efficiency of the

11 *Wen Wei Po*, 25 November 1986, p. BN2.

labour force and the level of knowledge and skills of the workers. In fact, a number of lower-and medium-level government officials have also been selected by public bidding rather than by the arbitary decisions of the higher-level authorities.

Fifthly, the traditional wage system has been reformed with the result that both the structure and rate of an employee's wages are determined in accordance with the work and service he provides. Employees in government agencies and public interest institutions earn a basic salary, a position subsidy (also in the form of a wage) and an annual bonus. The wages for staff and workers in manufacturing industries are determined on a floating basis plus annual bonus. Such a system has proved to be very successful in the zone.

Sixthly, in the area of capital construction, the traditional system of allocation of materials by the government, designation of the institutions to be in charge of design and construction, and management of construction enterprises, has been replaced with a market-oriented system. Currently, project designs as well as construction enterprises are selected by tender. Within each construction enterprise, each subdivision or group is subject to a subcontract and has to be responsible for the quality as well as punctual completion of the portion of project it has contracted for.

Seventhly, enterprises in the Shenzhen SEZ are more independent in decision-making. They are exclusively responsible for their losses and profits and have full power to make decisions regarding production, supply, marketing and recruitment of employees. Such enterprises are no longer regarded as being under the direct supervision and control of any particular department of the city government. Moreover, they are allowed to conduct business in more than one sector, a practice which was previously absolutely forbidden. These policies have effectively improved the economic returns of enterprises in the zone.[12]

Economic reforms

The reforms which have been carried out in the Shenzhen SEZ have yielded substantial economic results. In a short period of seven years, the Shenzhen SEZ has developed from a backward rural area into an industrial city. In 1979, there were only a small number of tiny enterprises processing products with materials and samples supplied by the purchasers. This rapid development has resulted from the introduction of advanced equipment, technology and management from abroad. The city now has more than 1,000 enterprises in light industry, textiles, chemicals, foods, machinery, building materials, medicines etc. In 1986, the Shenzhen SEZ's total gross value of industrial and agricultural output was over RMB3.5 m, 58 times as much as in 1979.[13]

12 *Wen Wei Po*, 26 November 1986, p. BN2.
13 *China Daily*, 8 April 1987, Supplement p. 1.

In addition, a number of export-oriented enterprises have been established, and their products are exported to 16 countries and regions including the United States, Africa, Oceania, Europe, South-east Asia and Japan. In 1986, the export value of the Shenzhen SEZ reached US$670 m.[14] This expansion in foreign markets was quite considerable, when one takes into account the fact that in 1985 the number of Shenzhen SEZ export markets was limited to five and the majority of its products were exported through Hong Kong. At present, many Shenzhen enterprises have established distribution systems in the United States, West Germany, Australia, Singapore etc, thus laying a foundation for further promotion of the SEZ's products in international markets.[15]

As regards the break-down of products exported, in 1986 manufactured products accounted for 60% of the total, a 36.6% increase over the figure for the previous year. In 1985, the export of manufactured products such as light industry goods, textiles, foods, clothing, art and crafts products, etc accounted for only 37.1% of the total industrial output of the Shenzhen SEZ. In 1986, exports of such products reached 51% of the total industrial output.[16] About 70% of the products exported by the Shenzhen SEZ in 1986 were manufactured by local enterprises using local components.[17] Furthermore, the Shenzhen SEZ assisted other domestic enterprises from interior areas to export their products.

The liberal economic policy adopted by the Shenzhen SEZ and the economic reforms carried out pursuant thereto have resulted in a substantial increase in foreign investment in the zone. As Table 1 shows, over the last eight years, the Shenzhen SEZ has concluded more than 5,000 investment agreements with a total investment value of US$3.87 b, of which US$1.27 b has been realized.

Although the number of new investment contracts concluded by the Shenzhen SEZ with foreign businesses in 1986 shrank significantly, with only 454 investment contracts signed and US$514 m worth of foreign investment contracted, down 9.9% and 50% from that of 1985, respectively, the zone had actually utilized US$489 m worth of foreign investment in 1986, up 48.6% from that of 1985. Of the total number of foreign-investment contracts signed by the Shenzhen SEZ in 1986, 31 were loan contracts with foreign financial consortia from Hong Kong, Japan, the United Kingdom, Canada etc, involving a total amount of US$225 m.[18] Drawings already made by 48 different Chinese units reached a total of US$108.6 m, accounting for 22.2% of the amount of foreign capital that the Shenzhen SEZ actually utilized in 1986. Of the Shenzhen SEZ's foreign debts outstanding at the end of 1986 (US$237 m), the Shenzhen Special Economic Zone Development Corporation is on the top of the list of borrowers with 22.8% of the total,

14 *Id.*
15 *Economic Reporter*, 9 March 1987, p. 20.
16 *Id.*
17 *Id.*
18 *China Economic News*, 9 March 1987, p. 9.

Table 1: Foreign investment in Shenzhen SEZ

Year	1979	1980	1981	1982	1983	1984	1985	1986	Total
Investment contracts signed	171	303	578	577	878	983	1203	454	5147
Increase or decrease (%)	—	+77.19	+90.76	−0.17	+52.17	+11.96	+22.38	−62.26	—
Amount agreed upon (including foreign loans) (US$ m)	29.84	271.22	863.60	180.28	334.51	645.64	1026.47	514	3865.56
Increase or decrease (%)	—	+808.9	+218.4	−79.12	+85.6	+93	+58.9	−50	—
Realized amount (including foreign loans) (US$ m)	15.37	32.64	112.82	73.79	143.93	210.50	193.40	489.33	1271.78
Increase or decrease (%)	—	+112.36	+245.65	−35	+95	+46	−8	+153	—

Sources: These figures were compiled by the author from various magazines, newspapers and yearbooks published in China and Hong Kong.

followed by the Shenzhen International Trust and Investment Co with 21.6%, and the Shenzhen Industrial Development Service Co and the Guangzhou-Shenzhen Railway Corporation with 9.7% and 8.4%, respectively.[19]

The decline in foreign investment in the Shenzhen SEZ is directly attributable to the central government's restraints on capital construction spending by the zone. The Shenzhen SEZ was forced to cancel a number of hotel, restaurant and high-rise construction projects in 1986. Although the SEZ recorded a hefty rise in terms of the foreign investment actually utilized in 1986, more than half of the investment went to the construction of the Shajiao Power Plant which started construction in 1985 and, by the end of 1986, had utilized US$286 m in foreign funds, of which US$278 m was used in 1986. Another relatively large-scale project is the Guangdong Float Glass Co which is a joint venture project between the PPG Industries (USA) and Thai interests on the one hand, and a consortium of Chinese interests on the other, with China Merchants Steam Navigation Co as the majority partner. The joint venture imported a US$57.6 m float glass production line from the United States in 1986.[20]

The role of foreign investment in Shenzhen's economy

Currently, foreign-investment enterprises in the Shenzhen SEZ play a major part in local industrial development. In 1986, such enterprises achieved a total industrial output of US$622 m, an increase of 37% over that of 1985.[21] Foreign-investment enterprises in the Shenzhen SEZ accounted for 65% of the SEZ's total industrial output and 60% of its exports.[22] According to statistics from the Shenzhen Financial Bureau, 75% of the zone's foreign-investment enterprises are making profits and most of those that have not made profits are newly-established companies. Since 1985, the Shenzhen government has paid particular attention to the balancing of foreign exchange when considering whether to undertake or approve a project. Of the 172 newly-signed industrial projects, most of them plan to export over 70% of their production as a means to generate hard currency income to balance foreign exchange accounts.[23] The city authority has also been cautious about the practicability of the products produced by enterprises with foreign participation and the technology employed by them.

Among the foreign investors, the Japanese businesses are still more interested in sales rather than investment in the Shenzhen SEZ. This can be seen in terms of the amount of direct investment contributed and, more important, the number of loan agreements made by Japanese

19 *Id.*
20 *Id.*
21 *Guangdong Business Monitor*, vol. 1, no. 8, 15 January 1987, p. 27.
22 *Id.*
23 *China Economic News*, 9 March 1987, p. 9.

enterprises. The Shenzhen SEZ signed 28 investment contracts worth US$487.9 m with Japanese businesses in 1986. Of the 28 contracts signed, 17 were loan agreements involving US$83.23 m or 94.8% of the total value contracted.[24]

Transformation of the other SEZs

The development of the Zhuhai SEZ has followed the Shenzhen pattern. Since 1985, the Zhuhai SEZ has tried to slow down capital construction and speed up the establishment of industrial projects. In 1986, it postponed and cancelled more than 60 capital construction projects and reduced consumer expenditures substantially. At the same time, more funds were allocated to manufacturing and productive projects. As a result, construction of most of the 45 major industrial projects was both commenced and completed in 1986.[25] The above measures made this possible.

By the end of 1986, the Zhuhai SEZ had contracted 213 projects with foreign businesses, worth a total contracted value of US$1.48 b, of which US$231 m has actually been utilized.[26] Since its establishment, the Zhuhai SEZ has attracted 112 foreign-investment enterprises. In 1986, the total industrial output of such enterprises amounted to RMB164 m and the total export value was US$34 m.[27]

Initially, the overseas capital which the Zhuhai SEZ brought in came mainly from Hong Kong and Macau. Since 1985, however, investors from more than ten countries and regions, including the United States and Europe, have established investment projects in the SEZ. Another feature of foreign investment in the zone is the growth of export-oriented projects negotiated and contracted with the Zhuhai SEZ. Among the 40 or more industrial projects established in the Zhuhai SEZ in 1986, more than 30 have the capacity to export more than 70% of their output.[28] Most of these projects use advanced technology and equipment of international standards.

The Shantou SEZ has benefited greatly from the experience Shantou City has had with foreign countries. Being traditionally a foreign-trade outpost, the value of Shantou's total exports, as early as 1949, was US$1.12 m, while in 1976 it reached US$100 m. By the end of 1986, the value of the city's total exports reached US$400 m, the highest in its history. Shantou City has had very good economic and technical cooperative relations with a number of foreign countries. From 1979 to 1986, the city signed 12,000 contracts valued at US$310 m, of which US$170 m was invested by foreign businessmen.[29] About 90% of these

24 *China Economic News*, 9 March 1987, p. 9.
25 *Wen Wei Po*, 11 March 1987, p. BN4.
26 *Id.*
27 *Id.*
28 *Id.*
29 *China Daily*, 8 April 1987, p. 3.

foreign-investment projects are industrial concerns which have upgraded the quality of goods produced and increased the capacity of the city to export its goods.

During the past few years, the Shantou SEZ has invested US$83.5 m in capital construction and built up an attractive investment environment by constructing reservoirs and roads and installing power cables, transformers and telephone exchanges. Equipment and technology imported by the Shantou SEZ have been mostly of the low investment, quick-return type. The SEZ currently hosts 96 industrial enterprises with foreign participation.[30] The main products manufactured are carpets, garments, furniture, plastics, construction materials, electrical and mechanical products, ceramics, toys and foodstuffs. The SEZ's industrial enterprises export about 75% of their products. In 1986, the total agricultural and industrial output of the SEZ reached US$39 m, an increase of 130% over 1985. Foreign exchange earnings through exports in 1986 were US$73.58 m, an increase of 31% over that of 1985.[31]

There were a number of factories in existence when the Xiamen SEZ was established in 1980. Accordingly, in developing itself, the SEZ has always attached more importance to the renovation and improvement of its old factories rather than to the building of new projects. By the end of 1986, the Xiamen SEZ had renovated and upgraded the equipment and technology of about 40% of its 'old' enterprises, and its gross industrial output grew by 10% per year from 1980.[32] The exports of the Xiamen SEZ also increased substantially in 1986.

In short, the four SEZs have established an adequate infrastructure for the further expansion of foreign investment. Manufacturing industries are developing satisfactorily in the SEZs with a total industrial output value of RMB6.8 b (about US$1.84 b) in 1986.[33] Most of the enterprises in the SEZs are able to export a portion of their products. At the same time, more and more export-oriented and technologically advanced projects are being introduced to the SEZs. The general approach of future Sino-foreign establishments or wholly foreign-owned enterprises would be to develop export-oriented and technology-and/or knowledge-intensive projects in order for the SEZs to be able to introduce foreign products and technology to inland areas.

II. Basic legal institutions

The SEZs are located in Guangdong and Fujian Provinces and are thus under the direct control and supervision of the respective provincial governments, although the State Council has set up an office at the

30 *Guangdong Business Monitor*, 1 March 1987, p. 50.
31 *Id.*
32 *Economic Reporter*, 2 March 1987, p. 29.
33 *Da Kung Pao*, 2 April 1987, p. 5.

national level which is responsible for the development of the SEZs. Laws and regulations governing activities within the SEZs are approved mainly by the Provincial People's Congresses of Guangdong and Fujian.

Purpose of the SEZs

According to the Regulations of the People's Republic of China on Special Economic Zones in Guangdong Province,[34] the establishment of the SEZs is to develop external economic cooperation and the transfer of technology, and to promote China's modernization programme.[35] In Guangdong Province, the authority which administers the SEZs is the Guangdong Provincial Administration of Special Economic Zones ('GPASEZ'). It exercises managerial power on behalf of the Guangdong provincial government. Some of its functions are as follows:

(1) drawing up development plans for the special zones and organizing their implementation;
(2) examining and approving investment projects in the special zones;
(3) dealing with the registration of industrial and commercial enterprises in the special zones and with land allotment;
(4) coordinating working relations among the banking, insurance, taxation, customs, frontier inspection, postal and telecommunications authorities and other organizations;
(5) administering labour matters;
(6) being responsible for educational, cultural, health and other public welfare facilities in the SEZs; and
(7) supervising the implementation and enforcement of laws and orders in the SEZs.[36]

Administration

The GPASEZ is directly responsible for the management of the Shenzhen SEZ. Other agencies have been set up in the Zhuhai and Shantou SEZs and these are under the direction of the GPASEZ. The Xiamen SEZ is under the direct control of Xiamen City.

34 Regulations of the People's Republic of China on Special Economic Zones in Guangdong Province were approved at the 15th Session of the Standing Committee of the 5th National People's Congress on 26 August 1980 (the 'Guangdong SEZ Regulations'). Prior to the establishment of the SEZs, the Guangdong provincial government drafted regulations on the estabishment of economic zones and submitted the same to the central government for approval. The central government eventually decided to set up certain areas for attracting foreign investment, to be named as special economic zones. The Standing Committee of the National People's Congress, in giving its consent to the regulations initially drafted by the Guangdong Provincial Government, authorized the Provincial People's Congress to adopt regulations in respect of the SEZs which would be reviewed and approved by the National People's Congress.

35 Guangdong SEZ Regulations, Article 1.

36 *Id*, Article 23.

In the SEZs, overseas investors are offered a wider scope of business and more favourable terms. They are permitted to invest in all sectors of industry, agriculture, livestock breeding, fish breeding and poultry farming, tourism, housing and construction, and research and manufacturing which involve advanced technology.[37] The essential condition for foreign investment is that it must have a positive effect on international economic cooperation and technical exchanges. So long as this prerequisite is met, foreign investors may invest in any economic sector in the SEZs. Another prerequisite for foreign investment, which is indirect in nature, is that the foreign-investment project should be export-oriented. Foreign-investment enterprises in the SEZs are required to sell their products in the international market. If any such enterprise wants to sell its products in the domestic market, it must first secure the approval of the GPASEZ and pay customs duties.[38] Although the relevant laws do not expressly state whether import-substitutes manufactured by foreign-investment enterprises in the SEZs can be sold domestically, the GPASEZ may resolve this issue on a case-by-case basis through specific authorizations.

Overseas investors wishing to undertake a certain project or economic arrangement are required to apply to the GPASEZ which will, upon examination and approval, issue registration licences and land use permits.[39] Such investors will need to open accounts with the Bank of China or with other banks set up in the SEZs with government approval.[40] The insertion of the term 'other banks' is very important. It implies that foreign banks are allowed to establish branches or subsidiaries in the SEZs and that these branches or subsidiaries may handle banking matters for foreign investors just like the Bank of China does.[41]

Investment incentives

Foreign investments in the SEZs are granted more favourable terms regarding land use, import and export, taxation and labour. Overseas investors in the SEZs are not permitted to acquire land by ownership but they may secure the right to use the land in accordance with their actual needs.[42] The terms of a land use contract such as the length of tenure, rent and method of payment are generally determined in accordance with the nature of the trade and use involved and are more favourable than those applicable to land in other parts of China.[43]

37 *Id*, Article 4.
38 *Id*, Article 9.
39 *Id*, Article 7.
40 *Id*, Article 8.
41 There were no regulations or laws governing foreign banks in China, including the Special Economic Zones, until 1985. For a discussion of foreign banking laws and regulations in the SEZs, see Chapter 7 of this book.
42 *Id*, Article 12.
43 *Id*.

Machinery, spare parts, raw materials, vehicles and other means of production of foreign-investment enterprises in the SEZs are exempted from import duties. The necessary consumer goods to be imported by such enteprises may be subject to higher or lower import duties or exemptions, depending on the merits of each case.[44] This provision, which is similar to the new rules which have been adopted by other provinces and cities since late 1986, has been of great benefit to foreign investors. As mentioned, other provinces and cities have adopted similar legislation, and appear to have benefited from the experience of the SEZs.

Overseas investors are encouraged to reinvest their profits in the SEZs and to use local components in the manufacture of their products. Investors who reinvest their profits in the SEZs for five years or longer are exempted from income tax on profits from such reinvestment.[45] Enterprises which use China-made machinery, raw materials and other goods are offered preferential prices on the basis of current export prices of similar Chinese commodities.[46] Nevertheless, foreign-investment enterprises are required to pay foreign exchange for the purchase of such items. This provision would have been much more attractive to foreign investors if it had provided that prices for such machinery and materials would be determined according to domestic market situations, for in general domestic prices are lower than export prices. The requirement of payment in foreign exchange also substantially reduces the appeal of the provision. If the provisions were otherwise, foreign investors would prefer to buy local components and machinery (which are cheaper than foreign ones) with Chinese currency and save their valuable foreign exchange to import parts and materials which are not readily available in China and to remit their profits overseas.

Initially, the rate of income tax payable by foreign-investment enterprises in the SEZs was set at 15%, which was much lower than the rate applicable in other parts of China.[47] In addition, preferential treatment was given to enterprises established within two years of the promulgation of the Guangdong SEZ Regulations. Enterprises which invested US$5 m or more and those which brought in advanced technology or had a longer cycle of capital turnover were also granted preferential tax terms.[48]

In December 1984, the State Council of China unified the tax systems in the four SEZs together with those of 14 other coastal cities and ports which were designated in November 1984 as 'open areas' for foreign investment. Under the Interim Provisions of the State Council, foreign-investment enterprises scheduled to operate for a period of ten years or more in industry, communications and transportation, agriculture, forestry, animal husbandry or other productive trades may, upon

44 *Id*, Article 13.
45 *Id*, Article 16.
46 *Id*, Article 17.
47 *Id*, Article 14.
48 *Id*.

approval by the tax authorities in the SEZs, be exempted from income tax in the first profit-making year and allowed a 50% reduction in the third to fifth years.[49] Enterprises which invest more than US$5 m and which are scheduled to operate for a period of ten years or more in service trades may, upon approval by the tax authorities in the special zones, be exempted from income tax in the first profit-making year and allowed a 50% reduction in the second and third years.[50] It is worth noting that according to Chinese legal concepts, banking business is not regarded as a service trade. Foreign banks in the SEZs are therefore not to be automatically accorded the tax reductions and exemptions provided in the Interim Provisions of the State Council.

Foreign investors in the SEZs are exempted from paying remittance tax.[51] Tax on income obtained from dividends, interest, rentals, royalties and other sources in the SEZs by investors who have no establishments in China is levied at a rate of 10%, except for the income exempted from income tax in accordance with the relevant Chinese law.[52] The local authorities of the SEZs are authorized to prescribe further tax reductions and exemptions regarding local income tax.[53]

As discussed earlier, starting from late 1984, China has concentrated on attracting foreign investment in manufacturing industries as well as in export-oriented projects. In order to achieve the goals of this policy, the Interim Provisions of the State Council stipulate that imports of machinery, equipment, raw materials, spare parts, vehicles and other means of production, which were previously liable to Consolidated Industrial and Commercial Tax, are exempted from taxation provided that the importation of these materials is for the purpose of production in the SEZs. Products for export manufactured by enterprises in the SEZs are also exempted from Consolidated Industrial and Commercial Tax except for a small number of products ear-marked for export by the State or subject to certain regulations. Foreign-investment enterprises in the SEZs which sell their products in the domestic market are granted a 50% reduction in Consolidated Industrial and Commercial Tax.[54] Quite surprisingly, this tax reduction on domestic sales by foreign-investment enterprises is not limited to import-substitutes. The level of technology involved is not specified either. Instead, the Interim Regulations grant such tax reductions to all kinds of products including mineral oil, cigarettes and liquor. This stipulation contrasts sharply with the preferential tax terms prescribed in the Provisions in respect of domestic sales by enterprises with foreign participation.

49 Interim Provisions of the State Council of the People's Republic of China on Reduction in or Exemption from Enterprise Income Tax and Consolidated Industrial and Commercial Tax for the Special Economic Zones and Fourteen Coastal Cities, effective from 1 December 1984, Article I(1).
50 *Id.*
51 *Id*, Article I(3).
52 *Id*, Article I(4).
53 *Id*, Article I(2).
54 *Id*, Articles I(5), (6) and (7).

Business management

By definition, enterprises in the SEZs which have foreign participation are allowed to operate their businesses more independently, to have access to the labour market and to have the right to determine the structure of their personnel and wage systems. The Guangdong SEZ Regulations authorize the establishment of labour service companies in each of the SEZs. The function of such a company is to recommend candidates for recruitment by foreign-investment enterprises.[55]

Potential employees should first be approved by the labour bureau in each of the SEZs and then, upon recommendation by the labour service companies, be tested and accepted for employment in accordance with the principle of selecting the best qualified.[56] The role of the labour service company is to assist the foreign investor who may have difficulty in recruiting qualified employees due to the poor communications system in China and the lack of skilled labour in the SEZs. In the early years, some foreign-investment enterprises tried to hire employees through direct recruitment. This, however, did not prove to be very successful. Nevertheless, at present, many foreign-investment enterprises still recruit employees directly from the public, without first consulting the labour service companies.

Staff and workers accepted for employment may be put on a three to six-month probation period.[57] Enterprises employing Chinese staff and workers are required to sign employment contracts with their employees. They are also required to provide employees with training courses at both managerial and general levels.[58] Since there is no specific requirement in respect of on-the-job training, foreign-investment enterprises in practice decide on the type and extent of training courses according to the needs of the enterprises.

Foreign-investment enterprises operating in the SEZs have an exclusive right to determine the wages, bonuses and subsidies etc for their staff and workers. The level of wages should be decided during negotiations on labour contracts and should take into account the nature of employment. Foreign-investment enterprises are required to increase their employees' wages at a rate of 5% to 15% per year according to the degree of technical proficiency of the employees concerned.[59] This provision is different in two aspects from the laws applicable nationwide. First, it does not require foreign-investment enterprises to pay their employees wages which are higher than those of staff and workers working in State-owned

55 Guangdong SEZ Regulations, Article 19.

56 Interim Provisions for Labour and Wage Management in Enterprises in the Special Economic Zones in Guangdong Province adopted by the 13th Session of the Standing Committee of the 5th People's Congress of Guangdong Province on 17 November 1981 and promulgated on 24 December 1981, Article 4.

57 *Id.*

58 *Id*, Article 6.

59 *Id*, Article 7.

enterprises in the same locality and which carry on the same trade.[60] Secondly, an index of wage increases is prescribed. The reason for the first departure seems to be that the wage level in the SEZs is already much higher than that in other parts of the country and even if wage levels were the same throughout the country, the foreign investors would still have difficulty recruiting qualified employees because of the competition from domestic Chinese companies.

There is no specific provision as to whether a foreign-investment enterprise should pay its employees both a direct wage and an indirect wage. It appears, however, that such enterprises must pay their employees a basic wage as well as a floating wage. Article 8 of the Interim Provisions of Guangdong Province on Labour and Wage Management provides that 70% of such employees' wages must go to the employees themselves (including basic and floating wages), 5% should be kept by the employer to subsidize the welfare fund for staff and workers, and the remaining 25% should be used for social labour insurance and to repay the various kinds of subsidies which the State provides to the staff and workers. This formula is different from that which is applied in other parts of China.

Foreign-investment enterprises operating in the SEZs are empowered to dismiss employees who have become redundant and are unable to perform even after re-training.[61] Such enterprises are required to pay the dismissed employees a certain amount of compensation based on their respective period of service. These enterprises may also dismiss employees who violate the rules and regulations of the enterprises and thereby cause harmful consequences. In such cases, the enterprises in question have to submit reports to the labour bureau of the SEZ which will then consider the matters.[62]

A member of staff or a worker who has been dismissed or sanctioned by an enterprise may object to the dismissal or sanction. He may propose to the enterprise that the matter be resolved through consultation. If the dispute cannot be resolved through consultation, he may request that the labour bureaus of the SEZs arbitrate the matter. If either party considers the arbitration by the labour bureau to be unreasonable, it may file a lawsuit in the local people's court in the SEZs.[63]

These provisions are aimed at protecting both employees' and employers' rights. They are nonetheless more restrictive than those certified

60 According to the Regulations of the People's Republic of China on Labour Management of Joint Ventures Using Chinese and Foreign Investment promulgated by the State Council on 26 July 1980, the wage level of the workers and staff members in a joint venture should be at 120% to 150% of the real wage of the workers and staff members of State-owned enterprises.

61 Interim Provisions for Labour and Wage Management in Enterprises in the Special Economic Zones in Guangdong Province, Article 16.

62 *Id*, Articles 16 and 17.

63 *Id*, Article 18.

by the Ministry of Labour and Personnel in late 1986.[64] Since foreign-investment enterprises are required to recruit their employees upon the recommendation of labour service companies (although, in practice, cases have been reported where foreign investors tried to employ employees by advertising in newspapers), it is evident that this multi-stage dismissal process is cumbersome to foreign investors and may reduce labour efficiency in the SEZs. Of course, this is not to say that employees' rights should be neglected altogether. In practice, there have not been any reports of a labour dispute being arbitrated or tried in court. However, there appears to be quite a bit of job-hopping among employees of foreign-investment enterprises.

The above-mentioned provision (Article 18) may be in violation of the Law of Civil Procedure of China, Article 193 of which provides that disputes which have been arbitrated must not be submitted to the people's court for legal process. Although Article 193 essentially applies to foreign trade and economic transactions, and arbitrations by Chinese foreign affairs arbitral organs, the general principle behind the provision should be observed by local legislative bodies so that Chinese laws at various levels can be enforced uniformly.

Regulations of the Shenzhen SEZ on foreign economic contracts

Another piece of legislation which has significant effect on the operations of Sino-foreign joint ventures and cooperative ventures, wholly foreign-owned enterprises and other types of establishments involving foreign investment in the SEZs, is the Provisions of the Shenzhen Special Economic Zone for Foreign Economic Contracts (the 'Shenzhen Economic Contract Law').[65] Although the Shenzhen Foreign Economic Contract Law applies only to the zone itself, transactions taking place in other areas occasionally make reference to the provisions of the legislation. This was particularly the case prior to the adoption of the National Foreign Economic Contract Law in March 1985. As a fore-runner of the National Foreign Economic Contract Law, the Shenzhen Foreign Economic Contract Law set out quite a few provisions which were later adopted by the national statute.[66]

Nevertheless, the Shenzhen Foreign Economic Contract Law still maintains its own characteristics which are significantly different from

64 For a discussion of the labour regulations adopted by the ministry of labour on 28 November 1986 and their impact, see Chapter 3 of this book.

65 The Provisions of the Shenzhen Economic Zone for Foreign Economic Contracts were adopted by the Standing Committee of the 6th People's Congress of Guangdong Province on 11 January 1984 and promulgated by the People's Government of Guangdong Province and effective from 7 February 1984.

66 For a comparative discussion of the National Foreign Economic Contract Law and Shenzhen Foreign Economic Contract Law, see Henry R Zheng, 'A Comparative Analysis of the Foreign Economic Contract Law of the People's Republic of China', *UCLA Pacific Basin Law Journal*, Spring/Fall, 1985, vol. 4, nos. 1 and 2, pp. 30–62.

those of the National Foreign Economic Contract Law. The Shenzhen Foreign Economic Contract Law applies to contracts, between Chinese enterprises or other economic organizations on the one hand and foreign enterprises and other economic organizations or individuals on the other, for the development of economic and technological cooperation. It is equally applicable to such contracts signed between wholly foreign-owned enterprises, Sino-foreign joint ventures and cooperative ventures, or contracts between such ventures and Chinese enterprises in the SEZ or other foreign enterprises.[67] The effect of this provision is to blur the statuses of Sino-foreign joint ventures and cooperative ventures as well as wholly foreign-owned enterprises which are registered in China and are thus Chinese legal persons. Since the aim of the Shenzhen Foreign Economic Contract Law is to regulate contractual activities between Chinese enterprises and foreign enterprises and individuals, the adoption of such a provision does not seem to be logical in theory although it may be plausible in practice. If the drafters of the law intended to make it uniformly applicable to all contractual transactions, domestic Chinese enterprises registered in the zone should not be excluded from its application. In this regard, the National Foreign Economic Contract Law is better drafted.

Another important provision of the Shenzhen Economic Contract Law is the requirement of approval of the local government. Article 5 of the statute stipulates that all contracts must be approved by the Shenzhen municipality before they become effective. Due to the fact that this provision does not distinguish between different types of contracts, a strict implementation of this approval requirement might constitute interference with the independent operations of foreign-investment enterprises in the zone, which are authorized under the Guangdong SEZ Regulations. For instance, when a joint venture concludes contracts on a regular basis with foreign enterprises for delivery of goods or for processing products, does it have to go to the Shenzhen government for approval each time a contract is concluded? If it does, such a venture may lose its business opportunities to its competitors from other parts of China or from other countries. Furthermore, the Shenzhen municipality is given three months to examine contracts submitted to it for approval. Such a lengthy period will not be in step with the ever-changing conditions in the international market. In view of the fact that other important contracts, such as joint venture agreements, are regulated by other national and local laws, the examination and approval requirements under the Shenzhen Foreign Economic Contract Law may not be necessary.

As with the National Foreign Economic Contract Law, the Shenzhen Foreign Economic Contract Law prescribes that contracts must be in writing and signed by the parties concerned. Modifications and extensions of such contracts should also be in writing and signed.[68] It also explicitly stipulates the main items that should be included in each type

67 Shenzhen Foreign Economic Contract Law, Article 2.
68 *Id*, Articles 7, 28 and 29.

of contract. In this regard, the stipulation regarding cooperative joint ventures is most important. Prior to the adoption of the Shenzhen Foreign Economic Contract Law, there was no specific provision in Chinese law regulating economic transactions and activities carried out by Sino-foreign cooperative ventures. Such ventures were not given any specific status although they are still the most popular vehicle for carrying out Sino-foreign economic ventures. Article 16 of the Shenzhen Foreign Economic Contract Law provides:

> A cooperative management contract constitutes a written agreement on the cooperative production, management or establishment of an enterprise or undertaking for which the special zone's side provides the right to the use of land and to the exploitation of resources, factory buildings, labour force and labour service, and the [foreign party] provides funds, equipment, materials and technology; as well as on the arrangements for profit-sharing and product-distribution among the parties concerned and their respective rights and obligations in connection with the cooperative production, including the liability for risk.

Thus, a cooperative venture is given the status of a Chinese legal person if the parties concerned wish this to be so. The intention of the statute, which gives a cooperative venture a status equal to that of a joint venture, is further clarified by the requirement that the main terms of a cooperative contract should include those that are applicable to joint venture contracts.[69]

69 Article 15 of the Shenzhen Foreign Economic Contract Law stipulates that joint venture contracts should include the following provisions:

(1) Names of the parties to the joint venture, their countries (or regions) of registration, official addresses, names of legal representatives and their functions and nationalities;
(2) Name of the joint venture, its address and purpose, area of land used by it, scope and size of its business;
(3) Total investment value and registered capital of the joint venture, amount and proportion of investment contributed by the parties to the joint venture respectively, mode of investment, time limit for payment of funds, and stipulation for handling the assignment of arrears of the payable funds;
(4) Main equipment and techniques to be used in production and their sources;
(5) Mode of purchasing raw materials and selling products;
(6) Schedule for the construction of the joint venture and the responsibilities of the parties to the joint venture in the fields of preparatory work, construction, production and management;
(7) Operational period of the joint venture, its dissolution, clearing procedures and the ownership of the properties after termination;
(8) Principles of handling finance, accounting and auditing;
(9) Stipulations for labour management, wages, welfare benefits, labour protection, labour insurance and other matters;
(10) The composition of the board of directors, its terms of office and functions;
(11) The procedures for the employment of the general manager and deputy general manager, the composition of personnel and their functions and limits of power;
(12) Sharing of profits or losses and the limits of responsibility;
(13) Guarantee and responsibility for violations of the contract;
(14) Arbitration agreement or other measures for the settlement of disputes;
(15) Place and date of signing of the contracts; and
(16) Other items which the two sides deem necessary.

With regard to the settlement of disputes, the Shenzhen Foreign Economic Contract Law has adopted quite a liberal attitude. Disputes arising between contracting parties during the implementation of a contract are to be settled through consultation or mediation, in line with the principle of equality and mutual benefit which is a common procedure for resolving disputes according to Chinese practice. If consultation or mediation cannot resolve the dispute, the parties concerned may request arbitration by an arbitration agency in accordance with an arbitration agreement.[70] This provision represents a formal departure from the Chinese tradition and practice of insisting that the dispute be arbitrated by a Chinese arbitral organ, or in China when a dispute involves a Chinese party. This digression, however, is not applicable to those contracts which involve China's sovereignty, such as the exploration of natural resources.[71] Such disputes must be arbitrated in China and by an arbitration agency established in the SEZ or by another agency agreed upon by the two sides.[72] By implication, such an arbitration agency can either be a Chinese institution or a foreign arbitral tribunal. So long as the arbitration is conducted in China, the requirements of this provision should be satisfied.

In any event, despite its shortcomings and defects, the Shenzhen Foreign Economic Contract Law has provided foreign investors with considerable certainty when doing business in China, and has also provided the Chinese central government as well as other provinces and cities with valuable experience in many different aspects of economic cooperation. If this were not the case, the national law regulating the same subject would not have been as successful and effective as it is. Pending the modification of the Shenzhen Foreign Economic Contract Law, those of its provisions which do not best serve China's open policy should not be enforced if they are in conflict with the National Foreign Economic Contract Law. At the same time, those provisions which are experimental but more effective in implementing China's current policies should continue to apply in the SEZ.

III. New provisions of the SEZs

After the enactment of the State Council Provisions in October 1986, the four SEZs adopted some new measures. Since several of the incentives set out in these Provisions had already been implemented in the SEZs by the time they were adopted, the measures taken by the SEZs were not as substantial as those adopted by other cities and provinces.

70 *Id*, Article 34.
71 *Id*, Article 35.
72 *Id*.

New measures adopted by the Shenzhen SEZ

To a large extent, the new preferential terms for foreign investors adopted by the Shenzhen SEZ in late 1986 were merely confirmatory of the existing laws and practices. Export-oriented enterprises, and investments with advanced technology,[73] are given more favourable terms under the new regulations. Although a 15% income tax rate is currently levied on all enterprises in the Shenzhen SEZ, businesses with investments of more than US$5 m, or which provide advanced technology or have long circulation (return) periods of capital, are entitled to a 100% income tax holiday for two years, followed by a period of three years where they will pay only half of their income tax.[74] This provision is more liberal than its predecessor in the sense that it does not require a specific operational period for the enterprises in question. Export Enterprises which were not directly addressed either in local tax laws or in the Interim Provisions of the State Council adopted in March 1986 are to pay income tax at a rate of 10% instead of 15%.[75] Technologically Advanced Enterprises can enjoy a further period of three years, where they need pay only half their income tax, after the two-year tax-free and 50%-reduction period have expired.

Products manufactured by Export Enterprises for export are exempted from export tax. Equipment and means of production imported by foreign-investment enterprises for production purposes are exempted from import tax. This policy of tax exemption also applies to articles imported for the foreign-investment enterprises' own use. Raw materials imported for the production of export products are exempted from Customs duties.[76]

As regards land use fees, the Shenzhen Municipal Government has reaffirmed the provisions, which have been in force since 1 January 1985, stating which parcels of industrial land should be charged at an annual rate of RMB1–1.6 per sq m. Projects which involve advanced technology (or Technologically Advanced Enterprises) are exempted from paying land use fees for a period of five years beginning from the day on which the use of land is approved. A 50% reduction in the land use fee for another three years will also be allowed after the expiration of the initial five-year exemption period. In addition, projects using especially advanced technology are granted a total exemption from land use fees.[77] However, the new provisions adopted by the Shenzhen SEZ do not lay down any criteria for the determination of the level of the technology in

73 In May 1987, the Shenzhen Municipality enacted a set of implementing rules which established concrete criteria for the examination and determination of export-oriented and technologically-advanced enterprises. The full text of the rules appeared in *Wen Wei Po*, 30 May 1987, p. BN2.

74 *China Economic News*, 10 November 1986, p. 1.

75 *Id.*

76 *Id.*

77 *Id.*

question. This matter will need to be dealt with by the administrative bodies in the SEZ.

The Shenzhen Municipal Government has also announced that all fees and charges must be charged according to government regulations. Foreign-investment enterprises may refuse to pay any unreasonable charges and may also appeal to the relevant authorities in charge of foreign investment in the zone.[78] This provision is apparently a reaffirmation of the State Council Provisions. Its significance is that it allows foreign investors immediate access to the municipal government to voice their complaints and problems.

In December 1986, the Shenzhen SEZ established a service centre to offer free services to potential foreign investors. The Shenzhen service centre currently offers the following four kinds of services, free of charge:

(1) Legal services in connection with investments by foreign investors;
(2) Liaison with government departments on behalf of potential foreign investors in Shenzhen;
(3) Provision of information on investment opportunities in Shenzhen; and
(4) Streamlining of bureaucratic procedures to facilitate investment.[79]

By April 1987, the centre had handled, among others, 48 complaints, 36 inquiries on the establishment of ventures in the SEZ, 87 consultancy cases and 72 other services.[80]

This service centre will offer substantial assistance to foreign investors. Unlike several years ago, there are currently more laws and regulations concerning foreign investment than ordinary foreign investors, perhaps including their lawyers, can possibly comprehend and appreciate. Since consultative opinions of foreign lawyers who are not qualified to practice Chinese law may not be relied upon by foreign investors, the legal services to be provided by the service centre will lend more certainty with regard to interpreting the local regulations, national laws and the interrelationship between the two. The provision of investment information is equally important in view of the relatively underdeveloped communications system in the SEZ.

For the purpose of implementing the State Council Provisions and the 'Procedures of the Customs of China for the Administration of Materials and Parts that Enterprises with Foreign Investment Need to Import in Order to Perform Product Export Contracts' adopted by the General Administration of Customs in November 1986, the Jiulong Customs located in the Shenzhen SEZ promulgated its own regulations to simplify the procedures for import and export by foreign investors in the

78 *Id.*
79 *Guangdong Business Monitor*, 1 March 1987, p. 47.
80 *China Economic News*, 8 June 1987, p. 3.

Shenzhen SEZ.[81] The Jiulong Customs Detailed Regulations and Measures are similar to those adopted by the General Administration of Customs of China. These provisions make it clear that the Jiulong Customs will rely on the Shenzhen municipal government's decisions in levying taxes on the import and export of goods by foreign-investment enterprises operating in the Shenzhen SEZ. Joint ventures, cooperative ventures and wholly foreign-owned enterprises are allowed to manage their import and export businesses themselves, provided they do not go beyond the scope of their authorized businesses. They can either clear the customs themselves or entrust other foreign trade companies to go through the procedures on their behalf.[82]

When a foreign-investment enterprise imports machinery, vehicles, raw materials, fuel, parts, components, packing materials etc for the carrying out of export contracts, it will be exempted from submitting any documents for approval[83], so long as it has signed a production and export contract which has been approved by the relevant authorities of the Shenzhen municipal government. For those without such export contracts, they can submit their annual or semi-annual production plans instead.[84]

The simplified procedures discussed above are for the convenience of export-oriented enterprises. When enterprises with foreign participation decide to sell their products in the domestic market they are required to secure import permission retroactively for the machinery and equipment which were imported without such certificates. Such enterprises are also required to apply to the relevant authorities, either in the Guangdong Province or in the central government, for approval.[85]

Zhuhai's preferential terms

The new measures adopted by the Zhuhai SEZ in early 1987 are more comprehensive and detailed than those of the Shenzhen SEZ. Its foreign investment incentive measures have a considerable impact on the operating costs of foreign investors, namely, income tax, land use fees and other charges. The standard income tax rate is 15% for enterprises with foreign participation. An income tax exemption for a period of two years, starting from the first profit-making year, is granted to enterprises which invest more than US$2 m, or employ advanced technology for which the capital recoupment time is relatively long, or whose contractual periods are for more than ten years. After the expiration of the two-

81 The Detailed Regulations and Measures of the Jiulong Customs in Implementing the Policy of Encouraging Foreign Investment (Chinese version) appeared in *Wen Wei Po*, 24 March 1987, p. BN4. No promulgation date or effective date was given in the regulations but it is understood that these regulations and measures have been effective since the beginning of 1987.

82 Detailed Regulations and Measures of the Jiulong Customs, Article 1.

83 *Id*, Article 2.

84 *Id*, Article 3.

85 *Id*, Article 6.

year tax exemption period, these enterprises will be granted a 50% tax reduction for another three years.[86]

Export Enterprises are given preferential treatment and pay income tax at a reduced rate of 10%. Technologically Advanced Enterprises are also entitled to a 50% tax reduction for an additional period of three years following the expiration of the preferential tax holiday stipulated by the State. In addition, all foreign-investment enterprises are exempted from paying local income tax for a period of five years starting from their first profit-making year.[87]

All foreign-investment enterprises in the Zhuhai SEZ are exempted from export duties. In addition, essential production equipment, other capital goods and consumer goods imported and used by foreign-investment enterprises are not subject to import duties. Raw materials imported for the production of export products enjoy the same treatment.

The Zhuhai SEZ Control Committee is required to assist foreign-investment enterprises in obtaining approval for their applications with regard to sales in the domestic markets of products whose importation is under State control. As for products which are not under State control, the Committee must give priority, subject to authorization by the State, to the examination and approval of the requisite applications submitted by the foreign-investment enterprises.[88]

The Zhuhai SEZ's foreign-investment incentives provide for reductions in land use fees. Previously, the land use fee was set at RMB5–15 per sq m per year. Under the new regulations, the land use fee has been lowered to RMB0.5–1 per sq m per year, a substantial reduction from the previous one. As an additional incentive, all industrial-specific foreign-investment enterprises are exempted from paying land use fees for a period of three years beginning from the date of their acquisition of the land use rights, followed by a 50% reduction in land use fees for another three years.[89] Although 'industrial-specific' projects are not defined in the regulations, they should include all manufacturing businesses in heavy as well as light industries.

Enterprises which employ advanced technology of international standards, or whose values of exports have exceeded 70% of the total output values for the current year, are entitled to land use fee exemptions for a period of five years beginning from the date they received approval to use the land. Following the expiration of the five-year exemption, these enterprises are entitled to a 50% reduction in land use fees for an additional five years. Enterprises which use exceptionally high technology do not have to pay any land use fees.[90] As in the case of the Shenzhen

86 *China Economic News*, 9 February 1987, p. 7.
87 *Id.*
88 *Id.*
89 *Id.*
90 *Id.*

SEZ regulations, such absolute exemptions must be approved by the relevant authorities of the municipal government of Zhuhai City.

In order for foreign-investment enterprises to operate efficiently, they are given priority in the supply of water and electricity. Any fees charged therefore will be at the same rates which apply to State-owned enterprises. This provision is obviously an improvement over the State Council Provisions which grant priority in the supply of water, electricity and other facilities only to Export Enterprises and Technologically Advanced Enterprises.

The new Zhuhai SEZ regulations strictly prohibit unreasonable fees to be levied on foreign-investment enterprises. These regulations provide that no administrative or operating expenses should be charged without the requisite approval of the provincial or municipal government, and that all fees payable by foreign-investment enterprises must be in line with the standards for State-owned enterprises. Foreign-investment enterprises have the right under these regulations to refuse to pay any charges or to complain to the municipal government or its authorized departments if such charges are levied without the formal approval of the provincial or municipal government.[91]

Another feature of the new Zhuhai SEZ regulations is the simplification of administrative procedures governing foreign investors. These regulations provide that the formalities for the establishment of foreign-investment enterprises must be simplified, and that the efficiency of the approving authorities must be raised. The authorities are required to examine and approve promptly the agreements, contracts and articles of association of the foreign-investment enterprises. To be specific, applications for the establishment of foreign-investment enterprises must be answered within one month from the date of receipt of the application documents, provided that the applications are within the scope of the approving authority of the municipal government.[92]

The import and export procedures for enterprises operating in the Zhuhai SEZ are now streamlined. Applications regarding the importation of equipment and raw materials by foreign-investment enterprises for production of export products or in respect of the export of such enterprises' own products must be attended to immediately upon their receipt, and decisions regarding such applications must be given within three days.[93] With these new provisions, the Zhuhai SEZ is now in a position to compete with the other SEZs, including the Shenzhen SEZ, the most developed of the SEZs.

Shantou's provisions

In late December 1986, the Shantou SEZ announced additional regulations designed to encourage foreign investment. These were aimed at

91 *Id.*
92 *Id*, p. 8.
93 *Id*, p. 7.

reducing the operating costs of foreign investment. According to these new regulations, labour insurance and subsidies for employees working in foreign-investment enterprises are set at 25% or less of their total salary.[94] Annual land use charges have been adjusted to between US$0.27 and US$3.79 per sq m, depending on the purpose for which the land is used. Foreign-investment companies are not subject to land use charges during their construction periods. Companies which export a substantially high percentage of production or which employ advanced technology are granted a 50% reduction in land use fees.[95]

Foreign-investment enterprises which export a major portion of their output or which use advanced technology, may pay land development charges in a single payment or on an annual basis, at their choice. Such charges will be determined on actual development costs. Originally, land development fees were between 3% to 5% of the total land costs. In addition, 9 out of 28 other administrative charges have been discontinued.[96]

Xiamen's rules

The Xiamen SEZ has not announced its own preferential terms for foreign investors. Instead, the Xiamen municipal government has promulgated new provisions which have simplified the import and export procedures for foreign investors. It has also provided special terms for foreign investments in the Xiamen SEZ. According to these new provisions, the Xiamen municipal government plans to turn the Xiamen SEZ into a free port gradually, and thus, any related policies will be implemented with this in mind.[97] At the present time, measures have been taken to set up special warehouses, factories and areas in which Export Enterprises will be exempted from paying duties.

Export Enterprises and Technologically Advanced Enterprises in the SEZ may apply to the Xiamen branch of the Bank of China, the Xiamen International Trust and Investment Co, or any other specialized banks for short-term loans or credits needed for production or distribution of products. They are entitled to priority in receiving such credits.

Under the Xiamen regulations, forcign investments are encouraged to be made in the Huli industrial zone. Foreign investments in the Huli industrial zone will be charged annual land use fees of RMB5 per sq m, and 10% reductions will be allowed on the sale prices of the factory sites as well as on rents. Foreign-investment enterprises may pay for their factories by instalments, with an initial down-payment of 30% of the sale price. The remaining amount may be paid within a period of one year.[98]

Foreign-investment enterprises in Xiamen are given considerable

94 *Guangdong Business Monitor*, 1 January 1987, p. 24.
95 *Id.*
96 *Id.*
97 *China Economic News*, 10 November 1986, p. 2.
98 *Id.*

freedom in hiring and dismissing their employees. They are allowed to recruit technicians and management staff directly from their locality, other areas in China as well as from abroad. This total freedom in labour management is a full implementation of the State Council Provisions and is different from the position in the Shenzhen SEZ.

These enterprises are also vested with exclusive rights to determine the prices of their products which are to be marketed, upon approval of the Xiamen municipal government, in the Chinese domestic market. This provision, however, is not applicable to circumstances where such products are under the State's unified pricing system.[99]

In order to improve 'the soft foreign investment climate', a special Foreign Investment Affairs Office has been established in Xiamen along with an Administrative Bureau for Enterprises Involving Foreign Investment. These two institutions are in charge of the examination and approval of foreign-investment contracts and other documents. Members of these institutions include representatives from the key departments of the municipal government.[100] Since the establishment of the above-mentioned foreign-investment institutions in Xiamen, administrative efficiency has improved considerably, for most of the foreign-investment matters can now be decided immediately by these institutions instead of by various departments. The Foreign Investment Office and the Administrative Bureau have also terminated seven items of charges which they considered unreasonable and ordered the reduction of another five items.[101]

Conclusion

Since their establishment seven years ago, the SEZs in China have built up a basic infrastructure and legal system for foreign investment. They have played, and will continue to play, a leading role in the implementation of China's open policy. They have experimented with new methods of attracting foreign investment, many of which have since been adopted by the central government as well as other local governments in China. Although the SEZs encountered various problems and difficulties in their initial years, they have successfully adapted their local economies to bring them in line with the country's overall economic development. Needless to say, further improvements still need to be made by the SEZs in order to maintain their status as fore-runners in attracting foreign investment and in carrying out domestic economic reforms. In the areas where the laws and regulations of the SEZs lag behind the national laws, the local authorities should consider applying the national laws pending the amendment of the local provisions. More liberal and creative measures should also be considered by the SEZs.

99 *Id.*
100 *Economic Reporter*, 2 March 1987, p. 29.
101 *Id.*

Chapter six

The corporate law of the SEZs

The SEZs are laboratories for the carrying out of China's open policy. Special legislation which initially was applicable exclusively to the SEZs has since been adopted by the national as well as provincial legislative bodies. Very often, major laws and regulations are first applied in the SEZs and then confirmed with modifications by the national legislature or the central government. The Foreign Economic Contract Law is a case in point. Currently, there is no formal and comprehensive corporate law at the national level governing either foreign-investment companies or domestic Chinese companies, although the Sino-foreign Joint Venture Law has been in existence for eight years. As far as the SEZs are concerned, however, Guangdong Province has not only adopted a formal corporate law but also in 1986 enacted a bankruptcy law. This chapter will discuss and analyze the main features of the legislation governing foreign-investment enterprises adopted by Guangdong Province, in conjunction with the Sino-foreign Joint Venture Law adopted by the National People's Congress in 1979. A comparative analysis of the Shenzhen SEZ bankruptcy law and the national bankruptcy law (which is applicable solely to State-owned enterprises) will be conducted. As these statutes were enacted only recently, materials concerning their interpretation and implementation are not readily available. As such, this chapter will focus on the wording of these statutes and discuss their operation and impact on foreign investment in China.

I. Essential requirements for the establishment of a 'direct foreign investment company'

According to the Regulations of Guangdong Province on Foreign-related Companies in the Special Economic Zones (the 'Guangdong Company Regulations'),[1] enterprises with foreign participation or direct foreign investment companies (also referred to elsewhere as 'foreign-investment enterprises') include Sino-foreign equity joint ventures, Sino-foreign

1 The Regulations of Guangdong Province on Foreign-related Companies in the Special Economic Zones were adopted at the 27th Standing Committee Meeting of the 6th People's Congress of Guangdong Province on 28 September 1986. The legislation went into effect on 1 January 1987.

contractual ventures, wholly foreign-owned companies and joint stock companies using Chinese and foreign investment (hereinafter referred to collectively as 'DFICs' and singly as 'DFIC') which are subject to the Guangdong Company Regulations. DFICs are not categorized as either private or public companies, which is often the case under other jurisdictions. They are limited liability companies and must be established in compliance with the procedures prescribed in the Guangdong Company Regulations. They must also be capable of assuming civil obligations independently upon registration with the Municipal Bureau of the Administration of Industry and Commerce where they are located.[2]

Before a DFIC can be established the following requirements must be met:

(1) There must be compliance with China's laws and regulations;
(2) The establishment of the DFIC must be beneficial to the development of the national economy;
(3) The registered capital of the DFIC must be not less than RMB1 m (or the equivalent amount in another currency) and the initial paid-up capital (in cash) must be not less than 25% of the amount of registered capital;
(4) The DFIC must be advanced in the areas of production technology, operational and management methods;
(5) All or most of the products manufactured by the DFIC must be for export and the products must be competitive in the international market.[3]

Clearly, the above requirements resemble, to a large extent, provisions of the Detailed Regulations Concerning Joint Ventures adopted by he central government.[4] Nevertheless, at least two requirements are novel and reflect the current development of the economies in the SEZs. The RMB1 m minimum registered capital requirement is apparently aimed at diverting foreign investment to manufacturing industries and discouraging such investment in small companies or service companies. The statutory minimum 25% paid-up capital requirement will ensure that a DFIC will have enough capital to start up initial operations. As discussed earlier, all the SEZs in China are required to readjust their economies into export-oriented ones. The requirement that DFICs export all or most of their products is a major effort in that regard and is one of the important measures introduced by Guangdong Province.

As is the case with the Joint Venture Regulations, the Guangdong Company Regulations stipulate that the establishment of a DFIC will not

2 Guangdong Company Regulations, Article 3.
3 *Id*, Article 7.
4 Article 4 of the Regulations for the Implementation of the Law of the People's Republic of China on Joint Ventures Using Chinese and Foreign Investment (the 'Joint Venture Regulations').

be approved if such a company is detrimental to China's sovereignty, violates Chinese laws and regulations, is not beneficial to the development of the national economy, or will cause environmental pollution.[5] The first three situations which are common features of the laws of many developing countries do not require comment. The inclusion of the environmental factor as a condition is absolutely important, when we take into account the current serious industrial pollution problems in China caused by domestic enterprises. Moreover, this factor also helps in the implementation of China's Seventh Five-year Plan (1986–1990) which has allocated RMB33 b for environmental protection.[6] In addition, if the agreement, contract or articles of association concerning a DFIC are obviously unfair and detrimental to the rights and interests of either party to the joint undertaking, the application by the parties will be rejected.[7] This is in accordance with the principle of equality and mutual benefit which has been practised by the Chinese authorities for a long time. The essential purpose of this provision is to encourage arms-length transactions. Its application should therefore be restricted to the few bona fide cases where one party is taking advantage of the other in concluding cooperation arrangements. Otherwise it would lose its practical meaning and significance.

As regards the setting up of DFICs, different kinds of DFICs are required to follow different procedures and submit different application documents. Equity joint venture companies, cooperative contractual companies and wholly foreign-owned companies must submit the following documents:

(1) a written application;
(2) a feasibility study report;
(3) the names of suggested members of the board of directors; and
(4) credit standing certificates of the parties concerned.[8]

Equity as well as contractual joint ventures must also tender the contract signed between the parties.

The credit standing certificate is a new item added by the Guangdong Company Regulations which was omitted from the Joint Venture Regulations.[9] The adoption of this provision was a direct result of China's past experiences in foreign investment where foreign investors were not asked to present any evidence of their credit standing even though, as it turned out, some were not financially sound. As a result, several joint establishments suffered heavy losses and the Chinese financial institutions which blindly provided 100% guarantees for the foreign investors had to repay the debts at the demand of foreign

5 Guangdong Company Regulations, Article 8.
6 *Wen Wei Po*, 11 May 1987, p. 1
7 Guangdong Company Regulations, Article 8.
8 *Id*, Article 12.
9 The documents required for the establishment of joint ventures in China are set out in Article 9 of the Joint Venture Regulations.

creditors. Thus, with this new requirement, the Chinese approving authority will be in a better position to assess the financial strength of foreign investors.

The Guangdong Company Regulations have also laid down specific rules for the preparation and composition of feasibility studies. In the past, several of the Sino-foreign economic cooperation failures resulted directly from poor feasibility studies. Very often, in preparing feasibility studies, both the foreign and Chinese parties aim at persuading the aproving authorities to believe that the venture in question has a bright future. In the absence of criteria, uneven standards have been adopted by various local authorities. Being aware of these problems, the Guangdong Company Regulations stipulate that a feasibility study report must include the following items:

(1) the scale and scope of production, operations or services;
(2) the nature of the company;
(3) the methods and forms of capital contribution (or conditions of cooperation), total amount of investment and time limit for making the capital contribution;
(4) the lifespan of the company;
(5) international market demand and the company's capacity;
(6) the marketing scheme for the products and the forms in which services will be provided, and measures for balancing foreign exchange accounts;
(7) a study report on techniques employed and the technology programme;
(8) the economic returns report;
(9) organization of the work force in production, the number of staff and workers and their training programme(s);
(10) an evaluation report on the impact on environment;
(11) an evaluation report on labour safety and hygiene;
(12) site selection and the area of land to be occupied;
(13) the amounts of capital, power and water supply, raw materials and labour needed for operations and infrastructure construction, and ways and means of providing for such inputs; and
(14) a comprehensive plan of the project.[10]

With these specific guidelines, the approving authorities are in a much better position to assess the suitability of an applicant. The effective enforcement of this provision will depend, of course, on the experience and knowledge of the officials in charge which will also need to be improved and upgraded.

The Guangdong Company Regulations also provide for repayment of investments made by foreign investors in cooperative contractual ventures (hereinafter referred to as 'CCV').[11] A CCV is permitted to

10 Guangdong Company Regulations, Article 13.
11 *Id*, Article 14.

repay the principal plus interest, in respect of the investment contributed by the foreign investor(s), by using the profits to be made or the products to be manufactured by the CCV.[12] The purpose of this provision is to ensure that the foreign investor(s) in question will be repaid for the investment made. In a case where the foreign party cannot recoup its share of investment due to an event of *force majeure*, which takes place during the operation of the CCV contract, an extension of the venture may be requested and approved.[13]

The CCV contract and the articles of association must also clearly provide for the settlement of the assets of the company after its termination. As there is no national law at the moment governing the establishment of CCVs in China and their activities, the Guangdong Company Regulations will no doubt establish some precedents for the laws to be adopted by the national legislative bodies and other local authorities on the same subject matter.

The establishment of a Sino-foreign stock limited company ('JSLC') requires a different procedure and different documents. Under the Guangdong Company Regulations, an application for the setting up of a JSLC must be submitted by at least five promoters. In addition, at least 50% of the promoters must be from the SEZ with the remainder from abroad.[14] The promoters are required to sign a formation contract and prepare the prospectus and articles of association of the company. In addition to these documents, the promoters will also need to prepare a written application, the credit standing certificates of the promoters and a feasibility study report, and present the same to the local municipal government for approval. The Regulations do not lay down any specific qualifications which the promoters must satisfy. Promoters can either be individuals (natural persons) or legal persons who carry corporate or other statuses.

The formation contract of a JSLC must include the following items:

(1) the objectives and scope of management of the company;
(2) the scope, aim and mechanics of the share issue;
(3) the total amount of shares to be issued and the face value of each share;
(4) the arrangement for the sharing of expenses among the promoters in respect of the inauguration of the company; and
(5) the benefits to the promoters in respect of work done.[15]

The promoters are required to bear, on a joint basis, all liabilities concerning the formation of a joint stock company. Before the company is actually formed, the promoters will not be allowed to negotiate or conclude legal obligations on behalf of the company and, if they do, they must bear all resultant losses or benefits personally.

12 *Id*, Article 35.
13 *Id*.
14 *Id*, Article 46.
15 *Id*, Article 48.

The prospectus to be submitted to the local municipal government for approval should contain:

(1) the total amount of shares to be issued;
(2) the type of shares;
(3) distribution methods for dividends and bonuses;
(4) notification procedures etc.[16]

The number of shares subscribed by each promoter must be specified in the prospectus. The promoters of a JSLC as a whole, must subscribe for not less than 25% of shares offered in the first share issue which should account for at least 25% of the total number of shares to be issued.[17] This provision serves to guarantee the minimum capital that a JSLC must have at its formation. The position of the Guangdong Company Regulations in connection with this matter is further clarified by the stipulation that such promoters are jointly liable for those shares which are not subscribed for by the public in the first share issue.[18] As a matter of comparison, the 25% subscription requirement for promoters is more liberal than that applicable to promoters of domestic Chinese enterprises who must pledge to take up 30% of the total share issue of a newly-established stock company.[19]

Within 30 days after completion of the first share issue, the promoters are to convene a company inauguration meeting. A written notification of the meeting should be sent to all subscribers 15 days prior to the date of the meeting. The purpose of meeting is to hear and examine a work report, prepared by the promoters, concerning the inauguration of the company, to amend and adopt the articles of association, and to elect the board of directors.[20]

The municipal government of the city where an SEZ is located is authorized to examine and approve the formation of DFICs.[21] The duration of operations of a DFIC should be specified in the relevant contracts or articles of association. Generally speaking, the life-span of a joint venture company or a wholly foreign-owned company is 5 to 30 years. A longer period may be allowed if the company contributes a large amount of investment, employs high technology, and has a long period of capital return or a low rate of return.[22] The life-spans of contractual joint ventures and joint stock companies are not specified in the Guangdong Company Regulations and are therefore left entirely to the parties concerned. For instance, a joint stock company can exist indefinitely

16 *Id*, Article 49.
17 *Id*, Article 52.
18 *Id*.
19 Provisional Rules of Guangdong Province on the Management of Shares and Bonds adopted by the Guangdong Provincial Government on 10 October 1986 (the 'Guangdong Shares and Bonds Management Rules'), Article 7.
20 Guangdong Company Regulations, Article 54.
21 *Id*, Article 6.
22 *Id*, Article 119.

unless and until it goes bankrupt or its members decide to wind it up. The silence of the Guangdong Company Regulations on this matter is clearly a step forward from the current national legislation which provides shorter life-spans for foreign-investment projects.

Upon the expiration of its operations, a DFIC may apply for an extension.[23] The application should be submitted to the municipal government 180 days prior to the date of expiration. The local authority must reply within 30 days upon receipt of such application.[24]

Once the establishment of a DFIC is approved, a certificate will be issued. Thereafter, the company will be regarded as having the status of a legal person under Chinese law. It must then go through the registration formalities with the tax bureau, local foreign exchange authorities and import and export administrative bodies. The DFIC is also required to open an account with a bank in the SEZ.[25] After the extension of its operations has been approved, the company in question must go through similar registration procedures.[26]

II. Internal organizational structure

The Guangdong Company Regulations provide that DFICs may have separate organizational structures, depending on their corporate nature. The internal organizational structure of wholly foreign-owned companies is not specified in the statute and is therefore left to the members of the company to decide. Joint venture companies ('JVC'), CCVs and JSLCs are each subject to different rules.

Following the principles established by the Joint Venture Law and the Joint Venture Regulations, the Guangdong Company Regulations provide that the highest authority of a JVC or a CCV is its board of directors which should consist of not less than three persons. The composition of the board of directors should be agreed upon by the parties concerned.[27] The chairman of the board of directors is to be appointed by the Chinese party while the vice chairmen (one or two) are to be appointed by the foreign party. Upon approval by the municipal government of the SEZ in question, however, the chairmanship of the board of directors can be shared on a rotation basis by the Chinese and foreign parties.[28] This provision is a major departure from the Joint Venture Law which provides that the chairmanship must be occupied by the Chinese party.[29] The latter provision, in general, effectively excludes non-Chinese citizens from being elected as chairman. Under the liberal provisions of the

23 *Id*, Article 120.
24 *Id*.
25 *Id*, Article 9.
26 *Id*, Article 121.
27 *Id*, Article 15.
28 *Id*.
29 Law of the People's Republic of China on Joint Ventures Using Chinese and Foreign Investment, Article 6.

Guangdong Company Regulations, the Chinese party can appoint an individual from the foreign party or a third party to be the chairman. This discretion is most welcome to foreign investors, as the chairman of the board of directors is the statutory legal representative of the company.

In addition to matters concerning amendments to the articles of association, additional capitalization, assignment of equity interest, and merger, discontinuation and dissolution of the company, the board of directors is vested with the authority to prepare the development plans, and operations and management programmes of the company. It may also exercise powers over matters concerning business operations, budget, settlement of accounts, employment of the general manager, deputy general managers, chief engineer, chief accountant, auditors and other senior managerial personnel, and wages of staff and workers etc.[30]

The board of directors must hold meetings at least once a year. Interim meetings may be called at the request of more than one-third of the directors. The quorum for a board meeting is 50% or more of the directorship. This provision deviates from the original requirement under the Joint Venture Regulations.[31] Board meetings should be called and chaired by the chairman.[32] Apparently, this power can be exercised either at the chairman's own initiative or at the demand of other board members. For instance, under normal circumstances, the chairman calls and chairs the annual meetings. At the same time, if more than one-third of the directors request an interim meeting, the chairman is legally bound to hold a meeting regardless of whether he consents to the convening of such a meeting or not. In extraordinary cases where the chairman refuses to convene an interim meeting, the issue of whether a vice chairman or another director, without authority delegated to him by the chairman, can call such a meeting has not been specifically addressed in the Guangdong statute. In accordance with the spirit of the legislation, however, in such cases a vice chairman or a director should be able to do so.

A JVC or CCV must set up a management office in its domicile, which should comprise a general manager and several deputy general managers who will be responsible for the day-to-day management of the company.[33] The general manager's functions include carrying out the decisions of the board of directors, organizing and conducting the day-to-day management of the company, and other duties authorized by the board. His authority in managing the external as well as internal affairs of the company should be defined, and delegated to him, by the board of directors.[34] As employees of the company, the general manager and

30 Guangdong Company Regulations, Article 16.
31 Article 35 of the China's Joint Venture Regulations provides that a board of directors' meeting requires a quorum of at least two-thirds of the directors.
32 Guangdong Company Regulations, Article 17.
33 *Id*, Article 19.
34 *Id*, Article 20.

deputy general managers can either be Chinese or foreign citizens. In any event, they must be full-time employees of the company, and are allowed neither to hold current posts in other companies in the capacity of general manager or deputy general manager nor to engage in any activities which compete with those of the company.[35] The general manager and deputy general managers are required to stay in the legal domicile of their company.

The board of directors and the general manager as well as the deputy general managers can be held responsible for losses suffered by the company as a result of corruption or serious dereliction of their duties. Nevertheless, the punishment for breach of fiduciary duties by the directors and managers may be different. The directors involved may be required to compensate for any losses caused but they cannot be removed from the board unless the party which originally appointed them decides to do so. However, the general manager or deputy general manager may be made to compensate the company for any losses suffered and may at the same time be removed from his post.[36]

Unlike a JVC or CCV, a JSLC's highest authority is its shareholders' general meeting which can be held either on a regular or special basis. The board of directors of a JSLC serves as the management, decision-making and execution body. The regular shareholders' general meeting, which is usually chaired by the chairman of the board of directors, must be held once a year, normally in the first quarter of the year.[37] Shareholders must be informed of the meeting by the board of directors 15 days in advance of the meeting. A special shareholders' general meeting may be convened at the request of the board of directors if it considers the meeting to be necessary or at the initiative of one-quarter of the shareholders.[38]

The principle of voting at the shareholders' general meeting is one vote per share. Any shareholder may appoint a proxy to represent him at the meeting and vote on his behalf. An appointment of proxy must be in writing.[39]

Shareholders' resolutions are subdivided into two categories, namely, ordinary and extraordinary. For any ordinary resolution to be valid, the shareholders attending the meeting must own more than 50% of the total number of shares of the company and the resolution must be supported by more than 50% of the votes of the shareholders attending the meeting.[40] For an extraordinary resolution to be adopted, the quorum is that the shareholders attending must hold two-thirds of the total number of shares and more than 50% of them vote in favour of the resolution.[41]

35 *Id*, Article 21.
36 *Id*, Article 22.
37 *Id*, Article 56.
38 *Id*.
39 *Id*, Article 59.
40 *Id*, Article 60.
41 *Id*, Article 61.

As a statutory requirement, the following matters must be decided by an extraordinary resolution:

(1) additional capitalization, bond issues, mergers, transfer of the entire or a substantial part of the assets of the company, and dissolution and liquidation of the company;
(2) amendments to the articles of association;
(3) appointment of the chairman of the board of directors where he is not a shareholder of the company; and
(4) other matters that require an extraordinary resolution as prescribed in the articles of association of the company.[42]

The provision implies that the chairman of the board of directors of a JSLC should generally be a shareholder of the company. In addition, the adoption and amendment of the articles of association as well as the assignment of the company's assets are not only subject to the authority of the shareholders' meeting but also require the affirmative vote of the holders of two-thirds of the shares. This is to provide minority shareholders with some remedies in case majority shareholders try to amend the articles of association at their expense.

Matters that can be decided by an ordinary shareholder vote include:

(1) the hearing and examination of the work report of the board of directors;
(2) the hearing and examination of the company's production and operations plans, budget report and account settlement report;
(3) the examination and approval of the proposals of the board of directors regarding such capital accounts as the reserve fund, employees' bonus and benefit fund, expansion fund, as well as plans for the distribution of dividends and bonus;
(4) the election and removal of board members and the determination of remuneration for the board of directors;
(5) the appointment and removal of, and the remuneration for, the person in charge of the reorganization or liquidation of the company; and
(6) decisions on other essential matters concerning the operations of the company.[43]

Although JSLCs are not restricted from issuing different classes of shares, it is quite surprising that this statute fails to prescribe whether shareholders of a JSLC who hold different classes of shares can appoint their own directors in accordance with the rights granted by their respective classes of shares. This right to appoint directors is common in other jurisdictions, eg, the US.

As regards shareholders' meetings, if the required quorum is not met at

42 *Id*, Articles 58 and 61.
43 *Id*, Article 58.

the scheduled date for the meeting, the meeting must be deferred for a period of 15 days at the expiration of which it should proceed regardless of the quorum.[44]

The chairman of the board of directors of a JSLC is the legal representative of the company and can exercise the functions and powers of the board of directors when the board is not in session.[45] As the management and execution body of the company, the functions of the board of directors include the following:

(1) convening the shareholders' general meeting;
(2) carrying out the resolutions adopted at the shareholders' general meeting;
(3) deciding all matters relating to the employment of the general manager, deputy general managers, chief engineer, chief accountant, auditors and other senior managerial personnel;
(4) deciding on the wages of staff and workers and formulating the reward and punishment scheme;
(5) preparing the production and management programmes, financial budget and account settlement report, dividends and bonus distribution plans as well as proposals relating to additional capitalization, merging and transfer of the property;
(6) managing important external corporate affairs; and
(7) exercising other powers as stipulated in the articles of association or authorized by the shareholders in general meetings.[46]

The exercise of several of the powers by the board of directors is, however, subject to the review and approval of the shareholders at shareholders' meetings. An obvious example would be any decision concerning salaries, bonuses and punishment systems.

Thirty days prior to the date of a regular shareholders' general meeting, the board of directors of a JSLC must have prepared and compiled the following financial statements:

(1) annual account settlement report and the annual budget;
(2) balance sheet of the company;
(3) profit and loss statement;
(4) inventory report;
(5) programmes regarding the withdrawal of capital from such capital accounts as reserve fund, employees' bonus and benefit fund, and expansion fund; and
(6) plans for the distribution of dividends and bonuses.[47]

The annual account settlement report, balance sheet and profit and loss statement must be verified by an accountant registered in China. The

44 *Id*, Article 62.
45 *Id*, Article 66.
46 *Id*, Article 65.
47 *Id*, Article 101.

above-mentioned documents must, before the date of a regular shareholders' general meeting, be placed at the principal place of business of the company for inspection and examination by the shareholders.[48]

The procedure for appointment of the general manager and deputy general managers of a JSLC is similar to that applicable to JVCs and CCVs. The functions of the general manager and deputy general managers are also more or less the same. All the directors, the general manager and deputy general managers are subject to removal and/or punishment for breach of fiduciary duties.[49]

III. Business operations and shareholding

The Guangdong Company Regulations have laid down specific standards regarding the operations of JVCs and CCVs whereas wholly foreign-owned companies and JSLCs are subject only to the general guidelines stipulated in that statute. Each JVC, CCV or wholly foreign-owned company is required to work out a production and operations plan based on its scope of business as approved by the local municipal industry and commerce bureau and its production scale.[50] The production and operations plan must be carried out by the company in question and should be reported to the relevant department of each municipality for record.

All DFICs have been granted rights to operate independently and to decide whether purchases of machinery, equipment or materials should be made in China or from abroad. JVCs and CCVs are required, however, to give priority to purchasing such items in China where the terms and conditions in respect of the purchase in China and from abroad are equal.[51]

JVCs and CCVs must prepare a procurement and inspection scheme for materials which includes the following items:

(1) The obligations of the person(s) responsible for the procurement and inspection of materials;
(2) Methods concerning how the procurement and inspection of materials should be conducted, with respect to variety, specifications, quality, quantity and packaging;
(3) Methods of checking and verifying the prices of materials purchased and confirmation of invoices;
(4) The scope of authority of members of the board and management (regarding the examination and approval of the procurement and inspection of materials); and
(5) A reward and penalty scheme.[52]

48 *Id*, Article 102.
49 *Id*, Article 68.
50 *Id*, Article 29.
51 *Id*, Article 30.
52 *Id*.

With the establishment of these specific criteria, JVCs and CCVs can better manage their procurement activities. The persons in charge of these activities will be rewarded or punished depending on their performance. This method will effectively reduce the potential conflicts or differences btween JVC or CCV parties, which in turn will significantly contribute to the smooth management of such companies. The Guangdong Company Regulations stipulate that in purchasing large quantities of materials or materials involving large sums, all the parties to the JVC or CCV must be consulted and the purchase should not be concluded unless an agreement is reached by all.[53] A JVC or CCV may purchase required materials through an agent who is acceptable to all the venture parties or through inviting tenders for such purchases.[54] The board of directors of a JVC or CCV is required to take legal action against anyone who commits a serious offence in respect of procurement or inspection.[55]

DFICs are required to sell all or a substantial portion of their products in the international market. When marketing its products abroad, the board of directors of a JVC or CCV may establish a minimum price for the product in question, taking into account the international market prices of similar merchandise over the relevant period of time. In such cases, the general manager and deputy general managers can jointly set a higher selling price. If they decide to market the products at a price below the minimum level decided by the board, the consent of the board of directors must be secured in advance, otherwise such general manager or deputy general managers may be held responsible for any economic losses suffered by the company as a result of their decisions.[56]

The above-mentioned scheme is entirely new to Chinese law. Its purpose is to ensure that the general manager and deputy general managers carry out the decisions of the board of directors strictly and effectively. Nonetheless, strict enforcement of this provision may reduce the efficiency of a JVC or CCV. For instance, international market conditions are often impredictable. If the general manager is or the deputy general managers are obliged to observe the minimum price requirement, they may lose marketing opportunities, for very often a slightly lower price may increase sales substantially. In practice, however, the operations of JVCs or CCVs will not be restricted in this way. Firstly, in most of the cases the general manager is a member of the board. As such, there should be no problems in communications between the board and him. Secondly, the board of directors can set the minimum price at a lower level in order to give the general manager and deputy general managers adequate discretion in making marketing decisions.

A DFIC is required to prepare its production, supply and sales

53 *Id.*
54 *Id.*
55 *Id.*
56 *Id*, Article 31.

statistics and report them to the relevant departments in the municipality where it is located.[57] It is also required to set up its own accounting unit and maintain its own set of books in the SEZ where the enterprise is established. Quarterly and annual financial reports are required to be submitted to the municipal tax bureau, municipal finance bureau, and other relevant departments.[58] The auditors of a DFIC are also responsible for the examination and auditing of the income, expenditure and other accounting items of the company, and must furnish their verification reports to the board of directors of the company.[59]

A JSLC is not required to follow the general guidelines set out in the Guangdong Company Regulations in respect of procurement and marketing. While JSLCs can operate independently, they must follow certain criteria in allocating their incomes. For instance, compensation for losses accrued in previous years of operation and payment of income tax must be paid out of the operational income of a JSLC first. Once this has been done, the company should then decide to use its current year's profits in the following order:

(1) repayment of matured liabilities;
(2) allocation of certain amounts for the reserve fund, employees bonus and benefit fund and expansion fund; and
(3) payment of dividends and bonuses.[60]

It should be noted that a JSLC is not permitted to distribute dividends and bonuses if it does not have a surplus in the current year. Nevertheless, if the company's reserve fund amounts to more than half of its registered capital, then upon resolution by the shareholders, 50% of the reserve fund may be withdrawn and distributed as dividends and bonuses to the shareholders.[61]

Except for the above-mentioned general principles, JSLCs are not subject to any other restrictions in the allocation of dividends. This is in sharp contrast to the situation of domestic Chinese enterprises in Guangdong Province which are not permitted to pay after-tax dividends and bonuses at rates exceeding 15% of their share capital.[62] The maximum rate of distribution for dividends and bonuses of the stocks of domestic Chinese enterprises is restricted to 20% of the annual interest rate offered by banks for time deposits taken by the public.[63]

The Guangdong Company Regulations have confirmed the methods of investment contribution by JVC parties which were set out in the Joint Venture Regulations. The parties to a JVC or CCV may contribute cash, buildings, land use rights, machinery, equipment, other materials,

57 *Id*, Article 32.
58 *Id*, Article 33.
59 See *Id*, Articles 34 and 104.
60 *Id*, Article 86.
61 *Id*.
62 Guangdong Shares and Bonds Management Rules, Article 11.
63 *Id*.

industrial property rights and proprietary technology either as investments or as part of the terms of cooperation.[64] Every party is required to pay its share of contribution within the period prescribed in the contract. The party which fails to carry out its obligations may be charged interest on the delayed amount or be asked to pay compensation for any losses suffered by the company.[65]

In several respects, the Guangdong Company Regulations have established more specific criteria for items to be contributed by JVC or CCV parties. The machinery or equipment provided by any party must be technically advanced, by international standards, and the materials provided must also be acceptable in international markets.[66] As regards the pricing of such items, the JVC or CCV parties are required to follow strictly the current international market prices for similar items. Moreover, such items must have passed an examination conducted by the China Import and Export Commodity Inspection Administration or its subordinate entities.[67] As a result of a previous unfortunate experience, the Guangdong Company Regulations further stipulate that any party to a JVC or CCV who contributes out-dated or worn-out equipment in order to deceive the other party or parties to the JVC or CCV is to be held responsible for any losses suffered by the company as a result.[68] This provision will help prevent the introduction of backward or unsuitable technology or equipment and help to ensure high standards of productivity and product quality.

The JVC or CCV parties may contribute their share of investment on a instalment basis. Under such circumstances, the parties concerned must have their investments verified by a China-registered accountant after each instalment is made.[69] The venture in question should not issue any investment certificate unless it has received a verification report by the accountant.

In comparison, the capitalization of a JSLC is much simpler. The paid-up capital collected for the shares issued by a JSLC in its first share issue is the registered capital of the JSLC.[70] All shares issued by a JSLC must be of equal value, although the face value of each share may be expressed in terms of Renminbi or other currencies. All shares must be registered and may be either common shares or preferred shares.[71] A JSLC can issue preferred shares in only one of the following circumstances:

(1) The issuance of common shares may cause difficulty;
(2) The company has financial problems which necessitate the raising of additional funds; or

64 Guangdong Company Regulations, Article 24.
65 *Id*, Article 28.
66 *Id*, Article 25.
67 *Id*.
68 *Id*.
69 *Id*, Article 27.
70 *Id*, Article 70.
71 *Id*.

(3) The company has insufficient funds to finance the introduction of advanced technology for its operations.[72]

Obviously, the Guangdong Company Regulations are not in favour of preferred shares being issued. This view is further clarified by the stipulation that every JSLC has the right to redeem its preferred shares in due course, in accordance with the terms and conditions specified in the articles of association.[73]

The specific rights of the preferred shareholders must be stipulated in the articles of association of the company. In the main, such shareholders are entitled to receive dividends higher than those paid to common shareholders, and to have priority in the distribution of dividends and the allocation of residual assets of the company.[74]

When additional funds are needed for the continued operation of a JSLC, it may raise new capital by issuing new shares. Such issues must be approved by an extraordinary resolution of a shareholders' general meeting.[75] No JSLC is permitted to issue new shares if it has not yet collected all the paid-up capital for shares already issued, or if it has suffered losses continuously for the previous two years.[76] However, JSLCs which take a longer period to recoup their capital but which have detailed and well-prepared operational plans and a high potential to generate profits, are not subject to this restriction on raising capital. The criteria for the application of this exception have been left to the local authorities in charge of share issues.

The Guangdong Company Regulations do not lay down any specific requirements for the transfer, assignment or mortgage of equity interests or other rights and interests of wholly foreign-owned companies. JSLC shareholders also face fewer restrictions when transferring or mortgaging their stocks. Shareholders of JSLCs are permitted to transfer their shares freely except that, from the date that notice of the shareholders' general meeting is given to the day the meeting ends, no share transfer registration application or other registration application in respect of changes of ownership will be accepted by the company.[77]

JSLC shares may be assigned, donated, inherited or used as collateral for bank loans.[78] Nevertheless, when a JSLC is undergoing a liquidation, its shares may not be assigned, mortgaged or transferred. In the case of promoters, their shares are not to be transferred within one year from the date of establishment of the company.[79] Transfers of shares owned by the directors of the company need to be approved and authorized by the board of directors.[80] As for shares which are jointly owned by more than

72 *Id*, Article 72.
73 *Id*, Article 74.
74 *Id*, Article 73.
75 *Id*, Article 87.
76 *Id*.
77 *Id*, Article 81.
78 *Id*.
79 *Id*, Article 83.
80 *Id*.

one person or entity, the transfers of these shares are subject to unanimous consent by the shareholders concerned.[81]

The transfer, in part or in whole, by one party to a JVC of the equity interests it owns to a third party must be authorized by the board of directors, and is subject to the approval of the local municipal people's government.[82] As regards such transfers, the other party to the JVC must be given priority in purchasing the shares which the other is intending to sell. Conditions for such transfers must not be less favourable than those for transfers to third parties. Share transfers which are in violation of the above-mentioned conditions may be regarded as invalid.[83] Transfers or assignments of rights and interests by the parties are also subject to similar conditions. However, land use rights or buildings contributed by the Chinese party to a CCV can be transferred only to a Chinese entity.[84] This provision applies only to CCVs, although joint venture parties may also contribute existing factories, buildings or work sites in return for equity interests.

The parties to a JVC or CCV may mortgage their equity interests or other rights and interests to third parties. Such transactions must be approved and authorized by the board of directors.[85] In addition, the proceeds of a mortgage, by a foreign investor in a CCV, of its rights and interests must not exceed the amount contributed or invested by the foreign party minus the amount that it has already recovered.[86] This provision is only necessary because CCVs are essentially contractual arrangements and the parties thereto are only entitled to what they have contracted for. If any party is allowed to mortgage its rights and interests for an amount larger than that which it is entitled to, the contractual venture in question may suffer losses.

IV. Reorganization and liquidation

DFICs operating in the SEZs which face financial difficulties may be declared bankrupt either voluntarily or compulsorily. Under certain circumstances, a reorganization of such companies may be allowed in order to save them from bankruptcy.

A DFIC facing bankruptcy may apply to have the enterprise reorganized. Such application should be made to a higher level department in charge of the DFIC which may approve the application if the DFIC:

(1) employs high technology and uses advanced equipment, produces products which are in great demand in the domestic market;
(2) contributes a large amount of investment; and
(3) takes a long period of time to recoup its investment.

81 *Id*, Article 84.
82 *Id*, Article 36.
83 *Id*.
84 *Id*, Article 38.
85 *Id*, Articles 37 and 39.
86 *Id*, Article 39.

In addition, if the bankruptcy of a DFIC will have unfavourable effects on society, a reorganization of the DFIC will most likely be allowed.[87]

While the first three conditions are easier to determine, the impact of a bankruptcy case on society may be difficult to assess. Presumably, if the DFIC in question plays an important part in the national economy or if its bankruptcy will have a substantial impact on domestic employment or the implementation of large contractual projects etc, the application for reorganization would be considered more favourably. This is better illustrated by the National State Enterprise Insolvency Law which provides that public enterprises and enterprises which are crucial to the national economy and to the people's livelihood may not be declared insolvent.[88]

Once an application for reorganization is approved,[89] the shareholders or the board of directors of the DFIC in question must appoint three to five persons to form a reorganization panel within 15 days of the approval.[90] The members of the panel can be shareholders, directors, or professionals who have no connection with the enterprise. The government department in charge and the creditors of the enterprise are each entitled to appoint one or two representatives to form a supervisory group to oversee the reorganization.

The functions of the reorganization panel include the following:

(1) exercising, in an acting capacity, the functions and powers of the board of directors;
(2) being in charge of all accounting books, certificates and documents relating to the business and financial activities of the DFIC;
(3) being in charge of the production and management rights of the DFIC;
(4) being in charge of the management and disposition of property;
(5) being responsible for the signing of contracts on behalf of the DFIC;
(6) drafting and implementing reorganization plans; and
(7) convening shareholders' general meetings, board meetings and creditors' meetings.[91]

87 *Id*, Article 107.

88 The State Enterprise Insolvency Law of the People's Republic of China was adopted at the 18th Meeting of the Standing Committee of the 6th Session of the National People's Congress on 12 December 1986 (the 'National State Enterprise Insolvency Law'). This statute is currently not in force and will take effect three months after the implementation of the Ownership of the Whole People Industrial Enterprise Law which is being drafted. Article 3 of the National State Enterprise Insolvency Law prescribes the circumstances under which State-owned enterprises may not be declared insolvent.

89 The higher-level department in charge must give an official reply to the reorganization application within 30 days upon receipt of all documents. See Guangdong Company Regulations, Article 110.

90 *Id*, Article 111.

91 *Id*, Article 113.

When a reorganization panel exercises its authority in respect of items 4, 5 and 6 above, the permission of the supervisory group is required. In addition, whenever members of the reorganization panel cannot reach agreement among themselves, the government department in charge of the company is authorized to make a final decision.[92]

The reorganization plans drafted by the reorganization panel should include suggestions regarding methods of disposition of property, collection of outstanding credits extended by the reorganized company, raising of additional capital, amendments to be made to the articles of association if necessary, and adjustments to the corporate structure of the enterprise in question.[93] All reorganization proposals and plans are subject to the approval of the shareholders or the board of directors, and should be submitted to the government department in charge for purposes of record. In any event, the reorganization of a DFIC must be completed within 180 days after the date the reorganization proposal is adopted.[94]

It is interesting to note that the reorganization of a State-owned enterprise which is facing a bankruptcy petition follows a similar pattern. Such an enterprise is not allowed to request for reorganization itself. Instead, the government department in charge of the enterprise may petition the court to have the enterprise reorganized.[95] This department would then be responsible for directing the reorganization. Representatives of the enterprise's employees are authorized to discuss the reorganization plans, and the employees themselves should be informed of the progress of the reorganization and their opinions solicited. Creditors are also entitled to be informed of the circumstances of the reorganization.[96] State-owned enterprises are given no more than two years to reorganize themselves.[97]

Under certain circumstances, a DFIC operating in a SEZ in Guangdong may be terminated. These circumstances include the expiration of the period of operations of the enterprise as stipulated in its contract or articles of association, the merger or assignment of all the property of the enterprise, the decision by the board of directors or shareholders to terminate voluntarily the operations of the enterprise, the occurrence of any event requiring dissolution of the enterprise as stipulated in the contract or articles of association, and the occurrence of any event of *force majeure*.[98] The board of directors or shareholders of a DFIC may also dissolve the operations of the enterprise by an extraordinary resolution. At the same time, if a DFIC has not resumed its operations

92 *Id.*
93 *Id*, Article 114.
94 *Id*, Article 115.
95 National State Enterprise Insolvency Law, Article 17.
96 *Id*, Article 20.
97 *Id*, Article 17.
98 Guangdong Company Regulations, Article 127.

after the approved adjournment period is over, it may be regarded as having been terminated automatically.[99]

The operations of a DFIC may be discontinued by a court order under the following situations:

(1) The DFIC in question has caused serious environmental pollution and ecological damage;
(2) A party to the enterprise has failed to honour its obligations and the normal operations of the DFIC are thereby seriously affected;
(3) A party has violated certain laws and this violation has substantial impact on the normal operations of the enterprise.[100]

A DFIC may also terminate its existence when an insolvency is declared either by itself, in which case consent of the municipality is required, or by court order. Under the Shenzhen SEZ Company Insolvency Regulations,[101] creditors may petition for a declaration of insolvency of their debtor.[102] The court must determine, within 10 days upon receiving a petition, whether or not it will accept the case.[103]

Once a dissolution decision is made either by the municipal government or by a court, the DFIC must be liquidated within a period of 180 days.[104] Under such circumstances, the DFIC in question must set up a liquidating committee, consisting of three persons, within ten days upon receiving the municipal government's decision or the court order.[105] The Shenzhen SEZ Company Insolvency Regulations, however, stipulate that if a Chinese court orders the insolvency of a DFIC, the liquidating committee may be formed by three to five persons including one China-registered accountant.[106] At the same time, Article 24 of the National State Enterprise Insolvency Law stipulates that members of the liquidating committee must be selected by the court from the government department in charge of the enterprise, the relevant government finance department and from among professonals. Although in cases of compulsory liquidation of a DFIC the court has the power to appoint the members of the liquidating committee, representatives from government departments may not necessarily be included.

The functions of a liquidating committee include convening creditors' meetings, board meetings and shareholders' meetings, being in charge of the property of the enterprise in question, preparing the balance sheet and the general inventory report, finalizing business dealings of the

99 *Id.*
100 *Id*, Article 128.
101 The Shenzhen Special Economic Zone Foreign Company Insolvency Regulations were adopted at the 23rd Meeting of the Standing Committee of the 6th Session of the Guangdong People's Congress on 29 December 1986, to be effective as of 1 July 1987 (the 'Shenzhen SEZ Company Insolvency Regulations').
102 Shenzhen SEZ Company Insolvency Regulations, Article 7.
103 *Id*, Article 9.
104 Guangdong Company Regulations, Article 129.
105 *Id*, Article 130.
106 Shenzhen SEZ Company Insolvency Regulations, Article 12.

enterprise, drafting liquidation plans and procedures, and deciding on the implementation of the liquidation plans and the distribution of company assets.[107] In addition to the duty of collecting outstanding credits extended by the insolvent enterprise, a liquidating committee must make calls on contributors of the insolvent DFIC for payment of such amounts as are acknowledged and unpaid.[108] The committee is also charged with the duties of allocating residual assets and acting on behalf of the DFIC in legal disputes or other activities.[109]

Under the National State Enterprise Insolvency Law, a liquidating committee is empowered to decide whether to rescind or continue to perform and discharge the contracts to which the insolvent enterprise is a party.[110] Where the liquidating committee decides to rescind a contract and where the other party to the contract suffers losses, the amount of such losses can be regarded as insolvency claims.[111] Neither the Guangdong Company Regulations nor the Shenzhen SEZ Company Insolvency Regulations has such a provision. Apparently, the basis for the adoption by the national insolvency law of such a provision is that a number of State-owned enterprises operate in accordance with mandatory State planning. If contracts signed by such enterprises cannot be carried out, the State plan may therefore not be fulfilled which in turn may have serious effects on the national economy. If a liquidating committee is vested with authority to determine whether certain contracts should be performed, the above situation can be effectively avoided. The reason for the omission in the Guangdong Company Regulations and Shenzhen SEZ Company Insolvency Regulations of any provisions regarding compensation for losses suffered by other parties to a contract involving the insolvent company is not clear, however, for the national statute and the Shenzhen SEZ Company Insolvency Regulations were adopted at almost the same time. In any event, the absence of these provisions may put such contracting parties in an ambiguous position.

As regards distribution of the properties of the insolvent company, secured creditors, such as providers of mortgage loans, enjoy a right of prior recovery against the item secured.[112] If the assets of the DFIC in question are insufficient to cover the claims, compensation should be made in the following order:

(1) liquidation expenses;
(2) wages, salaries and social insurance funds of workers and staff;
(3) taxes payable to the State; and
(4) other debts incurred by the DFIC.[113]

107 Guangdong Company Regulations, Article 133.
108 *Id*, and also see Article 43 of the Shenzhen SEZ Company Insolvency Regulations.
109 Guangdong Company Regulations, Article 133.
110 National State Enterprise Insolvency Law, Article 26.
111 *Id.*
112 Article 140 of the Guangdong Company Regulations and Article 39 of the Shenzhen SEZ Company Insolvency Regulations.
113 Guangdong Company Regulations, Article 40.

If the insolvent DFIC does not have sufficient resources to repay its debts of a particular category, creditors belonging to that category must share the amount allocated to that category proportionately.[114] The National State Enterprise Insolvency Law and the Shenzhen SEZ Company Insolvency Regulations have adopted similar provisions in this matter.

Both the National State Enterprise Insolvency Law and the Shenzhen SEZ Company Insolvency Regulations provide that certain actions taken by an enterprise, within 180 days prior to the declaration of its insolvency, are to be regarded as invalid. They include:

(1) concealment, illicit distribution or gratuitous transfer of property;
(2) provision of security to creditors who were originally unsecured;
(3) repayment of debts before their due date;
(4) abandonment of the company's own credits; and
(5) permission granted to third parties to occupy or remove property of the company gratuitously.[115]

A DFIC facing an insolvency petition may apply to the court for reconciliation. Upon approval by the court, the liquidating committee should convene a creditors' meeting to examine the reconciliation plans adopted by the enterprise. Such plans must be carried out strictly, otherwise the DFIC may be declared insolvent as a result.[116]

As a general principle, the Guangdong Company Regulations and the Shenzhen SEZ Company Insolvency Regulations do not recognize an insolvency which is declared according to the insolvency law of a foreign country, and thus the property of the insolvent situated in a SEZ will not be affected.[117] When a foreign party to a JVC or CCV or the foreign owner of a wholly foreign-owned company established in a SEZ is declared insolvent outside China, the said institution or individual may give opinions on the disposition of its assets in the SEZ.[118] The disposition of such property must take the form of a transfer of shares or an assignment of rights and interests which should be executed without adversely affecting the normal business and operations of the enterprise.[119] The proceeds of such transfer or assignment must be applied first to the costs of the verification of the assets, taxes payable and other domestic debts.[120] The disposal of the remainder of the proceeds will then be decided by the owner.

The board of directors of an insolvent DFIC is not liable for the insolvency of the enterprise unless a crime is committed by either the

114 *Id.*
115 See Article 35 of the National State Enterprise Insolvency Law and Article 11 of the Shenzhen SEZ Company Insolvency Regulations respectively.
116 For reconciliation, see Articles 19–26 of the Shenzhen SEZ Company Insolvency Regulations.
117 Shenzhen SEZ Company Insolvency Regulations, Article 5.
118 Guangdong Company Regulations, Article 40.
119 *Id*, Article 44.
120 *Id*, Article 45.

DFIC itself or any of its representatives. On the other hand, when a State-owned enterprise is declared insolvent, the supervisory government departments and auditing department must conduct an investigation into the cause of the insolvency. The legal respresentatives of the insolvent enterprise as well as the leaders of the government departments in charge, principally responsible for the insolvency, are subject to administrative punishment. If these persons have caused the insolvency of the enterprise through dereliction of duty, resulting in great losses to the nation, they may be prosecuted according to the provisions of the Chinese criminal law.[121]

To summarize, the corporate laws applicable to foreign-investment enterprises operating in the SEZs are more liberal and, to a certain extent, better defined than the relevant legislation at national level. These statutes incorporate many features contained in the corporate laws of foreign countries. The effective enforcement of these provisions will enhance foreign investment in the SEZs.

121 National State Enterprise Insolvency Law, Article 42. According to Article 127 of the Criminal Law of China, such persons may be sentenced to less than five years' imprisonment or detention.

Chapter seven

SEZ regulations on foreign banks

When the People's Republic of China was established in 1949, there were 15 banks with foreign capital and three banks with overseas Chinese capital operating in several of the major Chinese cities.[1] At that time, the Chinese policy in respect of foreign banking was that 'any bank of good standing with a sufficient amount of foreign funds, capable of operating foreign exchange business and which was willing to observe the laws and the decrees of the People's Republic of China might apply to the People's Bank of China for the position of an assigned foreign exchange bank dealing in foreign exchange business within the regulated scope'.[2] In accordance with these guidelines, 11 foreign banks and three overseas banks applied and were given approval to continue their business operations in China.

In the early 1950s, when China embarked on socialist reforms in the hope of establishing a system of private means of production, most of the banks with foreign capital applied for termination of their businesses. Only four banks decided to continue their operations in China. They were The Hongkong and Shanghai Banking Corporation, Chartered Bank, Overseas Chinese Bank and East Asia Bank, all of which operated in Shanghai City. In addition, Overseas Chinese Bank had a branch office in Xiamen City.[3]

As soon as China adopted its open policy in the late 1970s, which resulted in a rapid inflow of foreign capital, many foreign financial institutions explored the possibility of setting up representative offices, branches or even Sino-foreign joint banks in China. Foreign banks which had been operating in China since the 1950s also requested for permission to expand their scope of business. In order to cope with this situation and to further the open policy, the central bank of China, namely, the People's Bank of China ('PBOC') promulgated the Provisional Regulations for the Establishment of Representative Offices in

1 Chen Quangeng, 'Long Term Prospects for Banks in China', a talk delivered at the *New Era in China Finance and Banking* seminar sponsored by the Institute for International Research on 30 October 1986, Hong Kong, p. 1.

2 *Id.* The term 'an assigned foreign exchange bank' is a direct translation of the Chinese term. It means that a foreign bank must apply to the People's Bank of China for an authorization regarding the operation of its foreign exchange business.

3 Chen Quangeng, *op cit*, p. 2.

China by Overseas Chinese and Foreign Financial Institutions on 1 February 1983 (the 'Representative Office Regulations'). Two years later, the State Council enacted the Regulations Governing Foreign Banks and Joint Chinese-foreign Banks in the Special Economic Zones of the People's Republic of China on 7 April 1985 (the 'SEZ Foreign Bank Regulations').

From 1979 to 1986, 173 representative offices of 149 banks, seven stock companies, and 14 insurance companies, from 23 countries and regions, were established in China.[4] In addition, a number of foreign banks have set up various establishments in the SEZs since 1985. At the moment, three branches of foreign banks and one Sino-foreign joint bank have been established in Xiamen. They are the Bank of the Orient (of the United States), The Hongkong and Shanghai Banking Corporation, United Overseas Bank Limited (of Singapore), and Xiamen International Bank which was set up with both Chinese and foreign capital.

The Shenzhen SEZ has taken the lead in playing host to foreign banks. There are currently 13 branches of foreign banks operating in Shenzhen City, namely, Bank of Credit and Commerce Ltd, Bank of Tokyo Ltd, Banque Indosuez, Banque Nationale de Paris, Fuji Bank Ltd, Hokkaido Takushoku Bank Ltd, The Hongkong and Shanghai Banking Corporation, Kwangtung Provincial Bank, Nanyang Commercial Bank Ltd (with two branches), Sanwa Bank Ltd, Societe Generale and Standard Chartered Bank. In addition, the Shenzhen branch of the Bank of China and Takugin International (Asia) Ltd jointly established the Shenzhen Industrial Development Credit Fund in October 1985, each side holding 50%. The purpose of the Fund is to 'assist basic industries, offer various kinds of consultancy services, including making loans, introducing foreign funds, technology, equipment and to provide international market conditions for enterprises in Shenzhen'.[5] This chapter will examine the operations of foreign banks, study the SEZ Foreign Bank Regulations and the enforcement thereof, and survey the provisions relating to mortgage loans and the current development of the foreign banking system in the SEZs.

I. Business operations of foreign banks in China

'The introduction of foreign banks embodied China's policy of opening itself to the outside world which, now being implemented, contributes to the introduction of foreign capital and advanced management methods to China, the enlargement of economic and financial cooperation between China and other countries and the promotion of the economic

4 *Id*, p. 6.
5 Chang Hong Yi (general manager of the Bank of China, Shenzhen Branch), 'Foreign Bankers in Shenzhen', *Foreign Bankers in China*, edited by the Bank of China, Hong Kong: Kong Yuen Publiishing Co, 1986 , p. 120.

development of the SEZs.'[6] As to why foreign banks are permitted to set up branches in the SEZs, an official from the Bank of China stated that 'China is at present incapable of giving large amounts of finance for the development of the SEZs. The funds it needs for construction should come mainly from the introduction of foreign capital. Accordingly, the introduction of foreign banks will provide some urgently-needed foreign exchange for the economic development of the SEZs.'[7] Needless to say, as laboratories for the implementation of China's open policy, the SEZs, by inviting foreign banks, will provide the country at large with valuable practical experience and pave the way for the expansion of foreign banking in other parts of China.

Currently, various kinds of banking business are carried out by foreign bank branches and representative offices in China. Under Chinese law, representative offices and subordinate representative offices set up by overseas Chinese and foreign financial institutions are permitted to operate only within the scope of non-profit-making activities such as carrying out business negotiations, acting as liaison offices, and providing consultancy and other services.[8] Such representative offices must not engage in any direct profit-making businesses.[9] The 'other services' include collecting market information, establishing business relations, assisting customers to enter into international business and joint venture partnerships with China, providing financial assistance and acting as correspondent banks etc.[10] In practice, however, representative offices which are not authorized to operate as branches also actively offer loans and make investments through their offshore branches or head offices, thus providing funds to foreign investors in China.[11] They have played an important role in introducing foreign funds to China. Nevertheless, because of their limited business scope, such representative offices are not as active as foreign bank branches in carrying out financial transactions.

At the moment, foreign bank branches or joint Chinese-foreign banks can be established only in the SEZs. Such banks may, upon approval of the PBOC, engage in some or all of the following businesses:

(1) Granting loans in local and foreign currencies and discounting bills;
(2) Handling inward remittances from foreign countries and Hong Kong and Macau regions, and foreign exchange collections;
(3) Settling export transactions and outward documentary bills;
(4) Dealing in the exchange of foreign currencies and foreign currency bills;
(5) Handling local and foreign currency investments;
(6) Handling local and foreign currency guarantees;
(7) Buying and selling stocks and securities;

6 *Id*, p. 121.
7 *Id*, p. 120.
8 Representative Office Regulations, Article 8.
9 *Id.*
10 Chen Qangeng, *op cit*, p. 3.
11 Chang Hong Yi, *op cit*, p. 120.

(8) Providing safe deposit box, credit investigation and consultation services;
(9) Handling outward remittances by overseas Chinese enterprises, foreign enterprises, Chinese-foreign joint ventures and Chinese-foreign co-operative enterprises, and settling import transactions and inward documentary bills;
(10) Handling local and foreign currency deposits and overdrafts by overseas Chinese enterprises, foreign enterprises, Chinese-foreign joint ventures and Chinese-foreign co-operative enterprises; and local and foreign currency deposits and overdrafts by foreign nationals, overseas Chinese and Chinese compatriots in Hong Kong and Macau;
(11) Handling foreign exchange deposits and loans in foreign countries and Hongkong and Macau regions; and
(12) Other business operations.[12]

From the wording of this provision, foreign banks do not have to confine their operations to the SEZs, although they are restricted from taking deposits from domestic Chinese enterprises either in local currency or in foreign currencies. The handling of import transactions and inward documentary bills by foreign banks is also limited to overseas Chinese enterprises, foreign enterprises, Chinese-foreign joint ventures and Chinese-foreign cooperative enterprises. In short, foreign banks in the SEZs mainly serve foreign-investment enterprises.

In view of their narrow scope of business, foreign banks in the Shenzhen SEZ engage essentially in the wholesale banking business. Of the 13 foreign bank branches in the SEZ, only three provide retail banking services to their customers.

Since most of the foreign banks in the Shenzhen SEZ essentially conduct wholesale businesses, they are not particularly interested in offering savings accounts. It was reported that except for Nanyang Commercial Bank Ltd, Kwangtung Provincial Bank and the Bank of Credit and Commerce Ltd, no other foreign bank in Shenzhen takes deposits.[13] Most of the foreign banks obtain funds from their sister branches in Hong Kong which take either HK$ or US$ deposits on behalf of the former. The maturity dates of such deposits vary. The interest rates are generally higher than those applicable in Hong Kong for deposits with the same maturity. It is estimated that in 1986 the total amount of deposits taken by foreign banks in the Shenzhen SEZ was between HK$6–7 b, of which 90% was from Hong Kong.[14]

The types of loans made by foreign banks include investment loans, working capital loans, property mortgage loans and loans for import-export financing. Although foreign banks are permitted to advance loans secured by properties located in the Shenzhen SEZ, most of them do not carry on this type of business. There are several reasons for this. First, a business of this sort requires a large staff membership due to its complex nature. Secondly, the procedures and documentation for such loans are

12 SEZ Foreign Bank Regulations, Article 6.
13 *Wen Wei Po*, 20 February 1987, p. BN4.
14 *Id.*

far more complicated than those for other loan facilities. Thirdly, a few major legal issues still remain to be clarified. So far, the Nanyang Commercial Bank Ltd has dominated the property mortgage loan market in Shenzhen.

Foreign banks are also not very active when it comes to foreign-investment project financing in Shenzhen. Their branches commenced operations in Shenzhen in 1985 when foreign investment in the city was at a low. The construction of most of the foreign-investment projects, which are currently being built or already in operation, commenced prior to 1985, that is, before the foreign bank branches started operations in Shenzhen. As a result there are not many project-financing opportunities for foreign banks. Currently, most of the financing of foreign-investment projects being conducted by foreign branches has been allocated or delegated to them by their head offices in order to avoid withholding taxes in other countries or regions.

The funding of working capital for enterprises with foreign participation is more common and is more attractive to foreign banks. Currently, many of such loans are advanced by the banks which participated in the initial financing. The size of this market in Shenzhen, however, is not considerable, as most of the foreign-investment enterprises are not in the manufacturing sector.

As for import-export financing, there are inherent difficulties facing foreign banks in Shenzhen. By the end of June 1986, the Shenzhen SEZ had absorbed about US$1.1 b in foreign-investment capital, and established more than 400 enterprises with foreign participation.[15] Most of these enterprises were set up prior to 1985, that is, before foreign banks were allowed to operate in the SEZ. In general, most of these enterprises have established working relationships with the Bank of China and Nanyang Commercial Bank Ltd in connection with their import-export financing activities. This situation has effectively excluded foreign banks from foreign trade lending. In addition, a number of foreign-investment enterprises, which engage in the import and export business, use Shenzhen as their processing centre and Hong Kong as their export centre. When these enterprises ship their products to Hong Kong for re-export, they do not need to obtain loans, for most of such transactions are completed on cash-on-delivery terms.

In short, foreign banks in the Shenzhen SEZ currently conduct transactions mainly with foreign-investment enterprises. Although under the SEZ Foreign Bank Regulations, foreign banks are not restricted from carrying on business outside the special zone, it was not until October 1986, that such banks began to extend their operations, with the approval of the PBOC, to other parts of China. At the moment, such banking transactions are conducted only between foreign banks and their traditional or existing customers who participate or operate projects in other cities or provinces.

15 *Wen Wei Po*, 18 February 1987, p. BN4.

Another important aspect of foreign banking in the SEZs is the relationship between foreign banks and State-owned Chinese enterprises or collective enterprises. For many years, State-owned and collective enterprises have been using ony the Bank of China for provision of import-export financing as well as letters of credit. In late 1986, the Shenzhen Branch of the PBOC issued a directive which permitted State-owned and collective enterprises to open letter of credit accounts with foreign banks in the city, provided that such enterprises had previously obtained loans from these foreign banks. Up till now, this business still remains at a primitive stage. Nevertheless, foreign banks are happy to develop this market as it is comparatively less risky.

Under the SEZ Foreign Bank Regulations, foreign banks are permitted to make loans or advances to their customers.[16] The definition of 'customers' is open-ended and thus enables foreign banks to lend money to State-owned enterprises and other Chinese institutions. Foreign banks may make Renminbi loans to such Chinese enterprises at will, but the source of their funding is a major difficulty. There are several reasons for this. Foreign banks are only allowed to take Renminbi deposits from foreign-investment enterprises. In addition, Chinese enterprises which are interested in obtaining loans in foreign currencies must first apply to the local Foreign Exchange Administrative Bureau for approval. The Foreign Exchange Administrative Bureau of Shenzhen has established very restrictive standards and rules for the examination of such loan applications. The essential criteria include the urgency and cost-effectiveness of the project in question. The rigid application of this policy, coupled with the slow-down in capital construction in Shenzhen, has substantially reduced the business potential for foreign banks in this area.

Nevertheless, thanks to the more liberal policy adopted by the Shenzhen Branch of the PBOC, working conditions for foreign banks in the city are improving. For instance, according to previous practice, when a Chinese enterprise borrowed money from a foreign bank, the proceeds had to be drawn as soon as the loan contract was signed. If, which was often the case, the borrower did not make use of the entire loan at once, the unused portion had to be deposited with the Bank of China. Currently, Chinese enterprises in Shenzhen which borrow loans from foreign banks do not have to deposit the unused portion of the proceeds with the Bank of China. Such funds can be kept by the foreign creditor. This policy has contributed substantially to the lending activities of foreign banks in Shenzhen which grew rapidly in the latter part of 1986. Between May 1985 and June 1986, the growth in lending by foreign banks was nominal. However, by the end of 1986, the total amount of this business showed a three-fold increase over the total for the period prior to June 1986.[17]

16 SEZ Foreign Bank Regulations, Article 6(1).
17 *Wen Wei Po*, 20 February 1987, p. BN4.

The lack of an adequate tax system governing foreign banks is another factor which hinders the development of their business in the SEZs. When foreign banks first started operations in the SEZs they were taxed in accordance with the Sino-foreign Joint Venture Income Tax Regulations and the Consolidated Industrial and Commercial Tax provisions. Under these rules, foreign banks had to pay Consolidated Industrial and Commercial Tax at a rate of 3% whenever they made loans or advances. In addition, when foreign banks provided facilities to domestic Chinese state banks at interest rates higher than those which the Bank of China offered, the income generated therefrom was subject to a 20% withholding tax. These regulations were obviously very unfavourable to foreign banks.

In recognizing the difficulties which foreign banks in the Shenzhen SEZ were faced with, the Shenzhen municipality issued on 19 May 1986 supplementary regulations on tax reduction and exemption. Several of the provisions deal directly with taxation of foreign banks. Under these supplementary rules, foreign banks are exempted from the Consolidated Industrial and Commercial Tax for ten years from 1 July 1986; individuals or enterprises from Hong Kong, Macau or foreign countries who have made deposits with foreign banks in the Shenzhen SEZ are exempted from withholding income tax until the end of 1995; overseas banks which make advances to foreign banks in the Shenzhen SEZ at prime rates are exempted from withholding income tax; and foreign branches in the Shenzhen SEZ are allowed to treat interest payments to their head offices, in connection with working capital loans, as operating costs, thereby subjecting the head offices to withholding tax.[18]

The adoption of these tax measures has improved the banking system in the Shenzhen SEZ and has apparently contributed to the rapid growth of foreign banking business since July 1986. However, there are still several issues which need to be clarified. For instance, under the supplementary tax regulations of the Shenzhen municipality, overseas banks are exempted from withholding income tax when they make advances to foreign banks in the Shenzhen SEZ at a 'international interbank interest rate'. Such overseas banks are required to submit valid documents in support of their claims that the loans in question were made at prime rates. Since the interbank interest rate is frequently changeable and different financial centres have different interbank interest rates, an 'international interbank interest rate' is therefore difficult to determine. The current practice is to rely on the original contracts or certificates relating to funds borrowed by a foreign bank and on-lent to a foreign bank branch in Shenzhen. In other words, if an overseas bank can deliver a document indicating that the money was raised through an interbank arrangement and there is no change in the interest rate for the re-lending, it will be exempted from withholding tax.

Another issue is the duration of the Consolidated Industrial and

18 *Wen Wei Po*, 19 February 1987, p. BN4.

Commercial Tax exemption. Foreign bankers welcome the ten-year exemption, but they are concerned that this provision may prevent them from making long-term loans. In addition, two to three years prior to the expiration of this exemption, even medium-term loans may be difficult to arrange, for the application of the tax would increase the costs to potential borrowers and would therefore effectively reduce the competitiveness of foreign banks in the Shenzhen SEZ.

II. Establishment of foreign banks

Banks which are registered in foreign countries or in Hong Kong and Macau, in accordance with local laws, and have head offices outside China may establish branches in the SEZs in China.[19] Other institutions or individuals from foreign countries or Hong Kong and Macau may set up banks with head offices located in the SEZs. These individuals and institutions may also jointly form banks in the SEZs with Chinese banks or financial institutions.[20] The application for establishment of a bank or branch must be submitted to the head office of the PBOC in Beijing.

Once a foreign bank or branch is established, it is subject to the control and supervision of the branch office of the PBOC in the respective SEZ.[21] This supervisory and administrative structure is in accordance with the banking system in China, under which the PBOC, together with its branches at provincial, city and county levels, functions as the central bank in charge of formulating policies and directing the businesses of other banks such as China's Industrial and Commercial Bank, Agricultural Bank etc. The approval of the PBOC for the establishment of a foreign bank or branch does not cover foreign exchange transactions by such institutions. A foreign bank desiring to conduct foreign exchange business must petition to the State Administration of Exchange Control for a foreign exchange business licence.[22]

Different application documents will have to be submitted depending on whether a foreign bank, a foreign bank branch or a joint-Chinese foreign bank is to be established. A foreign bank which wishes to set up a branch in an SEZ must, through its head office, submit an application to the head office of the PBOC and furnish the following documents and information:

(1) A written application signed by the chairman or general manager of the bank with the authorization of its board of directors and certified by a notary public, giving the name of the branch to be set up, the amount of operating funds allocated to it by the head office, a brief personal history of, and a letter of authorization for, each of the key officers, and the kinds of business applied for;

19 SEZ Foreign Bank Regulations, Article 2.
20 *Id.*
21 *Id*, Article 4.
22 *Id.*

(2) The articles of association, a list of the members of the board of directors, and the balance sheets, profit and loss statements and business reports for the three years preceding the application;
(3) A copy of the business licence issued by the competent authorities of the country or region where the bank is located; and
(4) A written guarantee from its head office taking responsibility for its taxes and other liabilities.[23]

The registration of a new bank, to be set up exclusively or partially with foreign capital (joint Chinese-foreign bank), requires documentation similar to that for the establishment of a wholly foreign-owned enterprise or a joint venture. An applicant who wishes to set up a foreign bank with its head office in the SEZs must submit a written application containing the name of the head office to be set up, the registered capital and paid-up capital, a list of the chief officers and the kinds of business applied for.[24] In addition, a copy of the articles of association, the names of the chairman, vice chairmen and members of the board of directors, nominated by the applicant, and a statement of the assets and liabilities of the applicant certified by a notary public, must be submitted.[25] If such an application is for the establishment of a joint Chinese-foreign bank, a feasibility study report which is jointly prepared by all the parties must be submitted as well.

In comparison, the setting up of a representative office requires the foreign applicant (bank) to make an application directly to the president of the PBOC. This application letter can be forwarded to the addressee directly or through a branch of the PBOC at the provincial or city level or through other Chinese financial institutions.[26] A photocopy of the charter or business licence granted by authorities of the country or region in which the applicant bank operates, the articles of association and the by-laws of the institution, the names of the board of directors, the latest balance sheet and statement of the profit and loss of the applicant must be filed along with the application.[27] In addition, a power of attorney given to the chief representative and signed by the chairman of the board or the chief executive of the general management, and a *curriculum vitae* of the chief representative and other representatives must be submitted as well.

Clearly, the documents required for the setting up of a representative office, branch or head office are similar. However, a foreign bank applying to open a representative office does not need to take responsibility for the taxes and liabilities of its representative office. This omission follows from the non-profit-making nature of the business which representative offices are permitted to carry on.

As for the life-spans of these institutions, each representative office has

23 SEZ Foreign Bank Regulations, Article 5(1).
24 *Id*, Article 5(2).
25 *Id*.
26 Representative Office Regulations, Article 4.
27 *Id*.

a term of three years, upon expiration of which an extension may be requested and approved.[28] On the other hand, there is no specific life-span for a foreign bank branch or head office in the SEZs. As discussed earlier, at present, a representative office may be established in any part of China while a foreign bank branch can be set up only in the SEZs.

A foreign bank must, within 30 days from the date of its being approved, register with the Administration for Industry and Commerce and obtain from it a business licence.[29] Thereafter, within 30 days from the date of commencement of its operations, it is required to register with the local tax authorities. If any such bank fails to commence operations within 12 months from the date of approval, it will automatically become disqualified.[30]

Under the SEZ Foreign Bank Regulations, a head office or a joint bank must have a minimum registered capital in foreign exchange, equivalent to RMB80 m, and a paid-up capital of not less than 50% of the registered capital.[31] A branch office is required to hold a foreign exchange operating fund allocated to it by its head office abroad which is not less than the equivalent of RMB40 m[32] This minimum paid-up capital and working capital requirement have been criticized by foreign investors as being too high.[33] Based on the applicable exchange rate in early 1985, when the SEZ Foreign Bank Regulations were adopted, a sum of RMB40 m would equal US$14.1 m. According to some foreign bankers, most countries require a capital base of only US$1 m to US$2 m or its equivalent.[34] With the substantial devaluation of the Renminbi in late 1986, the current requirements for paid-up capital and operating funds have in fact been considerably reduced. This minimum capital requirement reflects China's desire to absorb foreign capital through foreign banks and its concern for the interests of depositors in the event of an insolvency of a foreign bank. Taking into consideration the unstable situation in the international financial market and the bank failures since the beginning of the 1980s, as well as China's inexperience in international financial matters, the cautious position taken by the Chinese government in this regard is not very surprising.

The SEZ Foreign Bank Regulations do not provide for the type of currency the paid-up capital and operating funds should be held in. The decision in this matter is deliberately left to the foreign banks. This does not mean, however, that such banks can keep their funds in whatever foreign currency they choose, for the borrowers in China, either domestic Chinese institutions or foreign-investment enterprises, may have a preference for a particular foreign currency or currencies.

28 *Id*, Article 7.
29 SEZ Foreign Bank Regulations, Article 8.
30 *Id.*
31 *Id*, Article 7.
32 *Id.*
33 *The Asian Wall Street Journal*, 18 April 1985, p. 3.
34 *Business China*, 9 May 1985, p. 70.

As a precondition to accepting local or foreign currency deposits within an SEZ, a foreign bank must keep with a branch office of the PBOC in the same zone a reserve fund against its deposits.[35] This provision is another safety measure for the protection of the public in the event that a foreign bank should run into financial difficulties. Currently, foreign banks in the Shenzhen SEZ which take deposits locally must deposit with the Shenzhen Branch of the PBOC an amount equivalent to 6% of the total amount of deposits they have taken.[36] The PBOC does not pay interest on deposits made by foreign banks.

Loans granted by a foreign bank's head office or a joint Chinese-foreign bank in an SEZ to any enterprise in the same zone must not exceed 30% of the aggregate of the bank's paid-up capital and reserve funds. In addition, the total investment in the SEZ by such bank should not exceed 30% of the aggregate of its paid-up capital and reserve funds.[37] The stipulation regarding the ceiling on lending is more liberal than that applicable in other countries or regions.[38] The purpose of this provision may be frustrated, however, by the scope of application of this provision. Foreign banks are permitted to make advances to Chinese enterprises or foreign-investment enterprises in other parts of China. Unless their lending to such enterprises can also be checked, the 30% ceiling which is only applicable to the SEZs may lose its force. The basis for the limitation on loans a bank may provide to enterprises in any one SEZ is more ambiguous. Some foreign bankers believe that this provision is to serve as a broad guideline for the operations of foreign banks.[39] So far, no specific interpretation concerning this Article has been given.

As discussed earlier, foreign banks are permitted to take deposits and make loans, overdrafts and discounts on bills in either local or foreign currencies. According to the SEZ Foreign Bank Regulations, the interest rate applied by a foreign bank to such transactions must be set up with reference to those prescribed by the PBOC in the same SEZ.[40] In practice, foreign banks in the Shenzen SEZ have been adopting their own interest rates because the Shenzhen Branch of the PBOC has not adopted any measures or methods which can be used as a reference by foreign banks in setting their interest rates. As a result, some foreign banks have adopted a floating interest rate in accordance with the prevailing rate in Hong Kong, while others have followed the interest rate adopted by the PBOC in Shenzhen, and still others have simply set up interest rates themselves in accordance with local market conditions. Since there are more foreign banks in the Shenzhen SEZ than needed by the local business community, the competition among foreign banks is very fierce. In the past,

35 SEZ Foreign Bank Regulations, Article 11.
36 *Wen Wei Po*, 27 February 1987, p BN4.
37 SEZ Foreign Bank Regulations, Article 9.
38 In the United States, the ceiling on lending by a bank is 15% while in Hong Kong it is 25%.
39 *Business China*, 9 May 1985, p. 70.
40 SEZ Foreign Bank Regulations, Article 10.

banks established high interest rates for deposits, while making advances at the prime rate for interbank lending in Hong Kong in order to attract business. The Japanese banks are well-known for such practices.[41]

Despite the keen competition among foreign banks, the PBOC in Shenzhen has not yet taken any action to regulate interest rates. There might be two reasons for the inaction by the Chinese central bank. First, fundamental reforms of the financial system in China are being carried out. The business operations of specialized State-owned banks which previously were strictly confined to the sectors they were respectively in charge of have now been expanded to cover other sectors of the domestic economy. State-owned banks are no longer cashiers for the State government or State-owned enterprises. Instead they are taking deposits, making loans and advances as well as carrying out other kinds of business. As regulation of domestic banks was more urgently needed than regulation of foreign banks, in 1986 the PBOC concentrated on establishing a domestic interest rate system as well as guidelines for other banking businesses. Secondly, the Shenzhen Branch of the PBOC regards its major function at the moment as assisting rather than supervising the operations of foreign banks, since the latter are not familiar with the local environment in the SEZ.[42] As a result, the interest rates offered by foreign banks remain unregulated. Nevertheless, since the interest rate system for domestic banks has been established, a similar scheme may soon be instituted for foreign banks operating in the Shenzhen SEZ. It is quite likely that maximum and minimum interest rates applicable to deposits and lending, respectively, will be set up. Foreign banks will be allowed to offer different rates within the margin to be prescribed by the PBOC.

Foreign banks which engage in foreign exchange transactions are required to use the exchange rate adopted by the State Administration of Foreign Exchange Control.[43] They are also bound by the relevant regulations governing foreign exchange transactions.

The branches of the PBOC in the SEZs have power to examine the business and financial positions of foreign banks.[44] Such branches may request foreign banks to submit or furnish information and data in connection with their business transactions or financial positions.[45] Officers of the PBOC may also be sent to foreign bank offices to examine their books, records etc.

As a statutory requirement, a foreign bank must submit to a branch of the PBOC in its locality the following reports on a regular basis:

(1) A balance sheet, as at the end of the previous month, to be submitted before the 10th of each month;

41 *Wen Wei Po*, 25 February 1987, p BN4.
42 *Wen Wei Po*, 10 March 1987, p BN4.
43 SEZ Foreign Bank Regulations, Article 10.
44 *Id*, Article 13.
45 *Id*.

(2) An analytical statement of deposits and loans, an analytical statement of outward and inward remittances and settlements of import and export transactions, and an analytical statement of investment items for the previous quarter; and
(3) The balance sheet, profit and loss statement, and statement of the balance of each accounting item for the previous year, along with an audit report by an accountant registered in China, to be submitted before the end of March of each year.[46]

The branches of the PBOC in the SEZs are empowered to issue warnings or impose fines on any foreign bank acting in contravention of the relevant regulations or provisions.[47] A foreign bank which does not consent to such punishment may appeal to the head office of the PBOC. Under the SEZ Foreign Bank Regulations, a foreign bank which commits a serious crime or carries out serious unlawful activities may be ordered to suspend its business operations or even to dissolve its institution.[48]

As with other foreign-investment enterprises, foreign banks are entitled to remit their after-tax profits.[49] This general rule is implemented with different criteria, depending on the nature of the foreign bank. A foreign bank branch in the SEZ is allowed to remit all its profits abroad so long as local tax been paid. At the same time, a foreign bank head office or a joint bank must allocate, in addition to a provision for taxation, a certain amount to the reserve fund, workers' bonuses, welfare fund and enterprise development fund, before remitting its profits. Thus, foreign bank head offices and joint banks are treated essentially as wholly foreign-owned enterprises, joint ventures or cooperative ventures in China.

III. Mortgage loans

In China, the concept of providing security for loans is a relatively new one. Since 1949, when the People's Republic of China was established, State-owned banks have been lending to State-owned enterprises, collective enterprises as well as individuals, without requiring any guarantee or security. Such financial transactions are regarded largely as administrative matters rather than commercial ones. Both banks and borrowers rely heavily on the approval of the relevant administrative authorities. Creditors are not entitled to declare insolvent any enterprise that is unable or has failed to repay its financial obligations. Since the start of its open policy, and with its increasing economic contacts with foreign countries, China has gradually accepted the common practices of international lending, including the provision of guarantees and security for the repayment of loans. This approach has directly affected the

46 *Id*, Article 12.
47 *Id*, Article 16.
48 *Id*.
49 *Id*, Article 14.

business activities of domestic Chinese banks and financial institutions. Various methods of borrowing and lending have been adopted in China step-by-step, with the SEZs spearheading the move.

As early as the beginning of 1985, the PBOC enacted the Interim Procedures for Banks' Mortgage Loans which was the first legislation of its kind since 1949 and marked the resumption of financial market operations in the country. The Interim Procedures for Banks' Mortgage Loans apply only to State-owned banks in the Shenzhen SEZ in relation to loans provided by such banks to State-owned and collectively-owned enterprises, enterprises jointly operated by the economic zone and other provinces in China, privately-owned enterprises, Sino-foreign joint ventures, Sino-foreign cooperative ventures and wholly foreign-owned enterprises.[50]

With the rapid establishment of foreign bank branches in the Shenzhen SEZ in 1985, on 25 December 1985, the Standing Committee of the 6th People's Congress of Guangdong Province adopted, at its 17th Session, the Provisions of Shenzhen Special Economic Zone on Administration of Mortgage Loans, which were promulgated by the Guangdong Provincial Government on 13 February 1986 (the 'Provisions on Administration of Mortgage Loans').

Unlike the Interim Procedures for Banks' Mortgage Loans, the Provisions on Administration of Mortgage Loans have a wider scope of application. Article 2 of the Provisions prescribes that these Provisions apply to the mortgage loan business carried on between banks and other financial institutions established in the SEZ pursuant to governmental approval, and Chinese-foreign joint ventures, Chinese-foreign cooperative ventures, wholly foreign-owned ventures, Chinese-foreign limited liability companies and individuals in the SEZ. Under this provision, parties to a mortgage loan transaction must reside in the Shenzhen SEZ. The mortgagor can be either an enterprise with foreign participation or an individual, while the mortgagee must be a bank or financial institution established with approval of the State Government. Therefore, State-owned Chinese banks, Sino-foreign joint banks, and foreign banks either with a head office or a branch office established in the SEZ, qualify to provide mortgage loans. The term 'other financial institutions' implies that investment companies and other organizations which conduct the business of lending are also permitted to make mortgage loans. At the same time, banks and financial institutions which are not located, or have no establishment, in the Shenzhen SEZ are excluded from carrying out such transactions with enterprises or individuals in the zone.

It is important to note that, under the Provisions on Administration of Mortgage Loans, State-owned enterprises and collectively-owned enterprises, as well as public interest institutions, do not qualify for mortgage

50 The Interim Procedures for Banks' Mortgage Loans adopted by the People's Bank of China were reprinted in the *China Economic News*, 21 January 1985. This piece of legislation does not have an adoption or promulgation date.

loans from foreign banks. This provision is in accordance with the Provisional Regulations on Borrowing Contracts adopted by the State Council in February 1985 which prohibit such enterprises and institutions from mortgaging their property to a foreign bank.

Assets which can be mortgaged as security collateral include both movable and immovable property. Immovable property refers to real property such as houses, materials, buildings, factories, equipment etc. Movable property that can be mortgaged may be in the form of securities, accounts receivable, and other rights. In general, the following rights-bearing and interest-bearing documents should be treated as security: government bonds, treasury bills, corporate bonds and debentures, shares, interest and dividend coupons etc.[51] Accounts receivable refer to such instruments as bills, drafts, cheques, bank deposit certificates, postal saving certificates etc.[52]

The term 'other rights' is an open-ended provision which is intended to embrace all kinds of rights or interests which are not included in the statute. Its immediate effect is to make the equity ownership of any party to a Sino-foreign joint venture a valid collateral for mortgage loans. At the same time, it is the drafter's intention that the rights or interests of a party to a Sino-foreign cooperative venture as set forth in the contract be mortgageable as well. In this regard, cooperative-venture parties may pledge either the venture's expected profits or the rights in the products to be manufactured by the venture.[53]

As a general rule, when joint-venture or cooperative-venture parties pledge their equity ownership, rights or interests as security, the approval of the board of directors of the venture in question must be obtained in advance and a certificate thereof must be issued by the venture.[54] With regard to foreign parties to such ventures, the consent of the board of directors should be adequate as far as execution of security documents is concerned. When the Chinese party to a venture is a State-owned enterprise or collectively-owned company and it wishes to pledge its shares or rights to obtain a loan, it may have to request for authorization from its higher authorities. Although the Provisions on Administration of Mortgage Loans do not contain any provision which is exclusively applicable to State-owned enterprises, such Chinese companies may nevertheless be subject to similar approval procedures. In practice, a Chinese party to a joint venture or cooperative venture will first secure the approval of the higher authorities and then report the matter to the board of directors of the venture so that the latter can decide whether the property, interests and rights should be mortgaged. Under such circumstances, the decision of the Chinese administrative authorities may not

51 Provisional Regulations for Exchange Control of the People's Republic of China adopted at the regular session of the State Council on 5 December 1980, Article 2.
52 *Id.*
53 *Economy and Law*, vol. 10, December 1986, p. 35.
54 Provisions on Administration of Mortgage Loans, Article 7.

carry any legal force. It only enables the Chinese party to make a request to the board of directors.

The Provisions on Administration of Mortgage Loans specifically stipulate the properties that may not be mortgaged as security. These include:

(1) land, mineral resources and other natural resources;
(2) goods, the purchase and sale of which are prohibited by the State; and
(3) property, the ownership of which is disputed.[55]

Among the three proscribed items, the exclusion of assets with disputed ownership is a common feature of the laws in many countries. The first two items are, however, novel to those who are not familiar with the Chinese legal system.

Under the Chinese Constitution, all minerals, waters and other natural resources in China belong to the State.[56] Land in urban areas belongs to the State, while land in the rural areas and urban suburbs belongs to the collectives except for the parcels which are owned by the State in accordance with law.[57] Land, waters, mineral resources and other natural resources are not considered as merchandise under Chinese law and they are therefore not subject to sale, purchase, lease, mortgage, pledge or other illegal transfers by any unit or individual. This situation is in sharp contrast to the situation in Western countries where land is a common and popular collateral for secured loans. Since enterprises or individuals can obtain only the right to use land, they can only mortgage the objects above the land. Apparently, this is similar to the present situation in Hong Kong where no individual or institution is entitled to own any piece of land.

Under Chinese law, certain goods are prohibited from being the subject of transactions by individuals or unauthorized institutions. In general, these goods include items of significant historical value, artistic merit, superior craftsmanship or scientific importance. Most of these goods are not allowed to be exported. Thus, the exclusion of such items from the list of security collateral is logical, for the mortgagee should have the right to sell the mortgaged property abroad eventually in the event of non-payment by the mortgagor.

The rights and obligations of the parties to a mortgage loan transaction should be specifically provided in the mortgage loan contract. The terms should include:

(1) use of the loan;
(2) amount of the loan and the currency in which it is to be made;

55 *Id*, Article 6.
56 The Constitution of the People's Republic of China adopted at the 5th National People's Congress on 4 December 1982, Article 9.
57 *Id*, Article 10.

(3) name, quantity, and value of the mortgaged property;
(4) term of the loan, the interest rate, the time schedule and the method of repaying the principal and interest;
(5) manner in which the loan is to be given;
(6) method of possession and control of, and responsibility for, the mortgaged property; and
(7) liability for breach of contract.[58]

A mortgage loan contract under the Provisions on Administration of Morgage Loans carries combined features of a loan contract and a security contract.

In giving the loan, the mortgagee can either obtain possession or be in charge of administration of the mortgaged property. It also has the discretion of not taking possession or being in charge of the administration of the property. This provision represents a more liberal and flexible stand from that of the Interim Procedures for Banks' Mortgage Loans which provide that banks should, in principle, take possession of the mortgaged property offered by the borrower.[59]

As a statutory requirement, once a piece of property is mortgaged, the mortgagor may not lease, sell, transfer, further mortgage or otherwise encumber the property unless the consent of the mortgagee is obtained in advance.[60] If a mortgagor violates this requirement, any encumbrance on

58 Provisions on Administration of Mortgage Loans, Article 11.

59 Interim Procedures for Banks' Mortgage Loans, Article 5. Since there is no law at present in China governing liquid assets and mortgage rights to fixed assets, banks are required to take possession of the mortgaged property with an undertaking in writing by the borrowers to transfer the same to the banks. The forms of transfer vary with the nature of the mortgaged property. In general, they take the following three forms:
(a) Commodities: When commodities used as collateral are stored in different places they are dealt with the different ways:
(1) If the commodities are stored in a licensed warehouse, the warehouse receipts, warrants and insurance policies of the commodities should be sent to and kept in the bank along with the completed transfer of ownership;
(2) If the commodities are stored in the warehouse(s) of a borrower enterprise, a contract should be signed between the borrower enterprise and the banks, whereby the warehouse is rented to the latter. A sign-board carrying the name of the bank is to be put up in front of the warehouse which will be guarded by men sent by the bank. The insurance policies are to be kept in the bank;
(3) If the commodities are stored in the borrower's own shops, the borrower enterprise should sign a 'trust receipt' in lieu of contract, specifying that the enterprise agrees to keep the commodities in the name of the bank. The enterprise should also be responsible for depositing with the bank, money obtained from sales of the commodities, to be used as payment for the loan. The bank has the right to make an inventory of the commodities every month.
(b) Negotiable securities: All bearer securities should be transferred to the bank. Registered securities are handed over to the bank after having been endorsed by the borrower enterprise and having gone through the necessary transfer formalities.
(c) Fixed assets: If a borrower enterprise raises a mortgage on a factory building or a house, the bank need not take possession of the building. However, the enterprise should register with the competent authorities to the effect that the building belongs to the bank, although it is used by the enterprise itself. Other assets such as large machines and equipment can also be mortgaged in the same manner.

60 Provisions on Administration of Mortgage Loans, Article 18.

the mortgaged property is without effect and the mortgagee is entitled to demand possession and administration of the mortgaged property immediately.[61] In addition, if the mortgagor or its successor or legatee refuses to repay the principal or interest of the mortgage loan, or if the mortgagor dies and there is no successor or legatee, the mortgagee also has the right to take possession and administration of the mortgaged property that was not originally possessed or administered by it.[62] When the mortgagee possesses or administers the mortgaged property following the occurrence of any of the above-mentioned events, it must notify the mortgagor, its successor or the legatee in writing. The latter is required, within 30 days upon receiving such written notice, to deliver the mortgaged property to the mortgagee.[63]

The party that has possession and control of the mortgaged property must properly protect and preserve the property and must not allow the mortgaged property to be lost or damaged. If the party intentionally or negligently causes damage to the mortgaged property, it must compensate for the loss (in the case of a mortgagee) or provide new mortgaged property or a guarantor (in the case of a mortgagor).[64]

In cases where a mortgaged property is required to be insured under Chinese law, the mortgagor must purchase insurance policies from an insurance company registered in the Shenzhen SEZ and the insurance certificate must be delivered to the mortgagee for safe-keeping. If, owing to *force majeure*, the insured and mortgaged property is damaged, the mortgagee has the right to recover from the indemnification proceeds to be paid by the insurance company, the loan principal and interest which it is entitled to.[65]

Under the Provisions on Administration of Mortgage Loans, if a mortgagor does not or is not able to repay the principal and interest of a mortgage loan when they fall due, the mortgagee may exercise the right to dispose of the mortgaged property.[66] As regards methods of disposing of the mortgaged property, in the case of a house and materials, the mortgagee may have the same sold by auction. If the mortgaged property is in the form of securities, accounts receivable or other rights, the mortgagee may transfer the title of such properties to itself directly.[67]

When a mortgagee sells mortgaged property by auction, it must obtain an auction sale certificate from the relevant authorities of the local government and then entrust a local auction organization to auction the property. The auction organization's functions include examining and verifying the mortgaged property and establishing a reserve price for the

61 *Id*, Articles 18 and 20.
62 *Id*, Article 20.
63 *Id*, Article 21.
64 *Id*, Article 17.
65 *Id*, Article 12.
66 *Id*, Article 22.
67 *Id*, Article 23.

sale.[68] Proceeds from the auction sale of a mortgaged property must be applied in the following order:

(1) payment of costs associated with the disposition of the property;
(2) payment of tax;
(3) repayment of the unpaid portion of the principal and interest on the loan; and
(4) return of the balance, if any, to the mortgagor.[69]

With regard to the disposition of mortgaged property there are still some unanswered questions. First, it is not clear whether the property can be paid for in foreign exchange. Secondly, if the mortgagee (a foreign bank) receives Renminbi from the auctioned mortgaged property, it is not clear whether it is entitled to change the local currency into foreign currency and repatriate the same overseas. Thirdly, there is no provision as to whether machinery and equipment sold can be shipped out of China without customs duties having to be paid. However, according to an official of the Shenzhen branch of the PBOC, so long as the issue of repatriation of currency or export of machinery is decided by a court in the SEZ, the Customs should obey the court ruling.[70]

Within 15 days after the signing of the mortgage loan contract, the parties to the transaction must register the mortgaged property with the relevant local authorities.[71] At the completion of a mortgage loan contract, the mortgagor and mortgagee are required, within 10 days, to cancel the security registration at the local bureaus in charge of the registration of mortgaged properties.[72] The scale of registration fees is established by the Shenzhen Municipality Pricing Bureau with the approval of the Municipal Government.[73] The registration fee is currently charged according to the value of the assets specified in the mortgage contract. The maximum fee for the service is US$1,351 and the minimum is US$5.40.[74] In addition, if mortgaged assets are contracted out or transferred, a fee of US$5.40 must be paid to alter the registration.[75]

IV. The position of foreign banks in the SEZs

The foreign banking community in the Shenzhen SEZ owes its rapid development not only to the special position of Shenzhen but also to the nation-wide reforms to the financial system. During the second half of

68 *Id*, Article 25.
69 *Id*, Article 26.
70 *Wen Wei Po*, 24 February 1987, p. BN4.
71 Provisions on Administration of Mortgage Loans, Article 13.
72 *Id*, Article 28.
73 *Guangdong Business Monitor*, vol. 1, no. 9, 1 February 1987, p. 36.
74 *Id.*
75 Provisions on Administration of Mortgage Loans, Article 30.

1985, China imposed further restrictions on industrial expenditure which resulted in a shortage of operating capital for companies in most of the regions in the country. This led in turn to the start of interlending between banks and the issuance of stocks and shares. This situation forced the Shenzhen SEZ to restructure its financial sector, thus benefiting the foreign banks in the zone. Over the last two years, foreign banks have made considerable progress but they still face various problems and difficulties. For instance, in China as well as in the Shenzhen SEZ, since credit facilities such as cheques and other drafts were not commonly used in a market where transactions were conducted mainly in cash, there was no universally acceptable standard in the SEZ regarding cheques and other securities. As a result, prior to the end of 1986 when the Provisional Provisions on the Administration of Securities of the Shenzhen Municipality[76] were adopted, the Shenzhen Branch of the PBOC and the foreign banks had adopted different standards. This statute has now clarified a number of issues concerning the operations of foreign banks and has paved the way for further financial reforms.

As regards deposit-taking in Renminbi, although Article 6 of the SEZ Foreign Bank Regulations permits foreign banks in the zone to accept local currency, this authorization is still only on paper. In practice, foreign banks are not allowed to take Renminbi deposits from local enterprises. Apparently, the reason for permission being withhold is the slow development of the local bank industry.[77] Even though a number of reforms have been made to China's financial system, the operations of Chinese banks are still backward and cannot be compared with the operations of foreign banks. The Chinese banks not only lack commercial experience but are also short of qualified personnel to carry out modern financial transactions. Under such circumstances, in order to protect the local banking industry, the PBOC has taken the position of not allowing foreign banks to take Renminbi deposits.

In fact, even if foreign banks were not prohibited from taking Renminbi deposits, they might still not be able to do so for the following reasons. First, in order to carry on this business, the foreign banks must enlarge their staff membership and add additional equipment. The shortage of qualified local staff and the limited scope of the business will effectively prevent foreign banks from expanding into this business. Secondly, over the last few years, Shenzhen City has been experiencing a shortage of funds. The increasing urgency to repay previous loans has further exacerbated the situation in the zone. As a result, the Chinese banks in the Shenzhen SEZ have taken huge interbank loans from inland areas. The cost of these loans is higher than the cost of taking deposits in

76 The Provisional Provisions on the Administration of Securities of the Shenzhen Municipality were adopted by the Shenzhen Branch of the PBOC and published by the Shenzhen Municipality on 20 December 1986. For the full text of the legislation, see *Wen Wei Po*, 20 January 1987 and 1 January 1987, p. BN2.

77 *Wen Wei Po*, 3 March 1987, p. BN4.

the SEZ, for the lending banks from the other areas will each charge a fee for such loans. Under such circumstances, foreign banks may not be able to compete with local Chinese banks which have good relations with Chinese banks in other cities and which are authorized to take local deposits. Thirdly, it is not certain whether foreign banks will be able to repatriate their Renminbi earnings from their local-currency deposit-taking business. For instance, there is no provision as to whether foreign banks can exchange their local Renminbi earnings at the foreign exchange centre for purposes of repatriation. The above difficulties by no means indicate that there is no need for foreign banks to take deposits in local currency. On many occasions, when foreign investors apply for financing, they not only need funds in foreign currencies but also funds in local currency, essentially for working capital purposes. But since the foreign banks do not have Renminbi funds, the foreign investors have to obtain local-currency loans from Chinese banks. The elimination of this parallel procedure will effectively increase the efficiency of foreign investment in China.

As regards deposit-taking in foreign currencies by local State-owned enterprises and individuals, foreign banks in China face problems similar to those relating to deposit-taking in local currency. Over the last few years, China has suffered from a shortage of foreign exchange. This situation is not likely to improve in the near future, for China will continue to import advanced technology and equipment in large quantities, using foreign exchange, in order to upgrade its existing enterprises and to develop new industries. In view of its intention to use foreign exchange in a planned manner, the Chinese government has exercised strict control over the foreign exchange earnings of State-owned enterprises and collectively-owned enterprises. As discussed earlier, the objective of permitting foreign banks to operate in China is to bring in foreign capital. Therefore, it is quite logical for the Chinese government not to allow foreign banks to accept deposits in foreign currencies by Chinese enterprises or individuals. If foreign banks were able to obtain sufficient foreign exchange locally, their interbank borrowings from Hong Kong, Macau or foreign countries would be reduced, and this would be contrary to China's intentions.

In the field of lending, the activities of foreign banks are largely unrestricted. State-owned enterprises can obtain foreign-currency loans from foreign banks, provided that the projects in question are for the purpose of introducing advanced technology or producing import-substitutes. In such circumstances, foreign banks can, upon the approval of the Foreign Exchange Administration, provide local Chinese companies with facilities in foreign currencies.

The smooth operations of foreign banks in the SEZs are also hampered by the lack of knowledge and inexperience of lower-level officials of the PBOC, and the lack of adequate legislation in respect of banking transactions. Although the key persons in the PBOC branches are experienced and have a good knowledge of banking, the junior officials are generally not familiar with banking business and are therefore not able to supervise foreign banks. For instance, in accordance with the SEZ Foreign Bank Regulations, foreign banks must submit monthly, quarterly as well as annual financial reports to the PBOC branches. However, so far, the Shenzhen Branch has not imposed any standard forms or other requirements for such reports. As a result, foreign banks prepare reports based on their own experience and practice. In addition, the PBOC in Shenzhen generally does not make any comments upon receiving such reports except for the occasional inquiry or request for further explanation of the contents of the reports.[78] Foreign bankers suspect that the silence on the part of the PBOC may reflect several things:

(1) The supervisory organ within the PBOC is unfamiliar with the matters involved;
(2) The officials are gathering information and experience to establish an effective system; or
(3) The supervisory organ has decided not to interfere with the business of foreign banks at this initial stage.[79]

Representatives from the PBOC Shenzhen Branch have openly admitted that the lower-level officials are not experienced or qualified to supervise foreign banks in the SEZ effectively. At the same time, they have stated that the policy of the PBOC is to assist rather than interfere with the business of foreign banks, and that this over-relaxed supervision of foreign banks would be improved in the future.[80]

On the legislative side, apart from the SEZ Foreign Bank Regulations and the Provisions on Administration of Mortgage Loans, there are no other detailed regulations governing the operations of foreign banks in the Shenzhen SEZ. This situation has caused some confusion in the foreign banking community. Under the current system, for instance, foreign banks may unintentionally help foreign investors to transfer foreign exchange out of China illegally. The reasons are as follows. Foreign banks in the Shenzhen SEZ are authorized to transmit capital, on behalf of foreign investors, from China to Hong Kong, Macau or other countries, without having to report this to any government organ or institution. And since there is no specific provision regulating such transactions, the foreign banks are not able to determine whether any particular transaction is legal or illegal and, thus, may unwittingly aid overseas investors in illegal foreign exchange transactions. There were reports of such cases last year.[81]

At present, the Shenzhen SEZ has not adopted tax legislation which is exclusively designed to deal with the earnings of foreign banks. Although foreign banks in the SEZ have been granted certain tax reductions and

78 *Wen Wei Po*, 7 March 1987, p. BN4.
79 *Id.*
80 *Wen Wei Po*, 10 March 1987, p. BN4.
81 *Wen Wei Po*, 7 March 1987, p. BN4.

exemptions under the current tax codes, foreign bankers still do not feel comfortable about being taxed on the same basis as other commercial institutions. In short, comprehensive legislation regarding the taxation of foreign banks in the SEZ is urgently needed to encourage the growth of these banks in China.

In spite of the somewhat arduous environment in which foreign banks in the Shenzhen SEZ operate, the future of foreign banking looks promising. The operations of foreign banks will benefit greatly from the current extensive financial reforms being carried out in China. At the beginning of 1987, 14 more cities were authorized to execute reforms in the financial sector on a trial basis. This brings the total number of such cities to 27. In addition, Guangdong Province has been confirmed as the 'testing ground' with regard to the implementation of the policies on financial reform.[82] The Chinese banks in Guangdong Province and in the 27 cities are to operate as business enterprises, and the presidents and general managers of these institutions will be the key decision-makers. These banks will be allowed to fix interest rates, make loans and advances in accordance with market situations and will be invested with the power to dismiss and hire officials and staff members as well as to determine wages and bonuses.[83] Thus, a more favourable financial system will be created for both Chinese and foreign banks.

The SEZs are taking the lead in domestic financial reforms. Three of them have established foreign exchange markets ie foreign exchange centres.[84] In addition, an extensive reform plan has been adopted by the Shenzhen branch of the PBOC. These reform measures, which apply to Renminbi services offered to enterprises by specialized banks and other Chinese banks in the SEZ, are designed to achieve four objectives:

(1) Establishment of an SEZ interest system based on the discount interest rates of the local branch of the PBOC, and the setting of maximum limits on interest rates for deposits and minimum interest rates for loans. Specialized banks to be allowed to float their interest rates within stipulated limits and the local branch of the PBOC to control the circulation of money in the SEZ through adjustments to the basic interest rate.
(2) Simplification of the various types of interest offered. Interest rates also to vary according to loan duration, with higher interest rates for longer term loans, thus enabling a better utilization of money.
(3) Preferential interest rates for commercial paper, thus speeding up the establishment of a market for commercial paper
(4) Bringing about of stable economic growth and a better flow of funds by way of interest reforms.[85]

82 *Wen Wei Po*, 15 February 1987, p. 3.
83 *Id.*
84 By mid-1987, the Shenzhen SEZ, Zhuhai SEZ and Xiamen SEZ had established foreign exchange centres in which foreign-investment enterprises as well as financial institutions could purchase or sell foreign exchange using the Chinese currency. Exchange rates for such transactions were determined by the parties involved.
85 *Guangdong Business Monitor*, vol. 1, no. 7, 1 January 1987, p. 19.

To be specific, loans by local Chinese banks will be subdivided into three categories, namely, provisional, short-term and long-term. The interest rate for each kind of loan will be calculated by adding a certain amount to the basic interest rate set by the PBOC. Companies will be allowed to raise funds through discounts on cheques and mortgages. There will be a penalty for late repayment of loans. These changes will provide foreign banks with a more comfortable environment to do business in.

Nevertheless, in the immediate future, foreign banks may have to keep their businesses essentially within the SEZs, for their primary customers are concentrated in such areas. With domestic economic reforms underway, the open and coastal cities are likely participants in the next phase of foreign banking in China. At the same time, it is certain that more foreign banks will be allowed to commence operations in China and carry on more diverse activities.

Chapter eight

Comparative analysis of the new laws

The new provisions on foreign investment adopted by the Chinese government are based on and, therefore, reflect China's current economic situation, and its policies particularly with regard to attracting foreign capital. Immediately following the adoption of the State Council Provisions, the provincial as well as city governments gave immense support to the new legislation by promulgating their own incentives for foreign investors. Even remote provinces and cities announced their own guidelines and special incentives to attract foreign investment. Although local rules may be less detailed than, or mere restatements of, national legislation, they do demonstrate the extent to which a national consciousness of foreign-investment issues has emerged. Taking into consideration the important part that local governments play in implementing national laws and policies, the proliferation of local legislation is far more significant than the laws themselves.

In order to illustrate the features of China's new foreign-investment laws, this chapter will analyze the new national incentives together with those which were in existence prior to 1986. Legislation which has been adopted by various provinces and cities as well as the Special Economic Zones will be examined on a comparative basis as well. Given the sporadic nature of published information and the limited scope of this book, the compilation of foreign-investment incentives herein cannot be exhaustive and covers only the most representative and important provinces and cities in the country.

I. National incentives – old and new

China's current position on foreign investment and its policies relating thereto can be summarized as follows: most of the enterprises with foreign participation that have so far been established in China are in light industries or the service sector and are aimed at the domestic Chinese market. This situation has not only frustrated China's hopes of introducing advanced technology and equipment into the country by attracting foreign investment but has also created problems for foreign-investment enterprises. For instance, in view of the non-convertibility of the Renminbi, a number of foreign-investment concerns suffer from a shortage of foreign exchange. The Chinese government cannot do much to improve this situation, for the volume of its foreign trade remains small and it needs to increase its purchases of advanced machinery, equipment and technology in order to realize its modernization programme. Furthermore, since China is essentially a planned-economy country, the problem of bureaucratic inefficiency proves to be one of the most serious difficulties that foreign investors have to face. Such inefficiency is also attributable to the existing less-than-perfect legal system and the lack of legal consciousness of many government officials in charge of foreign investment.

Tax reductions and exemptions

Having recognized the obstacles and difficulties facing foreign investors, and with the aim of diverting foreign capital to the productive or manufacturing sectors, the new laws adopted by the State Council in 1986 offer additional incentives to export-oriented enterprises or enterprises producing import-substitutes, and to productive concerns using advanced equipment or technology. As Table 1 indicates, Export Enterprises ('EEs') and Technologically Advanced Enterprises ('TAEs') are given preferential treatment in enterprise income tax reductions and exemptions. Export enterprises which export more than 70% of their production are treated preferentially. In addition, the reinvestment of profits by foreign investors in an EE or a TAE is encouraged and such foreign investors are entitled to a total refund on the tax paid on the reinvested amount. This measure taken by the Chinese government will also help to resolve the foreign exchange shortage faced by foreign investors.

Under this policy, foreign investors who suffer from a shortage of foreign exchange but have Renminbi surpluses generated from domestic sales may reinvest their Renminbi profits in an export-oriented enterprise in order to achieve a foreign exchange balance between the two enterprises. The most noticeable feature of this tax provision is that it focusses on the nature of the foreign-investment enterprises and not on their sources of investment. Therefore, investors from Hong Kong or Macau or overseas Chinese investors no longer enjoy any special treatment. The emphasis of the new provisions is on export-investment projects and hi-tech concerns. This represents a departure in policy from the previous legislation which encouraged foreign investment in low-profit making sectors or remote areas.[1]

1 The regulations described herein, concerning equity joint ventures, are in general equally applicable to contractual or cooperative ventures in China. In addition, unless it is otherwise indicated, the provisions discussed herein are also applicable to wholly foreign-owned enterprises.

Table 1: Existing laws and new provisions[2]

Existing laws

A. *Taxation of Sino-foreign ventures (JV)*[3]

Sino-foreign joint ventures subject to a flat tax rate of 30% on the total taxable income, plus a local income tax at a rate of 10% on the assessed amount of income tax, thus making the total tax rate, 33%; remittance tax at a rate of 10% to be levied on the amount remitted abroad. (Art. 3)

B. *Reductions and exemptions for JVs*

(1) New JV contracts for 10 years or more:
- — tax exempt for the first profit-making year. (Art. 5)
- — 50% tax reduction for subsequent two profit-making years. (Art. 5)

(2) JV with long-term capital recovery, or engaging in low-profit operations such as farming, forestry, animal husbandry, coal mining, or located in remote, economically underdeveloped areas:
- — 15–30% tax reduction for 10 years; further tax reduction allowed upon approval of Ministry of Finance. (Art. 5)
- — 40% refund on tax paid on income reinvested in China for five or more years by a foreign JV party. (Art. 6)

(3) JVs for construction of ports and wharves:[4]
- — income tax at 15%. (Art. 6)
- — if scheduled to operate for 15 years or more, tax exempt for the first five profit-making years and a 50% tax reduction for the subsequent five profit-making years. (Art. 6)
- — profit remittance tax exempt for a foreign JV partner. (Art. 7)

C. *Taxation of Wholly Foreign-owned Enterprises (WFOE)*[5]

WFOE's income taxed on a progressive scale, the lowest tax rate being 20%, the highest 40%, plus a 10% local tax on the taxable income, thus making the highest total tax burden less than 50% of any given income. (Art. 3)

D. *Tax exemptions and reductions for WFOEs*

WFOEs scheduled to operate for 10 years or more in farming, forestry, animal husbandry or other low-profit operations:
- — tax exempt in the first profit-making year. (Art. 5)
- — 50% tax reduction for subsequent two years. (Art. 5)
- — 15–30% tax reduction extension for 10 years after expiration of exemptions and reductions, with approval of Ministry of Finance. (Art. 5)

E. *Local income taxation*

JVs, WFOEs and Sino-Foreign Cooperative Ventures (CVs) may be exempted from paying income tax or may enjoy a reduction in local income tax at discretion of local governments concerned.[6]

New provisions

EEs and TAEs are defined in the State Council Provisions and receive preferential treatment:
- — remittance tax exempted for amounts remitted by foreign parties to JVs, WFOEs or CVs. (Art. 7)
- — An EE exporting 70% or more of production in value terms, entitled to a 50% tax reduction after the expiration of tax reduction or exemption period under relevant State provisions. (Art. 8)
- — A TAE entitled to a 50% tax reduction for three years after the expiration of tax reduction or exemption period under relevant State provisions. (Art. 9)
- — 100% refund on tax paid on income reinvested by a foreign party in a project for the establishment or expansion of EEs or TAEs for an operational period of five years or more. (Art. 10)

Import measures and Consolidated Industrial and Commercial Tax

With regard to imports and exports and the Consolidated Industrial and Commercial Tax ('CICT'), the effect of the State Council Provisions is to simplify the procedures that foreign-investment concerns have to go through for the importation of equipment and machinery for production purposes. In addition, convenient import procedures for the production of exports have been provided. Under the new laws, enterprises intending to export products must apply for export licences every six months. The reason behind this provision is that China has obligations towards other countries in that it has quotas on its exports. If exports by foreign-investment enterprises are not checked, China may violate its international obligations. In accordance with current Chinese policy, foreign investors are granted exemptions from CICT for their exports, while the tax on domestic sales remains unchanged. (See Table 2).

Management of business and management of labour

The autonomy that foreign-investment enterprises enjoy in business operations and in hiring and dismissing employees is endorsed by the State Council Provisions. These enterprises now have the right to make independent decisions regarding production matters, marketing, and organization of personnel. Needless to say, these measures are major steps, in the right direction, taken by the Chinese government and will not only greatly assist foreign investors in running their businesses but will also increase both labour and management efficiency. (See Table 3, on page 172).

Operating costs

In order to prevent local authorities and institutions from levying charges on foreign-investment enterprises indiscriminately, and in order to guarantee the smooth operations of such enterprises, the State Council Provisions explicitly stipulate that no unreasonable charges should be

2 The information contained under the heading 'New provisions' in this section is taken from the State Council Provisions, unless otherwise indicated.
3 The materials contained in A and B(1) and (2) of this Table are from the Joint Venture Income Tax Law of China.
4 The materials contained in this entry are from the 'Provisional Provisions on the Preferential Treatment of China-Foreign Joint Ventures for the Construction of Ports and Wharves' promulgated by the State Council of China on 30 September 1985.
5 The materials contained in C and D of this Table are from the Wholly Foreign-owned Enterprise Tax Law of China.
6 Article 4 of the Wholly Foreign-owned Enterprise Tax Law of China authorizes local governments to grant further tax reductions or exemptions to foreign investors. Although there is no specific authorization of such a nature in the Joint Venture Tax Law, local governments are in practice given a discretion in respect of local tax reductions or exemptions.

Table 2: Existing laws and new provisions

Existing laws

A. Under CICT Regulations, there are in existence 108 taxable items which are categorized according to products and trades, with 41 flat tax rates, the lowest being 1.5%, the highest 69%, an average rate of 5% applicable to ordinary industrial products.[7]

B. *Reductions and exemptions*

- — Exports of products manufactured by a foreign-investment enterprise, except for those on the State's export restriction list, exempted from CICT.[8]
- — Exempted from CICT: raw materials, semi-finished materials, components, spare parts and packing materials imported by a foreign partner for processing or assembly into finished products or for the production of exports.[9]
- —

Machinery, equipment, parts, components and materials imported by a JV partner as part of investment, exempted from CICT; for other foreign-investment venture partners, exemption subject to approval of tax authorities.[10]

C. *Import-export licences*

- — For importation or exportation of machinery, equipment, materials, products etc, import licences required.
- — JVs may, within the scope of operations stipulated in the contract, make an import plan every year for items which require import licences, and make an application for such licences every six months.[11]
- — For other foreign-investment enterprises (FIEs), import licences to be obtained on a case-by-case basis.[12]
- — Export licences required for JVs — to follow application procedures for import licences.[13]
- — Import-export licences in general to be issued by MOFERT.

New provisions

Export products of every foreign-investment enterprise enjoy a total CICT exemption, except for crude oil, finished oil and other products which are subject to special State provisions. (Art. 11)

Import-export licences

- — Every FIE is required to apply for import licences when importing equipment, materials etc as part of foreign investment. (Art. 12)
- — Import licences not required for importation of machinery, equipment, vehicles, raw materials, fuel, spare parts, accessories and components for export-oriented production if resultant products sold in domestic Chinese market, reapplication for licences required. (Art. 13)
- — Importation of machinery, parts, raw materials etc for domestic market production, import licences required — procedures similar to those already in existence. (Art. 13)
- — Importation of non-production goods for FIEs' own use — licences (issued by provincial or city authorities) required.[14]
- — Export licences for products of FIEs to be applied for and issued every six months. (Art. 12)

levied on foreign investors and that the latter have the right to challenge any such charges or even appeal to the central government for resolution of such disputes. This measure will remove some of the difficulties which foreign investors have encountered with local authorities. In addition, EEs and TAEs are entitled not to pay any land use fee which is above that fixed in the central government legislation. However, this provision may not have much practical effect at the moment as many cities and provinces have already lowered their land use fees. Nevertheless, the minimum standard set up at least reflects the Chinese government's determination to lower the operating costs of foreign investors in China.

As regards the balancing of foreign exchange accounts, the Chinese government does not have much to offer at this moment. Nevertheless, the mutual adjustment of foreign exchange surpluses and deficiencies among foreign investors at rates which are different from the official exchange rate is still encouraging and is in line with China's previous practice. The introduction of Renminbi mortgage loans is another new measure taken by the Chinese government. Thus, these new measures clearly demonstrate that the Chinese government is keen on helping foreign investors solve their difficulties.

The State Council Provisions, together with the regulations adopted by various ministries, have given foreign investors more freedom in decision-making and have offered new incentives to EEs and TAEs. They represent the current trend of Chinese policies on foreign investment and will, no doubt, have far-reaching effects in this area.

II. Measures adopted by the open coastal cities and SEZs

The 14 open coastal cities, together with the four Special Economic Zones in China, have attracted most of the foreign investment. These cities and zones enjoy equal freedom and authority as far as the tax terms

7 See generally the Regulations of the Consolidated Industrial and Commercial Tax of the People's Republic of China.

8 Joint Venture Regulations, Article 72.

9 *Id*, Article 71.

10 *Id.*

11 Joint Venture Regulations, Article 63.

12 See Article 3 of the Regulations Concerning the Supervision and Control Over and the Levying and Exemption of Duties on Imports and Exports for Chinese-Foreign Contractual Ventures, promulgated by the General Administration of Customs, Ministry of Finance and Ministry of Foreign Economic Relations and Trade on 31 January 1984, effective as of 1 February 1984.

13 Joint Venture Regulations, Article 63.

14 Article 5 of the Rules for Application of Import and Export Licences promulgated by the Ministry of Foreign Economic Relations and Trade on 24 January 1987.

Table 3: Existing laws and new provisions

Existing laws

A. *Management of business*

- JV to work out production and operating plans in accordance with the scope of operation and scale of production stipulated in the contract.[15]
- Business plans of JVs require approval of the board of directors and have to be filed with the department in charge.[16]
- The department in charge of JVs, and planning and administration departments at all levels, restrained from issuing compulsory directives to JVs on production and operating plans.[17]
- WFOE to work out production and operating plans which must be filed with the department in charge for purposes of record.[18]
- The business operations of a WFOE, if in accordance with its articles of association approved by the Chinese government, not to be interfered with by anyone.[19]

B. *Management of labour*[20]

- Matters pertaining to employment, dismissal and resignation of staff, wages, awards, punishment, labour insurance and welfare, labour protection and discipline stipulated in labour contracts. (Art. 2)
- JVs have right to punish and dismiss employees; punishment by discharging employee required to be reported to the department in charge and the labour management department for approval. (Art. 5)
- Discharged employees have the right to challenge decision of management. (Art. 6)
- Wage level of workers in JVs 120% to 150% of the real wages of similar employees in State-owned enterprises carrying on the same trade. (Art. 8)
- JVs to pay for Chinese workers' labour insurance, medical expenditure and government subsidies. (Art. 11)
- Workers to be employed upon recommendation of local labour authorities or at the initiative of JVs with consent of labour authorities. (Art. 3)

New provisions

A. *Management of business*

- The government at all levels in China and the relevant department in charge required to guarantee the right of autonomy of FIEs and to support such enterprises' internationally-advanced scientific management. (Art. 15)
- FIEs have the right, within the scope of approved contracts, to determine independently production and operating plans, and to raise and use funds, to purchase production materials and to sell products at discretion. (Art. 15)

B. *Management of labour*

- FIEs entitled to determine wage levels, forms of wages and bonuses and allowance system for their employees. (Art. 15)
- FIEs enjoy the right to determine independently their own organizational structure and personnel system, the recruitment or dismissal of senior management personnel, and any increase or reduction in staff and workers. (Art. 15)
- Staff and workers who break the rules and regulations subject to disciplinary action depending on the seriousness of the case. (Art. 15)
- Names of dismissed employees filed with local authorities for record only. (Art. 15)
- Employment of workers either from the locality of an FIE or elsewhere; Chinese concerns required to release employees wanting to work for FIEs. (Art. 15)

terms for foreign investors and the policies concerning foreign investment are concerned. In general, foreign-investment income in these cities (particularly, the original urban districts and the economic and technology development zones) and in the SEZs is taxed at a reduced rate of 15%. Moreover, income tax reductions and exemptions may be granted to enterprises bringing in large amounts of foreign investment, or advanced technology, or with operational periods of ten years or more. This policy also applies to the levying of CICT in these cities and the SEZs.

Each of the coastal cities has been delegated the power of authorizing and approving foreign investments up to a certain limit. For instance, Shanghai and Tianjin are authorized to approve foreign investments up to US$30m, while Dalian and Guangzhou have the power to authorize projects involving less than US$10m. The approval limit of the other coastal cities is in general US$5m, although they must also seek official approval from the respective provincial governments.

This section will compare and analyze the new measures which have been adopted by most of the coastal cities and SEZs in implementing the national laws. Since Beijing is a prime location for foreign investment, its rules and regulations will be discussed together with those of the coastal cities.

Business autonomy and administrative efficiency

The right of foreign-investment enterprises to make decisions independently is crucial to their success. China is a planned economy country and, thus, has not had much experience in corporate management. Due to the imperfect nature of the Chinese legal system, the administrative authorities very often interfere with the business operations of foreign-investment enterprises, although such actions may not done with malice. At the same time, because of the poor infrastructure and shortage of supplies, such as water, power, fuel, skilled workers etc in the country, foreign investors must, to a large extent, rely on the assistance of the bureaucracy, for administrative organs are still the most important authorities in China. This situation makes it inevitable that the success of any foreign-investment project depends, on the one hand, on the autonomy of the enterprise in question, and on the other, on the assistance of administrative authorities at all levels. Therefore, the

15 Joint Venture Regulations, Article 56.
16 *Id.*
17 *Id.*
18 Article 11 of the Law of the People's Republic of China on Enterprises Operated Exclusively With Foreign Capital adopted on 12 April 1986.
19 *Id.*
20 The materials contained in this entry are from the Regulations of the People's Republic of China on Labour Management in Joint Ventures Using Chinese and Foreign Investment, promulgated by the State Council on 26 July 1980.

Table 4: Existing laws and new provisions

Existing laws

A. *Land use fees*

— No national or uniform rules.
— Preferential treatment at discretion of local authorities – usually provided for cultural, educational, scientific or public welfare enterprises; varied rules adopted by local governments giving land use fee reductions or exemptions to projects which use high technology, make low profits, have long-term capital return, or are overseas-Chinese investment projects.

B. *Other charges*

— No national law or standard in respect of other operating charges of FIEs;
— Local authorities often change or raise fees concerning FIEs.

C. *Balancing of foreign exchange*[21]

— JVs required, in general, to maintain balance between foreign exchange income and expenditure. (Art. 75)
— In certain circumstances, relevant provincial and city governments help JVs with unbalanced foreign exchange accounts by injecting foreign exchange from the government's reserves, if the unbalance was foreseen in feasibility studies. (Art. 75)
— The central government provides foreign exchange in extraordinary cases. (Art. 75)
— Foreign exchange or RMB loans to be provided by BOC to FIEs under certain circumstances. (Art. 78)

New provisions

A. *Land use fees*

— The maximum land use fees prescribed for EEs and TAEs, except for those located in busy urban sectors of large cities, are as follows:
a) at RMB5 to RMB20 per sq m per year in areas where development fees and site use fees are computed and charged together;
b) at not more than RMB3 per sq m per year for areas where development fees are computed and charged on a one-time basis, and for areas developed by the users themselves. (Art. 4)
— Local governments allowed to provide further reductions in or exemptions from land use fees at their discretion. (Art. 4)

B. *Other charges*

— Local governments required to curb indiscrimate levying of charges and to formulate specific methods to strengthen general supervision and to administer central government's directives in this regard. (Art. 16)
— FIEs have right to challenge and not to pay unreasonable fees, and to appeal to local authorities or the central government regarding such charges. (Art. 16)

C. *Balancing of foreign exchange*

— FIEs permitted to make mutual adjustments to their foreign exchange surpluses and deficiencies (exchange rates different from the official ones – allowed in practice). (Art. 14)
— RMB loans secured by foreign exchange to be provided by Chinese banks or other authorized financial institutions. (Art. 14)
— Direct lending by Chinese banks in either foreign or local currencies.[22]
— Priority given to EEs and TAEs in fund-raising. (Art. 6)

D. *Additional information*

— EEs and TAEs entitled to priority in supply of water, electricity etc. (Art. 5)

efficiency of the bureaucracy, and the right of autonomy of foreign-investment enterprises, must go hand in hand.

In order to improve the investment climate, the State Council Provisions sanction the absolute autonomy of enterprises with foreign participation in the following areas: production, procurement of materials, hiring and dismissal of employees, determination of wage systems and levels, fixing of product prices etc, so long as what they do is within the scope of the approved contracts. Local governments are also required to raise their efficiency and assist foreign-investment projects in their operations.

The legislation enacted by the open coastal cities and SEZs represent a more liberal trend. While freedom of production and distribution has been unanimously acknowledged at local level, many city governments have also offered new incentives for the better management of foreign-investment enterprises. For instance, a number of cities have established supply and service companies to assist foreign investors. Many pieces of local legislation provide that production facilities needed by foreign investors must be charged at rates similar to those applicable to State-owned enterprises. Decision-making procedures have also been simplified or improved at local level. In addition to shortening the response-time for an official reply, several city governments have adopted a 'joint-office' method, that is, key officials from various departments in charge of foreign investment work together in the same office to improve efficiency. (See Table 5).

Tax reductions and exemptions

At the initial stage, taxation will not be the primary concern of international investors. The issue of tax-saving will not arise until a later stage when the project in question is agreed upon by the parties. This does not mean, however, that any reduction in or exemption from tax is not important to foreign investors for, after all, these factors are pertinent particularly to reinvestment. For one reason or another, the Chinese government, at all levels, is most keen on offering preferential tax terms. As indicated in Table 2, the coastal cities and SEZs have attached enormous importance to tax incentives in encouraging the inflow of foreign capital and, in particular, have granted considerable tax breaks to EEs and TAEs. In addition to the reductions in and exemptions from enterprise income tax provided for by national legislation, many statutes adopted by the city governments provide for exemptions from local surtax, CICT and customs duty. The general trend is to encourage productive investment and the introduction of advanced technology.

21 The materials contained in this entry are from the Joint Venture Regulations.

22 Article 6 of the Regulations of the Bank of China on Providing Loans to Foreign-invested Enterprises promulgated on 24 April 1987.

Table 5: Measures to improve business autonomy and administrative efficiency

Location	Management of labour	Supply of materials and funds	Approval procedures
Beijing[23]		— Service companies established to provide foreign investors with materials and equipment at prices applicable to State-owned companies. (Art. 6)	— Planning Commission solely responsible for approving projects. (Art. 1) — Projects under US$1m to be approved by district or county government instead of city government. (Art. 1) — All decisions to be made within one month. (Art. 2)
Dalian[24]		— Preferential working-capital loans available to successful foreign investors; — Loan application procedures simplified.	
Fuzhou[25]		— Issuance of debentures and bonds allowed. (Art. VI) — Mortgage loans available. (Art. VI)	
Guangzhou[26]	— Wage system and levels decided by board of directors, report not necessary. (Art. 15) — Employees' insurance and subsidies same as those applicable to State-owned companies. (Art. 15) — Both long-term and temporary employment allowed. (Art. 16)	— Priority to foreign investors in supply of water, electricity, coal, oil and transportation and communications facilities, at prices applicable to State-owned companies. (Art. 19) — Service and supply companies established. (Art. 20)	— Foreign-investment matters to be handled by a leadership group. (Art. 21) — Decisions to be made within two months or less. (Art. 21)

	recruitment of personnel.	investors in supply of raw and supplementary materials, at rates applicable to State-owned enterprises; — Establishment of materials supply centres by foreign investors allowed.	
Ningpo[28]	— Wage level 120–150% that of local employees. (Art. 4) — Insurance fee equal to 20% of direct salary. (Art. 4) — Welfare fund set up in accordance with State provisions. (Art. 4) — RMB25 per month housing allowance for each employee retained by the employer for improvement of employees' housing conditions. (Art. 4) — Other subsidies exempted. (Art. 4)	— Supply companies established. (Art. 3) — Supply of water etc to be coordinated. (Art. 3) by the city government. — EEs and TAEs to pay prices applicable to State-owned companies. (Art. 3)	— Joint approval procedure (meeting of all the relevant departments in the city) established. (Art. 1) — A joint approval office to be established in future so that investment projects can be approved within the office. (Art. 1)
Qingdao[29]	— Freedom in determining wage system and levels, and in hiring and dismissing employees. (Art. 2(1)) — Subsidies granted in accordance with State regulations. (Art. 2(1)) — Expatriates' accommodation, urban transportation, postal services, and communications within city, charged in RMB at domestic rates. (Art. 2(3))	— Priority guarantee to the EEs and TAEs in supply of operating facilities. (Art. 7(1)) — City supply department in charge of supply of materials at reasonable prices. (Art. 7(2))	— Written reply in 30 days re project and feasibility matters. (Art. 6(1)) — Registration and licences, within 10 days. (Art. 6(1))

Table 5: Measures to improve business autonomy and administrative efficiency (cont'd)

Location	Management of labour	Supply of materials and funds	Approval procedures
Qinhuang-dao[30] (ETDZ)	— Total freedom in every employment matter. (Art. 7) — Foreign investors' relatives from rural areas allowed to settle in the city. (Art. 7)	— Priority in supply of operating facilities at prices applicable to State-owned companies. (Art. 2) — Assistance in fund-raising. (Art. 3) — Supply company in charge of providing materials within or without the locality. (Art. 3)	— One department solely responsible for investment matters. (Art. 6) — Determination of project proposals, within 15 days. (Art. 6)
Shanghai[31]	— Public or open recruitment allowed. (Art. 6) — Labour Department to assist foreign investors. (Art. 6) — Housing allowance retained by employer for improvement of accommodation of employees. (Art. 5)	— Priority in supply of operating facilities to EEs and TAEs at domestic prices. (Art. 7) — Priority in loans. (Art. 8) — Supply companies established. (Art. 11)	— Approvals for project proposals, contracts, feasibility studies, within 30 days. (Art. 13) — Approval certificates to be issued within 10 days. (Art. 13) — Foreign-investment service leadership group established to provide consultancy services. (Art. 9)
Tianjin[32]	— Labour service, labour insurance companies, and a labour dispute commission to be established for the benefit of foreign-investment enterprises in recruiting and dismissing employees.[34]	— Supply companies to be established.[33]	

Wenzhou[35]	— Freedom in setting up personnel and wage structures. (Art. 1) — Free recruiting within the city. (Art. 1) — Cross-region recruiting requires approval of local authority. (Art. 1) — Except for labour insurance, medical and welfare fund, and housing allowance, no other subsidy to be paid. (Art. 13) — Foreign investors who experience financial difficulties, may upon approval, be exempted from paying all subsidies. (Art. 13) — Expatriates to pay domestic rates for food, housing etc. (Art. 14)	— Priority in supply of operating facilities to export and hi-tech enterprises at domestic prices. (Art. 6) — Assistance in supply of materials provided. (Art. 7) — Loans will be provided. (Art. 8)	— System of joint approval established. (Art. 16) — Approval of project proposals, articles of association, feasibility studies, within 30 days. (Art. 16) — Certificates or licences to be issued within 10 days. (Art. 16)
Yantai[36]	— Housing subsidies to be retained by employers for improvement of accommodation of employees. (Art. 1) — Expatriates, including temporary foreign employees, to pay domestic rates for food, housing etc. (Art. 1)	— EEs and TAEs to enjoy priority in supply of operating facilities. (Art. 2) — Loans and materials will be provided to EEs and TAEs. (Art. 2)	— Coordinating leadership team in charge of foreign investment established. (Art. 8) — Approval of documents, within 20 days. (Art. 8)

Table 5: Measures to improve business autonomy and administrative efficiency (cont'd)

Location	Management of labour	Supply of materials and funds	Approval procedures
Zhanjiang[37]	— Independent determination by FIEs of structure of staffing, wages, bonuses and allowances. (Art. 4) — Right to employ and dismiss workers and staff. (Art. 4) — Support by local enterprises required. (Art. 4)	— EEs and TAEs to enjoy priority in supply of raw materials, fuel, water, electricity and communications facilities, at rates applicable to domestic enterprises. (Art. 5) — Loans will be provided to FIEs on priority basis. (Art. 7) — Issuance of bonds and stocks by FIEs allowed. (Art. 6)	— Decision on agreements, contracts, articles of association, within one month. (Art. 10) — Decision on other matters, within one week. (Art. 10)
Shantou (City)[38]	— Freedom in determining wages and bonuses. (Art. 9) — Labour insurance and welfare fund determined according to the rates applicable to domestic companies, currently not more than 27% of the wage. (Art. 9)	— Priority in provision of funds to all foreign investors, EEs and TAEs. (Art. 4)	— Approval authorities to improve coordination of work (Art. 10) — Replies to all applications, within one month. (Art. 10)
Xiamen[39]	— Full freedom in hiring and dismissing employees, including recruiting them from other cities or regions.	— EEs and TAEs to be given priority in provision of loans.	— Leadership group in charge of foreign investment established.
Zhuhai[40]		— Priority in supply of water and electricity to foreign investors, at domestic rates.	— Approval of agreements, contracts, articles of association, within one month. — Determination of other matters, within 10 days.

23 The materials herein concerning Beijing City are from the Stipulations for Improving the Investment Environment and Encouraging Foreign Investment in Beijing issued by the Beijing Municipality on 12 October 1986.

24 The measures for the encouragement of foreign investment issued by Dalian Municipality in late 1986 were summarized in *China Economic News*, 29 December 1986, pp. 4–5. The materials herein regarding Dalian City are from the above summary.

25 The materials herein concerning Fuzhou City are from the Preferential Measures of Fuzhou Municipality on Enterprises with Foreign Investment adopted by the Standing Committee of the Sixth Fujian Provincial People's Congress on 12 December 1986.

26 The materials herein concerning Guangzhou City are from the Implementing Measures of Guangzhou Municipality for the Encouragement of Foreign Investment adopted on 30 October 1986.

27 The materials herein regarding the Foreign Investment Incentives of Natong are from a summary of the report of the preferential term package carried in *China Economic News*, 2 March 1987, pp. 7–8.

28 The materials herein concerning Ningpo City are from the Implementing Measures for the Encouragement of Foreign Investment in Ningpo. These Measures were announced after the enactment of State Council Provisions, but no specific date of promulgation is available.

29 The materials herein concerning Qingdao City are from the Regulations for the Implementation of the Provisions for Encouraging Foreign Investment of the State Council promulgated by the Qingdao Municipal Government on 16 October 1986.

30 The materials herein concerning Qinguangdao ETDZ are from the Regulations of Preferential Treatment on Encouragement of Foreign Investors to the Economic and Technical Development Zone announced by the Qinguangdao Municipal Government in November 1986.

31 The materials herein are from the Provisions of the Shanghai Municipality for the Encouragement of Foreign Investment which have been in force since 11 November 1986.

32 Unless otherwise indicated, the materials herein concerning Tianjin are from the Preferential Measures for Foreign Investment in the ETDZ promulgated by the Tianjin Municipal Government on 20 November 1986.

33 *Economic Reporter*, 19 January 1987, p. 26.

34 *Economic Reporter*, 12 January 1987, pp. 36–37, *Da Kung Pao* (Chinese version, Hong Kong), 18 March 1987, p. 11.

35 The materials herein concerning Wenzhou City are from the Preferential Terms for the Encouragement of Foreign Investment adopted by the Wenzhou Municipal Government on 4 December 1986.

36 The materials herein concerning Yantai City are from the Preferential Measures for Encouraging Foreign Investment adopted by Yantai Municipal Government in November 1986.

37 The materials herein concerning Zhanjiang City are from the Certain Preferential Provisions for Foreign Funded Enterprises adopted by the Zhanjiang Municipal Government in March 1987.

38 The materials herein concerning Shantou City are from the Certain Preferential Measures for the Encouragement of Foreign Investment promulgated by the Shantou Municipal Government on 5 January 1987.

39 The materials herein concerning Xiamen are from a summary of the report on the Preferential Measures for the Encouragement of Foreign Investment promulgated by the Xiamen Municipality which was carried in *China Economic News*, 10 November 1986, p. 2.

40 The materials herein concerning Zhuhai are from a summary of the report on the Incentives for the Encouragement of Foreign Investment promulgated by the Zhuhai Municipality which was carried in *China Economic News*, 9 February 1987, p. 7–8.

Table 6: Tax reductions and exemptions

Location	Local surtax incentives	Consolidated industrial and commercial tax (CICT)	Customs duties
Beihai	— For manufacturing projects, upon approval, exemption from surtax for the first three profit-making years, thereafter, a 50% reduction for subsequent five years. (Art. 7) — For non-productive projects involving US$5m or more, exemption from surtax for the first two profit-making years, thereafter, a 50% reduction for the subsequent three years. (Art. 7) — Enterprises which enjoy national income tax exemption are automatically exempted from local tax for the same period. (Art. 8) — Enterprises which export more than 50% of their production are exempted from surtax for the year in which this occurs. (Art. 8) — Projects involving US$3m or more and having annual profits of less than RMB1m exempted from surtax, upon approval, after expiration of the period for which reductions or exemptions are given. (Art. 10) — Total exemption from remittance tax. (Art. 16)	— Exports exempted from CICT. (Art. 11) — Imports of equipment, materials, machinery etc for export production exempted from CICT. (Art. 12) — Domestic market-oriented projects exempted from CICT if facing difficulties at initial stages. (Art. 15)	— Imports of equipment, machinery, materials etc for export production exempted from customs duties. (Art. 11) — Imports of goods for enterprises' own use exempted from customs duties. (Art. 14)

Beijing	— Hi-tech or export projects exempted from surtax upon approval of tax authorities. (Art. 7) — 50% surtax reduction for projects whose annual incomes are less than RMB1m. (Art. 7) — Exemption from surtax for projects whose profit rates are lower than 20% of their total sales. (Art. 7)	— CICT exemption for export products manufactured. (Art. 9)	— No customs duty on import-substitutes, imported parts, fittings etc put under care of bonded warehouse. (Art. 5) — If such imports are sold to domestic end-users who enjoy duty exemptions or reductions, same terms applicable to such imports. (Art. 5)
Dalian	— Exemption from surtax for the first seven profit-making years. — EEs or TAEs enjoy additional one to five-year exemptions, upon approval of local authorities. — Additional exemption from surtax for projects in energy, communications and port construction. — Projects scheduled for 10 years or more enjoy 50% enterprise income reduction for three years. — 40% refund on reinvestments in EEs or TAEs wth three to five-year life-spans.		
Fuzhou	— Total exemption from local surtax. (Art. I(B)) — Total refund of reinvested amounts in EEs or TAEs which are scheduled to operate for not less than five years. (Art. I(A) (9))	— Imports of machinery, means of transportation and equipment for production in old urban areas exempted from CICT. (Art. I(C) (1))	— Imports of machinery, means of transportation and equipment for production in old urban areas exempted from duties. (Art. I(C) (1))

Table 6: Tax reductions and exemptions (cont'd)

Location	Local surtax incentives	Consolidated industrial and Commercial tax (CICT)	Customs duties
Fuzhou (Cont'd)		— Imports of parts, raw materials etc for export production exempted from CICT. (Art. I(C) (2)) — Enterprises facing difficulties exempted from CICT, upon approval of local authorities. (Art. I(C) (6))	— Imports of parts, raw materials, etc for export production exempted from duties; for domestic sales production, no exemption. (Art. I(C) (2)) — Imports of goods for enterprises' own use exempted from duties. (Art. I(C) (4))
Guangzhou	— EEs and TAEs exempted from surtax. (Art. 3)	— Refunds on portions of CICT relating to local parts or materials, if such parts and materials later used for export production. (Art. 4)	— Imports of parts or materials used for production of import-substitutes exempted from duties, if the imports of the final products enjoy exemptions. (Art. 6)
Nantong	— EEs and TAEs exempted from surtax for the period for which national income tax reductions or exemptions are allowed. — Other FIEs enjoy a three-year exemption from surtax and a 50% reduction for subsequent three years.		— Production of import-substitutes exempted from duties.

Ningpo	— EEs and TAEs enjoy exemption from surtax for the first five profit-making years. (Art. 5) — Enterprises exporting 70% of production enjoy exemption for seven years. (Art. 5)	
Qingdao	— Total exemption from surtax for EEs and TAEs. (Art. 3(1)) — Three-year 50% national income tax reduction for EEs and TAEs after expiration of the reduction or exemption period under national law. (Art. 3(1)) — Exemption from remittance tax for EEs and TAEs. (Art. 3(2))	— Exports exempted from CICT. (Art. 3(4))
Qinhuang-dao (ETDZ)	— Total exemption from surtax. (Art. 1) — Reduction and exemption of enterprise income tax upon approval of local authorities. (Art. 1)	— CICT reduction or exemption upon completion of necessary formalities. (Art. 1)
Shanghai	— Exemption from surtax for EEs and TAEs for the same period for which national income tax reductions and exemptions allowed; thereafter, will enjoy three-year exemption from surtax and a 50% reduction for subsequent three years. (Art. 2)	

Table 6: Tax reductions and exemptions (cont'd)

Location	Local surtax incentives	Consolidated industrial and commercial tax (CICT)	Customs duties
Shanghai (Cont'd)	— Enterprises which export 70% of production exempted from surtax. (Art. 3)		
Tianjin (ETDZ)		— Imports of production equipment and construction materials exempted from CICT. (Art. 3) — Imports of parts, materials, etc for export processing or production exempted from CICT. (Art. 3) — Exports of FIEs' own products, except for those restricted by State, exempted from CICT. (Art. 4) — FIEs facing difficulties at initial stages exempted from CICT upon approval of authorities. (Art. 4)	— Imports of equipment and construction materials for production exempted from duties. (Art. 3) — Imports of parts, materials etc for export processing or production exempted from duties and licence requirements. (Art. 3) — Exports of products manufactured by FIEs, except for those restricted under State regulations, exempted from duties. (Art. 4)
Wenzhou	— Total exemption from surtax till 1990; for EEs and TAEs till 1995; extension of exemption allowed upon approval of local government. (Art. 3)	— Exports exempted from CICT. (Art. 4) — Domestic market-oriented enterprises having financial difficulties exempted from CICT upon approval of local government. (Art. 4)	

Yan Tai	— Overseas-Chinese investment enterprises and Hong Kong, Macau and Taiwan investment enterprises exempted from enterprise income tax for the first three profit-making years, plus a 50% reduction for subsequent four years upon approval of local authorities. (Art. 6) — EEs and TAEs enjoy exemption from surtax for ten years. (Art. 6) — Refund on the portion of surtax and national income tax paid and reinvested in an EE or a TAE scheduled to operate for five years or more. (Art. 6)	— Total CICT exemption for exports. (Art. 6) — EEs and TAEs having difficulties at initial stages exempted from CICT upon approval of local authorities. (Art. 6) — Purchases of local products by foreign investors for export in lieu of remittance of profits exempted from CICT. (Art. 6)	— Imports of parts, raw materials, etc for production of import-substitutes, put under care of bonded warehouses, exempted from duties, if imports of the same by domestic end-users enjoy exemptions. (Art. 6)
Zhanjiang	— EEs and TAEs exempted from local tax for seven years plus a 50% reduction for subsequent three years. (Art. 3) — FIEs exempted from local tax for five years plus a 50% reduction for subsequent two years. (Art. 3)	— Purchases of local components for export production by FIEs exempted from CICT. (Art. 3) — Import-substitutes exempted from CICT. (Art. 3)	— Imports of materials or parts for production of import-substitutes exempted from customs duties, if imports of same products exempted from duties. (Art. 3)
Shantou (City)	— EEs and TAEs exempted from surtax and remittance tax. (Art. 8)		— Imports of parts, raw materials etc for production of import-substitutes, put under care of bonded warehouses, exempted from duties if imports of the same by domestic end-users enjoy exemptions. (Art. 5)

Table 6: Tax reductions and exemptions

Location	Local surtax incentives	Consolidated industrial and commercial tax (CICT)	Customs duties
Shenzhen	— Projects involving US$5m or more, using advanced technology or with long recoupment periods enjoy income tax exemption for two years plus a 50% reduction for subsequent three years.		— Products exported exempted from duties. — Imports of machinery, equipment for production exempted from duties. — Imports of parts or raw materials for export production exempted from duties. — Imports of parts or raw materials for local sales production enjoy a 50% reduction in duties.
Xiamen			— Imports of machinery, equipment, vehicles, parts, raw materials, etc for production do not require licences.
Zhuhai	— Exemption from national income tax for the first two profit-making years allowed for projects involving US$2m or more, using advanced technology or scheduled to operate for ten years or more. — Total exemption from surtax for the first five profit-making years.		— Imports of raw materials for export production exempted from duties. — Imports of raw materials for local sales production enjoy a 50% reduction in duties.

Operating costs and balancing of foreign exchange

The city governments of the coastal cities and SEZs have adopted a more liberal policy as regards business expenditure and balancing of foreign exchange. Site development and use fees are, in general, much lower than those drawn up by the central government. A number of cities exempt EEs and TAEs from land use fees. Such enterprises are also given priority in obtaining foreign-currency loans and are authorized to charge foreign exchange for the sale of import-substitutes. Several cities have also decided to allocate foreign exchange quotas to productive enterprises, particularly those with promising export potential. Almost all of these local governments authorize foreign investors not to pay any charges which are levied indiscriminately by local departments without the explicit approval of the provincial or city governments. The general policy is again to boost foreign investment in advanced-technology areas and in the manufacturing sectors. (See Table 7). These measures are very significant when we take into consideration the power and discretion that local governments have in setting the policy in these matters.

III. Incentives adopted by the provinces

A number of provincial governments in China have enacted their own provisions in the hope of attracting foreign capital and advanced technology. These provincial regulations, like those of the coastal cities and SEZs, provide for preferential terms to be granted to foreign investors. Among the representative provinces located in the coastal areas and hinterland, Jiangsu and Heilongjiang Provinces, which have relatively good industrial bases and experience in attracting foreign capital, concentrate on investments in export projects or in projects using advanced technology. Anhui and Shandong Provinces have, in general adopted all the incentives sanctioned by the State Council Provisions, although they also offer some additional preferential terms. In fact, to a large extent, Shangdong's regulations have been borrowed directly from the State Council Provisions. The measures offered by Hunan Province are particularly worth noting. They not only offer clear-cut reductions in operating costs but also make direct references to the competing incentives adopted by the coastal cities and other areas. Tibet, as a latecomer on the scene, with only one Sino-foreign joint venture, offers, among others, favourable terms to foreign investors in respect of the division of profits and losses. (See Table 8, on page 200).

Table 7: Operating costs and balancing of foreign exchange

Location	Land use fees	Other fees	Balancing of foreign exchange
Beihai	— Term of land use generally for 10–30 years; extension allowed by contract. (Art. 7) — Land use fee charged at RMB1 per sq m per year. (Art. 17) — Land development fee charged at RMB30–60 per sq m depending on the area and trade. (Art. 17) — EEs and TAEs exempted from land use fees and enjoy land development fee reductions. (Art. 17)		
Beijing	— EEs and TAEs exempted from land use fees or given reductions therefrom, upon approval of city government. (Art. 8)		— Import-substitutes manufactured in China to be charged in foreign exchange upon approval of local foreign exchange administration. (Art. 4) — Domestic companies selling parts or raw materials for production of import-substitutes not permitted to charge foreign exchange. (Art. 4)
Dalian	— EEs and TAEs which do not need to increase their supplies of water electricity, gas, or which have not constructed transportation	— Water, electricity, gas, fuel, transportation and communications facilities for production	

	or communications facilities, need only pay land use fees (annual rate not higher than RMB3 per sq m. — Reductions in or exemptions from land use fees for TAEs which export 70% or more of production permitted for three to five years.	and operations charged at the same levels as for State-owned enterprises.	
Fuzhou	— Fees for building infrastructure exempted. (Art. II) — Standard charge of land use fees at RMB5–15 per sq m per year depending on use and geographical conditions. (Art. II) — Annual land use fees not exceeding RMB2 per sq m in cases where the site development fee is charged in a lump sum or the site is developed by the user. (Art. II) — Exemption from land use fees allowed for EEs and TAEs upon approval of local government. (Art. II)		— Adjustments to be made by enterprises themselves. (Art. III(A)) — Sales to SEZs or ETDZs and charging of foreign exchange allowed. (Art. III(C)) — Upon approval, sales to other regions and charging of foreign exchange allowed. (Art. III(C)) — Reinvestment in Renminbi in foreign exchange-earning projects encouraged. (Art. III(D)) — Mortgage loans in foreign exchange to be provided. (Art. III(E)) — Direct foreign exchange borrowing to be provided to enterprises with foreign exchange earning ability but suffering temporary deficiencies. (Art. III(f))

Table 7: Operating costs and balancing of foreign exchange (cont'd)

Location	Land use fees	Other fees	Balancing of foreign exchange
Guangzhou	— Site development fees charged at 5% of the total cost. (Art. 17) — EEs and TAEs exempted from site development fees and to pay not more than RMB2.50 per sq m per year for land use, except in busy urban areas. (Art. 17)	— Foreign-investment concerns entitled not to pay any charges not approved by the State, provincial government or city price administration bureau. (Art. 17)	— Adjustments to be made by enterprises themselves. (Art. 10) — TAEs to be provided with foreign exchange by local authorities in case they suffer foreign exchange deficiencies. (Art. 11) — Mortgage loans provided. (Art. 12) — Raising funds by issuing bonds or stocks allowed. (Art. 14)
Nantong	— Except for those located in downtown districts or business hubs, a four-year site use fee exemption granted to all FIEs.	— Exemptions from 'collective' charges for the supply of water and electricity imposed by departments concerned. — All departments prohibited from collecting extra or unreasonable charges.	— Sale of import-substitutes for foreign exchange allowed. — Compensation arrangements encouraged.

Ningpo	— EEs and TAEs to pay standard fees for site development and land use, set at RMB5-20 per sq m per year. (Art. 4) — In ETDZs, RMB5–6 per sq m per year. (Art. 4)		
Qingdao	— Except for busy urban areas, land use fees are as follows: old urban areas, RMB12–15 per sq m per year; newly-developed areas, RMB10–12; counties, RMB8–10; towns, RMB5–6. (Art. 2(2)) — If site development fee is paid in a lump sum or the site is developed by the user, land use fee set at RMB1.20 per sq m per year. (Art. 2(2)) — Projects started before 1990 enjoy a 20% reduction in land use fees. (Art. 2(2))	— Priority in construction and installation, fees at the same levels as those for State-owned enterprises. (Art. 7(5))	— Adjustments to be made by enterprises themselves. (Art. 7(6)) — Mortgage loans provided. (Art. 7(6))

Table 7: Operating costs and balancing of foreign exchange (cont'd)

Location	Land use fees	Other fees	Balancing of foreign exchange
Qinhuang-bao (ETDZ)	— Exemptions from site development and use fees during construction of foreign-investment projects. (Art. 2) — EEs and TAEs set up in 1987 and 1988 to pay land development and use fees at rates of RMB2.5 per sq m per year for two years after start of operations. (Art. 2)		— Adjustments to be made by enterprises themselves. (Art. 4) — Those having sold large sums of foreign exchange to State banks and suffering deficiencies to be provided with foreign exchange by State banks upon approval. (Art. 4)
Shanghai	— Except for those located in busy urban sectors, EEs and TAEs exempted from land use fees for three years after establishment. (Art. 4) — Starting from the fourth year, fees at 50% of the minimum level prescribed by law but not higher than RMB2.5 per sq m per year. (Art. 4)		— Foreign exchange adjustment agency established to assist foreign investors in swapping foreign exchange. (Art. 10)

Tianjin (ETDZ)			— Upon approval, products manufactured with advanced techniques, knowhow, technology or equipment provided by foreign investors to be allowed for sale in domestic market to replace imports of similar products, provided the quality of such products is higher than that of other products made domestically, and the same or similar products are badly needed in China. (Art. 6)
Wenzhou	— For EEs and TAEs, site development and use fees set at RMB5–15 per sq m per year if site development and site use fees calculated together. (Art. 2) — If land development fee is paid in a lump sum or the site is developed by the user, land use fee charged at RMB0.5–2.5 per sq m per year. (Art. 2) — A 30% reduction in land development fees and exemptions from land use fees offered to foreign investors till the end of 1990. (Art. 2)	— FIEs authorized not to pay any fees not in accordance with State regulations, and may appeal to local authorities. (Art. 1)	— Adjustments to be made by enterprises themselves. (Art. 9) — Mortgage loans provided. (Art. 10)

Table 7: Operating costs and balancing of foreign exchange

Location	Land use fees	Other fees	Balancing of foreign exchange
Yantai	— For EEs and TAEs, site development and use fees set at RMB5–10 per sq m per year if site development and use fees calculated together. (Art. 1) — If land development fee is paid in a lump sum or land is developed by the user, maximum land use fee set at RMB3 per sq m per year. (Art. 1) — Enterprises with especially advanced technology or which export not less than 60% of production enjoy total land use fee exemptions for 5–10 years upon approval of the city government. (Art. 1)	— Enterprises with foreign participation authorized not to pay charges levied indiscriminately. (Art. 1)	— Adjustments to be made by enterprises themselves. (Art. 3) — Compensation arrangements allowed, ie foreign investors purchase local products with local currency for their own use abroad. (Art. 3) — Domestic companies prohibited from charging foreign exchange for sales of materials or parts to foreign investors. (Art. 3) — Sale of import-substitutes by foreign investors for foreign currency allowed. (Art. 3)
Zhanjiang	— FIEs to pay annual land use fees between RMB5 and 15 per sq m if land development and use fees calculated together:		— RMB mortgage loans provided. (Art. 6) — Production of import-substitutes encouraged. (Art. 8)

	For EEs, TAEs and FIEs in scientific research, education and health sectors, RMB5 per sq m. (Art. 2) For productive FIEs, RMB8 per sq m. (Art. 2) For enterprises in commercial and service sectors, RMB15 per sq m. (Art. 2) — FIEs scheduled to operate for 16 years or more exempted from land development fees. (Art. 2)		
Shantou (City)	— Total exemption from land development and land use fees for all foreign investors. (Art. 3)		— Adjustments will be made in foreign exchange centre in the city. (Art. 7) — Foreign investors permitted to establish materials supply centres in the city to earn foreign exchange. (Art. 7)
Shenzhen	— Land for industrial use and for building warehouses charged at an annual rate of RMB1–1.6 per sq m. — A five-year land use fee exemption plus an additional three-year 50% reduction for companies using internationally-advanced technology.	— All fees and charges to be levied according to government regulations. — FIEs authorized to refuse to pay unreasonable charges, and to appeal to the city government.	— Adjustments will be made in foreign exchange centre in the city.

Table 7: Operating costs and balancing of foreign exchange (cont'd)

Location	Land use fees	Other fees	Balancing of foreign exchange
Shenzhen (Cont'd)	— Land development fees computed and charged essentially on actual site development cost.		
Xiamen	— Preferential land use fees granted to enterprises in the Huli industrial zone. — Land use fees charged at an annual rate of RMB5 per sq m. — 10% reductions in the sale prices and rents of general-purpose factories. — Purchases of land by instalments allowed with 30% down-payment.		— Adjustments will be made in foreign exchange centre in the city.
Zhuhai	— Industrial land use fees charged at RMB0.5–1 per sq m per year. — Industrial-specific enterprises exempted from land use fees for three years plus a 50% reduction for subsequent three years.	— Indiscriminate charges strictly prohibited. — All fees charged in line with standards for State-owned enterprises.	

— Enterprises using internationally-advanced technology or exporting 70% or more of production enjoy a land use fee exemption for five years plus a 50% reduction for subsequent five years. — Total exemption from land use fees granted to outstanding TAEs as extra incentive. — Land development fees charged according to actual cost.	— FIEs authorized to refuse to pay charges not approved by the provincial or city governments.

Table 8: Incentives adopted by the Provinces

Location	Tax incentives	Land use fees	Supply and charges	Balancing of foreign exchange	Administration
Anhui[41]	— Enterprises established in sectors of energy, transportation, raw materials and infrastructure enjoy, subject to the approval of local authorities, a 50% reduction in enterprise income tax at the expiration of the exemption period under national law. (Art. 3 and 4) — Low profit-making projects enjoy a 30% reduction in enterprise income tax for ten years at the expiration of the exemption period under national law. (Art. 5)	— For EEs and TAEs, RMB3–10 per sq m per year, for other FIEs, RMB5–20 if land development and use fees computed together. (Art. 2) — For EEs and TAEs, if land development fee is charged as a lump sum or the land is developed by the user, total exemption from land use fees for five years and thereafter at a rate of not more than RMB1 per sq m per year; for other FIEs, not more than RMB3. (Art. 2)	— All facilities and materials necessary for production to be provided to FIEs on a priority basis and to be included in the provincial plans. (Art. 7) — Charges for such supplies at rates applicable to State-owned enterprises. (Art. 7)	— Loans to be provided. (Art. 8) — Sales of import-substitutes to be paid for wholly or partially in foreign exchange. (Art. 9) — Domestic suppliers of materials or parts prohibited from charging FIEs in foreign currency. (Art. 9)	— Replies to project proposals to be within 15 days. (Art. 11) — Reviews of feasibility study to be within 30 days. (Art. 11) — Approvals of contracts, articles of association, regis-tration and licences to be within 20 days. (Art. 11)

	— Exemption from surtax for all foreign-investment projects. (Art. 6)				
Heilongjiang[42]	— For EEs and TAEs and projects in energy, agriculture etc and in low-profit sectors: (1) Enterprises which export 50% of production exempted from surtax. (Art. 3) (2) TAEs and other low-profit companies enjoy eight-year exemption from surtax after expiration of tax reduction and exemption period under State regulations. (Art. 3)	— For EEs, TAEs and projects in low-profit sectors: (1) Five-year land use fee exemption. (Art. 4) (2) RMB5–10 per sq m per year if land development and use fees computed together. (Art. 4) (3) RMB1.5 per sq m per year if land development fee paid in a lump sum or land developed by the user. (Art. 4)	— Priority given to FIEs in supply of materials, parts and other facilities. (Art. 6) — Local supply companies to be set up to provide FIEs with material needed for production. (Art. 6) — Labour subsidies exempted according to State provisions. (Art. 8) — Housing subsidy of RMB30 or less to be retained by FIEs for improvement of housing of their employees. (Art. 8)	— Tax to be paid in RMB. (Art. 5) — Mortgage loans provided. (Art. 5) — Adjustments to be made by FIEs. (Art. 5) — Sales of import-substitutes for foreign exchange upon approval of local authorities. (Art. 5) — Under certain circumstances, local government may lend or provide foreign exchange to foreign investors. (Art. 5)	— Replies to any matter within the jurisdiction of the province to be within 30 days.

Table 8: Incentives adopted by the Provinces (cont'd)

Location	Tax incentives	Land use fees	Supply and charges	Balancing of foreign exchange	Administration
Heilong-jiang (Cont'd)	— All FIEs exempted from surtax for the same period for which there is enterprise income tax exemption or reduction under national law. (Art. 3)		— FIEs authorized not to pay charges levied indiscriminately. (Art. 9)	— Other loans. (Art. 7)	
Hunan[43]	— Total exemption from surtax for 5–10 years for all FIEs. (Art. 5) — EEs, TAEs and low-profit enterprises: five-year exemption from enterprise income tax plus a subsequent reduction of 50%. (Art. 5)	— EEs and TAEs: 50% reduction in fee imposed by national regulations. (Art. 3) — Enterprises in low-profit sectors: total exemption for 5–10 years with subsequent 50% reduction in fee imposed by State regulations. (Art. 3)	— Labour cost is 70–80% of that in coastal cities and areas. (Art. 2) — Priority to FIEs in supply of materials and facilities. (Art. 3)		— Replies regarding any matter within the jurisdiction of the province to be within 30 days. (Art. 8)

Jiangsu[44]	— EEs and TAEs exempted from surtax for period in which such enterprises are exempted from enterprise income tax under the State regulations. — FIEs which export 50% or more of production exempted from local surtax. — FIEs with annual net earnings of less than RMB1m enjoy a 50% reduction in surtax.	— EEs and TAEs exempted from land use fees for five years, and thereafter to a 50% reduction calculated at the lowest applicable rate. — Other FIEs enjoy a 50% reduction, for five years, calculated at the lowest applicable rate. — Additional preferential terms to be provided by local authorities to FIEs in low-profit sectors.	— Supply of materials and facilities to FIEs to be included in the provincial plans, priority given and supplies charged at rates applicable to State-owned enterprises. — EEs and TAEs to pay preferential prices fixed by the State for materials etc. — Supply institutions to be established.	— Mortgage loans to be provided. — Sales of import-substitutes for foreign exchange upon approval of local authorities. — Other loans.	— Explicit approval of each level of government needed for foreign-investment projects. — 30-day maximum for reply to any matter. — Certificates and licences to be granted within 10 days. — No tour by government officials to FIEs without consent of the FIEs.

Table 8: Incentives adopted by the Provinces

Location	Tax incentives	Land use fees	Supply and charges	Balancing of foreign exchange	Administration
Shandong[45]	— FIEs which export 70% or more of production enjoy a 50% enterprise tax reduction after expiration of exemption period under State regulations, and also enjoy surtax exemption for seven years. (Art. 4) — TAEs enjoy a 50% enterprise tax reduction for three years after expiration of exemption period under State regulations.	— For EEs and TAEs: (1) RMB5–20 per sq m per year if land development and use fees calculated together. (Art. 2) (2) RMB3 or less per sq m per year if land development fee paid in a lump sum or land is developed by the user. (Art. 2)	— EEs and TAEs enjoy priority in supply of materials and facilities and at rates applicable to State-owned enterprises. (Art. 3) — Construction fees charged at standards applicable to local companies. (Art. 12)	— Compensation trade or purchase of local products. (Art. 10) — Adjustments to be made by enterprises themselves. (Art. 11)	

	— Exemption from remittance tax. (Art. 6) — Refund of tax on reinvested amount in EEs or TAEs. (Art. 7)	— Upon approval, TAEs and FIEs which export 60% or more of production exempted from land use fees for five years or more. (Art. 2)		
Tibet[46]	— FIEs taxed at rates applicable to local enterprises. — FIEs which develop new products exempted from CICT. — JVC parties to divide profits prior to paying tax, and 50% enterprise income tax reduction or total exemption for the first five years.		— Priority in supply of raw materials and construction materials, electricity, transportation etc at rates applicable to local companies.	— Loans provided to JVCs and CVs at rates applicable to local enterprises. — Loans provided to WFOEs at 20% discount on rates established by the State.

Table 8: Incentives adopted by the Provinces

Location	Tax incentives	Land use fees	Supply and charges	Balancing of foreign exchange	Administration
Tibet (Cont'd)	— As regards dividends, foreign parties allowed to take amount 5–10% more than proportion given by investment ratio. — As regards losses, foreign parties allowed to assume amount 5–10% lower than proportion given by investment ratio.				

41 The materials herein concerning Anhui Province are from the Provisions of the Government of Anhui Province for the Encouragement of Foreign Investment promulgated on 24 November 1986.

42 The materials herein concerning Heilongjiang Province are from the Provincial Provisions for Encouraging Foreign Investment in the Province promulgated on 8 December 1986.

43 The materials herein concerning Hunan Province are from the Certain Preferential Measures for Encouraging Foreign Investment adopted by Hunan Provincial Government. (No specific date of promulgation is available).

44 The materials herein concerning Jiangsu Province are from a summary of the report on the Supplementary Guidelines to Implement State Council's Incentive Package adopted by the Jiangsu Provincial Government which was carried in *China Economic News*, 12 January 1987, pp. 6–7.

45 The materials herein concerning Shandong Province are from the Preferential Measures of Shandong Province for Encouraging Foreign Investment promulgated on 14 October 1986.

46 The materials herein concerning Tibet are from a summary report on the Preferential Measures of Tibet for the Encouragement of Foreign Investment which was carried in *Wen Wei Po*, 31 May 1987, p. 16.

Chapter nine

Practical significance of the new laws

The enactment of the State Council Provisions, together with the mushrooming of local laws, has elicited mixed reactions from foreign investors and commentators. The majority of foreign investors have welcomed the new laws cautiously, while acknowledging the sincere efforts made by the Chinese government to improve the investment environment. These investors believe that although 'many questions remain to be answered, China's investment climate is going to get better – may be significantly better . . . particularly for companies interested in manufacturing import-substitutes for the Chinese domestic market'.[1] In the first four months of 1987, foreign-investment contracts in China, totalling US$550m, were made by 382 newly-approved firms; both the total investment amount and the number of projects are higher than those for the same period in 1986.[2] In 1986, China approved 1,462 foreign-investment projects with a total investment value of US$1.37 b. It appears that the effects of the new laws on foreign investment are beginning to be felt. This chapter will discuss and analyze the implications of these pieces of legislation on current and potential foreign investors, as well as on the interrelationship of the coastal cities, SEZs, inland cities and provinces.

I. Effect on foreign investment

Balancing of foreign exchange

In the realm of international investment, a shortage of foreign exchange results chiefly from the non-convertibility of local currency on the one hand, and the domestic-market-oriented production strategy of foreign investors on the other. As is the situation in other developing countries, a number of foreign-investment enterprises in China suffer from a shortage of foreign exchange. Put simply, the problem is that virtually all domestic sales are paid for in non-convertible Renminbi, unless special permission

1 *China Business Review*, January-February 1987, p. 10.
2 *Wen Wei Po*, 26 May 1987, p. BN4.

is obtained under the relevant regulations. In addition, foreign-investment concerns often find that the domestic market is hungry for their products or that domestically-manufactured products are not yet up to world standards, with the result that in either case, the enterprises in question would prefer to sell their products domestically, thereby encountering difficulties in balancing their foreign exchange accounts. Meanwhile, foreign-investment enterprises sometimes have to inject foreign exchange periodically to pay for the import of raw materials, components, and other items not readily sourced in China. In general, projects in non-manufacturing industries such as hotels, office complexes and taxi services etc are not faced with this difficulty. It is the investment projects in manufacturing industries which are the chief victims.

In order to cope with this situation, the Chinese government has over the last few years introduced several measures to tackle the problem. First, where products turned out by foreign-investment enterprises are capable of introducing advanced and key technology and are urgently needed in China, they may be sold in the domestic market. Secondly, if these products or items are those which China will need to import for a long period of time, distribution contracts may be signed with domestic end-users and, upon approval, payment may be made in foreign currency. Thirdly, sales to the SEZs and ETDZs may be settled in foreign exchange. Fourthly, foreign investors may purchase with local currency and export, in lieu of repatriating profits, products manufactured by domestic Chinese concerns. Under such circumstances, the exportation of products which are exclusively handled by the central government or which require export licenses or fall under export quotas must be approved by the Ministry of Foreign Economic Relations and Trade.

Another method permitted by the Chinese government is the balancing of foreign exchange accounts among sister companies. Under this method, a foreign investor may set up a parent company in China which holds equity interests in two or more enterprises (either exclusively foreign-owned, joint ventures or cooperative ventures). If enterprise A has a surplus of foreign exchange and B suffers from a shortage, foreign exchange will be allowed to flow between the enterprises with the consent of all the venture parties and the approval of the State Administration of Foreign Exchange Control. Some Hong Kong investors use this method, especially for tourism projects which earn foreign exchange. Hotels and travel agencies are the most common form of additional ventures set up to generate foreign exchange. Nevertheless, since many companies lack the ability to run both industrial and tourist ventures efficiently, this method has not proved to be very effective.

One other permitted method is the reinvestment of Renminbi earnings by foreign investors in projects which will be able to generate or increase foreign exchange earnings. A foreign investor is entitled to a partial refund of income tax paid and can share a larger portion of foreign exchange generated by the enterprise it has invested in.

Without careful analysis, one may conclude that the new laws have not offered any concrete measures to resolve the problems relating to the balancing of foreign exchange accounts. It is true that most of the new regulations are merely confirmatory of previous practices. However, such confirmation is in itself very significant, for without it, foreign investors would have to rely on the discretion of government officials and the bureaucracy. In giving legal force to these scattered practices, the Chinese government has shown its sincerity in attempting to resolve the foreign exchange shortage problem. It has also given foreign investors the lawful right to conduct transactions permitted under the law, without having to obtain the further approval of any government authority.

In fact, several provisions are not mere confirmations of existing practices. For instance, prior to the adoption of the State Council Provisions, and in particular, before the mushrooming of local legislation, it was not clear what treatment should be accorded foreign-investment enterprises which produced import-substitutes, and each local government treated the matter according to its own standards. The State Council Provisions now accord both Export Enterprises and Technologically Advanced Enterprises, including those producing import-substitutes, equal treatment and require local governments and authorities to confirm the status of each kind of enterprise. This has not only set up some guidelines for local governments but has also encouraged the latter to adopt supplementary regulations. Without such a specific stipulation, local governments might not have adopted their own measures requiring domestic companies to give priority to the purchase of products produced by foreign-investment enterprises and imported by China. In effect, local regulations have carried the principles contained in the State Council Provisions a step further. Several of them unequivocally prohibit domestic companies from charging foreign exchange when making sales to foreign-investment enterprises. At the same time, foreign-investment enterprises are authorized to sell their products for foreign exchange in local markets, with the approval of the local authorities. When we take into account the enthusiasm shown by the provincial and city governments and the scope of their supplementary provisions, it is not beyond hope that these new measures will go a long way towards solving the foreign exchange problem.

The Renminbi mortgage loan is another novel method which can be especially beneficial to newcomers to the China market.[3] Loan guarantee regulations have also offered specific and detailed guidelines to Chinese guarantors, foreign creditors as well as borrowers. These measures have provided foreign investors with clear guidelines as to where they should invest and how they should invest.

Nevertheless, taking into consideration the current status of China's foreign trade, the foreign exchange shortage problem will remain unresolved in the near future. The coming into being of foreign exchange

3 For the specific operation of a mortgage loan and its significance, see Chapter 3 of this book.

centres in China will not furnish the final solution either, although they represent by far the most important new options. The main obstacle to the operation of these centres is that foreign-investment ventures which have hard currency, such as hotels, are obligated to pay back bank loans and dividends and are therefore not able to swap sizeable amounts in the centre. At the same time, foreign investors regard foreign exchange centres as places of last resort because of the tight restrictions under which the latter operate.[4]

In the final analysis, the problem of balancing foreign exchange is virtually an outgrowth of different and, sometimes contradictory, expectations of foreign investors and their Chinese hosts. Foreign investors are attracted by the enormous potential of the Chinese market (the low domestic production costs being one essential factor), while the Chinese parties hope to import advanced technology and to increase foreign exchange reserves by strengthening export industries and producing goods domestically which would otherwise have to be imported. 'All too often, however, both parties to a potentially lucrative foreign-equity investment in China have been frustrated by their inability to harmonize their respective goals.'[5] In order to resolve the foreign exchange situation in the long run, the State Council Provisions, together with other laws at both central and local government levels, have given export and hi-tech enterprises particularly strong incentives in various aspects. With the establishment of more 'productive enterprises' and the expansion of exports by foreign-investment enterprises, foreign investors will eventually be freed from the inconvenience of foreign exchange shortages. At the same time, by singling out Export Enterprises and Technologically Advanced Enterprises, the new laws will not have an adverse effect on non-productive foreign-investment projects, such as hotels, taxi companies, 'since these [ventures] have tended to proliferate and sometimes even to prosper despite well-known difficulties and occasional government discouragement'.[6]

Management autonomy and administrative efficiency

Management autonomy and administrative efficiency are two sides of the same coin. They are interrelated and interdependent. Many foreign investors who are familiar only with market economy systems are often awed by the Chinese economic and legal systems. Once they enter the Chinese market, they realize that they have to communicate and cooperate not only with their counterparts but also with the bureaucracy,

4 *South China Morning Post,* 22 April 1987, p. BN1.
5 Mao Baigen, 'China: New Provisions to Encourage Foreign Investment', *International Business Lawyer,* May 1987 p. 204.
6 Jerome Alan Cohen and Ta-kuang Chang, 'New Foreign Investment Provisions', *China Business Review,* January-February 1987, p. 11.

regarding the procurement of materials, parts, components etc, decisions relating to production, distribution of final products, and the hiring and dismissing of employees. In reality, the Chinese partners present fewer problems. It is the bureaucratic government which interferes, rather than cooperates, in the business operations of these enterprises. Many of the government officials, especially those at the lower level, are not familiar with modern methods of business management and lack knowledge of international markets. They may therefore unintentionally interfere with normal decision-making by commercial enterprises. In addition, leftist ideology is still very influential in China. There are people who are not in favour of the current open policy and hold, in general, a negative attitude towards foreign investment. They have been trying to suppress the current reforms, including areas of Sino-foreign economic cooperation. For instance, successful Sino-foreign ventures often become targets of criticism, or are asked to make donations.

At the same time, since China is a developing country and its domestic market is still in a state of infancy, foreign investors are often astonished at the system for the supply of raw materials and the distribution of products. The scarcity of raw materials in the domestic economy makes their supply a serious problem which cannot be resolved by foreign investors without the assistance of administrative organs. With regard to domestic distribution, selling in China is basically similar to selling elsewhere in Asia in that one must do the necessary market research and then identify, meet and negotiate with the buyer. 'Selling in China, however, differs from selling elsewhere in much of Asia in that market information on organizations, price and quality is not as readily available; in that the decision-making process must go through layers of bureaucracy.'[7] Very often, domestic distribution by foreign-investment enterprises has to be arranged by government authorities or specialized corporations.

A similar problem arises in building up an effective labour force in that well-trained employees, especially senior managerial personnel, are scarce in China. Under the previous rules, in order to recruit such persons, foreign-investment enterprises had to face certain restrictions. First, the approval and recommendation of the local labour authorities had to be obtained. Secondly, the enterprises could employ staff only from their locality. Thirdly, the original employers ie domestic enterprises, were not always willing to let their employees leave.

The new laws enacted by the central government and the provincial as well as city governments have established a legal framework under which the authorities at all levels are required to guarantee the business autonomy of foreign-investment enterprises subject to the scope of the relevant contracts. Foreign investors now have the authority to decide independently the organizational structure for production and manage-

7 *China Trade Report,* 21 October 1986, p. 6.

ment, and the wage and bonus system. As regards the hiring of workers and staff members, some cities as well as provincial governments have authorized foreign-investment enterprises to hire employees from within and without their localities, and have also informed domestic Chinese employers to lend their support. Several cities have also allowed foreign-investment enterprises to recruit workers directly from the public or through other means commonly used in Western countries.

As some commentators have pointed out, 'this legal guarantee of autonomy will provide strong ammunition – though certainly no guarantee of effectiveness in practice – when foreign-investment enterprises assert their right to make decisions relating to the enterprises'.[8] The function of government authorities is to assist rather than interfere with the operations of foreign-investment enterprises. Under the legal systems of several cities and provinces, local authorities must guarantee priority for foreign-investment projects, particularly export and hi-tech enterprises, with regard to the supply of raw materials, components etc. To achieve this purpose, companies supplying materials have been established in some localities. In addition, foreign investors may, with the assistance of local authorities, conclude contracts directly with domestic users. These measures will prove to be very useful, for, in China, doing business is still hampered by a lack of information, and difficulties in identifying buyers and negotiating terms.

In order to tackle the complex bureaucratic problems, and in response to the growing presence of foreign businesses in China, time limits for the approval of foreign-investment matters have been laid down by statutes enacted at both the central and local government levels. Leadership groups and joint approval apparatus have also been set up in various governments. The major role of these authorities is to coordinate the work of local departments which deal with foreign-investment matters.

To be sure, this institutional structure is not new in China's history of foreign investment. For instance, prior to 1983, at the central government level, there was a Foreign Investment Control Commission which coordinated the work of several ministries and local governments. Unfortunately, the Commission was merged into the Ministry of Foreign Economic Relations and Trade in that year and became the Foreign Investment Administration Bureau of the Ministry. As a result, the lack of coordination often delayed problem-solving. 'Some projects could be delayed for years before getting approval and even routine matters could take an unreasonably long time to be approved.'[9] This situation resulted chiefly from the extremely complicated investment review procedures. 'Even after both partners to a joint venture reached an agreement to proceed with a project, it was still necessary to secure clearance from, among others, the General Taxation Bureau of the Ministry of Finance,

8 Cohen and Chang, *op cit* at p. 13.
9 Mao, *op cit* at p. 205.

the Customs Administration, the General Administration for Exchange Control, and the Bank of China, before proceeding with the project.'[10]

The re-establishment of the leading team in the central government will better coordinate and hasten the decision-making process in relation to foreign investment. The joint-office working method adopted by several local authorities will also help to increase the efficiency of the government and ensure that foreign-investment matters are responded to without delay. In short, the new legislation has offered more concrete measures for guaranteeing the business autonomy of foreign-investment enterprises and for simplifying the regulatory procedures of the government.

Tax incentives and reduction of costs

Several new and favourable income tax incentives stipulated in the new pieces of legislation apply especially to export and hi-tech enterprises. For instance, foreign investors in such ventures are exempted from paying the 10% profit remittance tax on amounts remitted overseas. Hi-tech enterprises will have their existing two-year tax exemption and three-year 50% reduction extended by an additional three years at half the tax rate. Almost all coastal cities and provinces which are major hosts of foreign investment have granted foreign investors tax reliefs from local tax.

Income tax reductions and exemptions may draw mixed reactions from foreign investors. The effectiveness of such measures depends on the nationality of the foreign investors concerned. In order to benefit from the low income tax rate in China, a foreign investor's home country must grant it a tax credit for the tax paid in China. Hence, unless the income tax rate of a foreign investor's home country's is lower than that in China, the reduction of income tax will constitute a transfer of funds from China's Ministry of Finance to the treasury of the foreign investor's home country. As a result, the beneficiaries of the low income tax rate in China are largely those who make reinvestments. This does not mean, however, that tax incentives will lose their weight, for none of the corporations or individuals wants to pay a higher income tax rate even though the incentives given may represent only a postponement of the tax liability. Nevertheless, exemptions from the Consolidated Industrial and Commercial Tax are very helpful to foreign-investment enterprises because they help to lower the costs of imported materials and machinery. The prices for the resultant products can therefore be set at lower rates.

The provisions for land development and land use fees as well as other operational costs prescribed by the new laws are significant and substantial. In practice, foreign investors are generally attracted by the potential market of a host country when making overseas investments.

10 *Id.*

Apart from the market element, low production costs, which include salaries, cost of raw materials and land use fees, are the things which appeal most to foreign investors. Thus, unless one can benefit from the overseas local market or low production expenditures, the overseas investment may not be sound and viable. Until the promulgation of the State Council Provisions, land use fees in China were subject to local regulations and their rates varied widely from location to location. Moreover, abuses of such rights by local authorities were occasionally reported.

Following the lead of the central government in establishing maximum land development and land use fees for Export Enterprises and Technologically Advanced Enterprises, a number of city and provincial governments have established their own standards either for such enterprises only or for all foreign-investment projects. These actions are particularly important in helping foreign investors to work out their budgets. In the past, when starting a project in China, foreign investors, together with their Chinese partners, were charged not only for land use fees but also for the costs of acquiring the project site (such as relocation of the area's inhabitants and including sometimes alternative employment for those affected.) Beyond that, local authorities sometimes made arbitrary decisions as to how much each foreign-investment enterprise had to pay. As one observer commented, a local government of the suburb of Beijing charged foreign-investment enterprises land development fees at RMB10 per sq m, although according to the relevant regulations of the Beijing Municipality, the fee should not have been more than RMB3 per sq m.[11]

The public pronouncement by the city and provincial governments of the maximum land development and land use fees will effectively prohibit the lower-level authorities from levying charges on foreign investors indiscriminately. This is further guaranteed by the double-benefit provision under the new legal framework which, on the one hand, formally requires governments at all levels not to levy unreasonable charges on enterprises with foreign participation and, on the other hand, authorizes foreign investors not to pay any fees which have not been clearly approved by the central government, or the provincial or city governments. A number of local laws contain a similar provision. In addition, foreign-investment enterprises may appeal, if necessary, to the local authorities and then all the way up to the State Economic Commission of the Central Government. These measures will prove to be crucial in reducing investment costs and guaranteeing the smooth business operations of foreign-investment enterprises.

Another promising move by several city and provincial governments is to charge foreign investors for essential facilities such as fuel, electricity, water etc at rates which are applicable to State-owned enterprises.[12] In

11 *Economic Reporter*, 1 December 1986, p. 9.
12 For detailed provisions on charges for operating facilities, see Chapter 8 of this book.

addition, several local regulations stipulate that expatriates working for foreign-investment enterprises, either on a permanent or temporary basis, need only pay domestic prices for their accommodation, transportation, food etc. This is an obvious departure from the previous practice in China where non-Chinese individuals were required to pay higher prices for their personal consumption needs, resulting in serious frustrations and extreme inconvenience both for them and for the Chinese. The proliferation of local rules in this regard may bring about an eventual abolition of the differential treatment between local residents and foreigners which is still applied on a nationwide basis.

In any event, efforts made at both the central government and lower levels to reduce operating costs are encouraging and will have major effects on foreign investment.

Import and export regulations

The newly-established investment framework does not offer any real benefit to foreign enterprises which deal purely in the import and export business. This is, however, not surprising for China is a developing country. In the international community, there is currently a general belief that developing countries have the need to protect their domestic industries which are in the process of industrialization. If this were not done, the weak domestic economy might experience stagnation or reversal, in the face of competition from abroad. Taking into consideration the continuing foreign exchange shortage suffered by China, its tight control on the import and export business is understandable.

The new laws, however, have introduced several changes to the import and export mechanism which are of fundamental importance. Currently, with the exception of oil-related products, exports by foreign-investment enterprises are all exempted from the Consolidated Industrial and Commercial Tax as well as customs duties. Foreign investors can export their products either directly through their own channels or through agents, either Chinese or foreign, appointed by them. In addition, export licences need only be applied for every six months. Most significantly, approvals and import licences are not required for the importation of equipment and machinery, as well as raw materials for performing export contracts, including those items whose importation is restricted by the government. Such imports are not subject to the Consolidated Industrial and Commercial Tax or customs duties.

The above measures virtually constitute reforms to China's import and export system. They also have a cost-saving effect on the operations of foreign-investment enterprises, for import and export duties can sometimes be enormous, and the imposition of the Consolidated Industrial and Commercial Tax often makes certain products uncompetitive in both the domestic and international markets. The simplification of import procedures is all the more meaningful to foreign investors, since it will enable them to cut through bureaucratic red tape which may otherwise delay the importation of equipment and machinery for months. These new import-export provisions will make China a more attractive place for foreign investment. At the same time, they will enable foreign investors to compete in the international market. Since foreign-investment enterprises may apply for and be issued export licences for a period of six months, it is quite unlikely that their export contracts will be frustrated. Of course, these liberalized import-export regulations need to be strictly implemented in order to prevent abuses from taking place.

II. Attracting foreign investment: some consequences

The competitive legislation enacted by various open cities and provinces for the encouragement of foreign investment has substantially improved the investment environment in these areas while at the same time mounting a challenge to the SEZs. The SEZs are, by definition, designed to offer foreign investors terms which are more favourable than those available in other parts of China. Nevertheless, with the establishment of ETDZs in the 14 coastal cities and ports, foreign investors now have a wider choice when making investment decisions. With the assistance of preferential tax terms, these 14 coastal cities, to some extent, have been able to attract foreign capital at the expense of the SEZs. This does not mean, however, that the SEZs have lost their status as laboratories for the implementation of China's policy on foreign investment.

In general, being the pioneers of China's economic reforms, the SEZs will continue to play a leading role in converting China's current economy into a planned market economy, and in experimenting with new methods and measures for carrying out Sino-foreign economic exchanges. Currently, the SEZs have the necessary infrastructure for that purpose. For instance, after several years of cooperation between Chinese and foreign parties, the Shenzhen SEZ has constructed the necessary basic facilities for large-scale foreign-investment projects. Although transportation and communications facilities in Shenzhen are not as efficient as those of Hong Kong, they are nonetheless very much better than those of other Chinese cities.

In addition, the special status of Shenzhen in China's domestic economic reforms has attracted many well-qualified people from other cities and provinces. Over the last few years, domestic Chinese companies, managers and government officials in the SEZs have gained abundant experience through their dealings with foreign businesses. These factors which are crucial to the success of joint ventures are not readily available in other areas. At the same time, a legal system for the SEZs is being set up, comprising several statutes of great importance to foreign investors. The Foreign Bank Regulations, the Shenzhen SEZ Foreign-investment Enterprise Bankruptcy Regulations and the Mortgage Loan Regulations are just a few examples.

As regards the range of permitted foreign investments, the SEZs still maintain their attractiveness, for in the SEZs, foreign investments can be made in all industries, including the banking and insurance sectors which are sensitive areas. This is not the case in other parts of China where certain industries are not yet open to foreign investment.

It appears that the Chinese government contemplates delegating more of its powers to the SEZs in order to maintain their attractiveness to foreign businesses. It has been reported that the procedures for obtaining export and import licences might be simplified to facilitate foreign investment in the SEZs.[13] The Chinese government is currently considering whether it is possible to delegate the power of issuing import and export licences to the Shenzhen SEZ so that investors will not have to go to the trouble of travelling to Beijing to obtain approval.[14] Some government officials are of the view that the SEZs should introduce additional measures, outside the scope of the State Council Provisions, to implement the national foreign investment policies.[15]

The success of the special policies relating to foreign investment in the SEZs will depend on the domestic economic reforms. In this regard, the steps taken by the governments of the SEZs have been encouraging. For instance, at the beginning of 1987, the Shenzhen Municipality issued directives permitting engineers, scientists and other specialists to form their own enterprises to research and develop technology, and to apply it to the production process. Such persons may also form consultancies or other service concerns. Their existing employers, including government departments or entities, are required to give them support in forming their own companies.[16] Policies like this will undoubtedly help create a more competitive environment which in turn will improve the conditions for foreign investment in the locality.

To summarize, under the new foreign-investment framework created by the State Council Provisions and the supplementary regulations adopted by the city and provincial governments, the foreign-investment environment in China has improved considerably. The most noticeable changes that these new laws have brought about include guaranteed autonomy for foreign-investment enterprises, total freedom in hiring and dismissing employees, reductions in and exemptions from land use fees and other fees, faster decision-making process of governments at all levels, prohibition on governmental interference in the normal operations of foreign-investment enterprises and on the levying of charges on such enterprises indiscriminately, lower tax rates, and priority in obtaining production facilities. Although certain privileges are limited to export-oriented and hi-tech companies, almost all foreign-investment

13 *South China Morning Post*, 11 February 1987, p. BN2.

14 *Wen Wei Po*, 11 February 1987, p. 1.

15 A summary of the speech by State Councillor Gu Mu at the National Conference on SEZs. *Wen Wei Po*, 11 February 1987, p. 1.

16 *Wen Wei Po*, 8 February 1987, p. 1.

enterprises directly benefit from the new laws, in particular, the supplementary regulations enacted by the local governments. Nevertheless, these provisions do not work miracles and therefore cannot resolve all the foreign-investment problems at once. For instance, with regard to the balancing of foreign exchange accounts, foreign investors will have to rely mainly on their own efforts, despite the several options offered by the new laws. Any increase in labour efficiency and any improvement in infrastructure will also take time. With the assistance of these provisions, however, foreign investors in China will face fewer difficulties. As discussed earlier, a more competitive environment for foreign investment has started to emerge in different cities and provinces, with the SEZs still as the leading hosts. This state of affairs will provide foreign investors with more choices when making business decisions.

Chapter ten

Alternative policies

China's current policy and laws on foreign investment are, in general, sound. Many impediments to foreign investment which are deeply rooted in China's history, and its economic and social systems, such as lack of information, power shortages, bureaucratic obstructionism, inadequacy of foreign exchange etc, can be overcome only through time and effort. However, the government is aware of most of these issues and, thus, measures for their resolution are being taken. This chapter will put forward some considerations for furthering China's current open policy on foreign investment.

I. Strategic planning

In order to attract foreign investment (and domestic investment, at least in some countries) a nation must provide an economic and social environment which is conducive to investment by overseas investors. This requires a fundamental understanding of the philosophy of multinational corporations.

Every multinational corporation possesses certain 'assets', such as technology and know-how for the production process, finance, marketing, classification of products, organization of operations and management etc. If it can maintain these advantages, it will be able to strengthen its competitive position in the market and maintain its profitability. Thus, multinational corporations, in having to protect their own interests, try hard to prevent other companies from obtaining their trade secrets. Moreover, in order to maintain their competitive positions in the international market, multinational corporations will also have to make overseas investments so as to give full play to their business potential. Therefore, when a multinational corporation selects locations for overseas investment, it must determine whether the environment of the prospective host country is conducive and whether production costs in that country will be lower.

With this general approach in mind, multinational corporations from different countries or economic sectors, or at different stages of development, will require different conditions for overseas investment. Generally, the fundamental factors include the adequacy of natural resources, geographical location, degree of governmental interference and control, taxation, government subsidies, degree of industrialization of the host economy, legal systems, institutions, infrastructure etc.

Multinational corporations are, as a rule, interested in long-term investments. In view of the increasing role of administrative authorities in foreign-investment projects, most multinational corporations regard the political situation of the host country as a decisive element, particularly for technology-intensive or capital-intensive projects. Political risks include governmental interference and administrative interruption of normal business operations, in addition to nationalization which is now not common.

Any analysis of China's existing environment for foreign investment and any suggested improvements thereto should take into consideration the investment strategies of foreign investors. Over the last eight years, foreign investment in China has had the following features:

(1) There are more unsuccessful negotiations than there are successful ones. For instance, in 1985, about 70% of the total projects negotiated in Shanghai failed to come to anything although Shanghai is considered the most sophisticated and experienced foreign-investment host in China;[1]
(2) There are more small-sized foreign-investment projects than there are large ones;
(3) The majority of foreign-investment projects are in the service sectors rather than in manufacturing industries;
(4) There are fewer technology-intensive projects than there are hotel and office complexes; and
(5) The life-spans of foreign-investment projects are relatively short, with most being for approximately ten years.

There are various reasons for the above state of affairs. The most important ones include: high political risks, low educational levels of the public, a largely closed domestic market, lack of market consciousness, poor infrastructure and over-strict control of foreign exchange.

As a result of the unfortunate events and turbulent periods in China's history, foreign investors are not yet convinced that they can make long-term plans or large-scale investments, although their lawful interests are protected by the Chinese Constitution and other laws. Furthermore, Chinese officials have, on numerous occasions, stated that the current open policy will continue for many years. But frequent policy changes in the past have left most people suspicious about the continuity of the open policy. As a result, any change in China's leadership may cause alarm among foreign businesses. In addition, China's legal system has yet to be perfected and individual officials often make discretionary decisions which do not conform to the law. When a government official at medium

1 *Wen Wei Po*, 7 May 1987, p. BN2.

or lower level is transferred to a different department or is promoted, a given project may be shelved. These risks plus the inefficiency of the bureaucracy make short-term and small investments convenient and feasible choices.

In view of the current educational and technological standards of Chinese society, it is not hard to see why there are not many technology-intensive projects. China does not have an adequate supply of skilled workers and well-educated managerial staff. However, to operate projects with sophisticated technology and equipment requires high educational standards. Thus, China's cheap but poorly-educated labour force loses its appeal to foreign investors who would not be enthusiastic about spending a lot of time and money to train unskilled workers. This is particularly so since other countries and regions in Asia are able to provide higher-skilled labour. Thus, investment projects involving advanced technology are usually located in neighbouring countries and regions such as Hong Kong, Taiwan, South Korea or Singapore.

The local market of the host country is always important to foreign investors. China has a huge market but its purchasing power is still very weak. In addition, most sectors of the market are not open to foreign investors. Foreign businesses have relatively good access to the tourism and hotel industries as well as the consumer goods markets, but they are virtually shut out of the market for manufactured products. This situation, coupled with the government's restrictive controls on foreign exchange, induce foreign capital to move to the non-productive sectors where the domestic market is less restricted and foreign exchange accounts easier to balance.

So, what alternative policies should China adopt? The current domestic economic reforms should be broadened and intensified by introducing more market elements into the domestic economy. For instance, the restructuring of the price system and the establishment of labour markets, which are emerging in some cities, should prove attractive to foreign investors. With labour markets in existence, individuals can quit their present jobs and take on new ones. This will not only give foreign investors easier access to the labour force but will also speed up technology and know-how transfers from foreign-investment enterprises to domestic companies. A market for foreign exchange and other financial transactions must also be set up. Without the necessary access to capital and foreign exchange, the current difficulties facing foreign investors in this regard cannot be overcome. In the long run, it will be necessary to open the domestic market to products manufactured by foreign-investment enterprises as this would raise the corporate efficiency of domestic companies and guarantee the quality of domestic products. Of course, this sort of open market can be achieved only on a gradual basis.

The government should also urgently tackle the issue of educating the public. The nature of knowledge, including management methods, and the cause of investment problems must be examined further. There is apparently a misconception about the nature of social science. Many people in China think that natural science and technology have no national boundary and can therefore be universally employed. However, even if modern measures, methods and institutions for production and management, which are social science subjects, are introduced or adopted by China, there will always be people who will question their nature ie whether they are socialist or capitalist in nature. These people are obviously ignorant of the simple fact that every item of knowledge or technology is the property of mankind and should be used by everyone. As long as this item of knowledge or technology can help China achieve its economic goals, it should be adopted by the government without hesitation. The realization of the country's modernization programme should be the sole standard for judging the appropriateness of the item of knowledge or technology. For instance, since the leasing of State-owned or collective enterprises to private individuals, and the system established whereby the State government contracts with employees with regard to production responsibilities and profit distribution, have brought about the growth of the economy, their use should be more widespread.

As for problems relating to foreign investment, there are some who see the main cause as being the wide scope of the open policy.[2] This opinion is groundless, for it overlooks the fact that any given investment environment will not become perfect without constant improvements and refinements, and that no country in the world would first perfect domestic conditions before allowing foreign capital to enter. In fact, it would be impossible to achieve a perfect foreign-investment environment as this environment must be constantly modified to keep pace with the changing attitudes of international investors, the development of the world economy and the advances in science and technology.

The crux of the matter lies in educating the people. China should plan to train not only university graduates but also managerial and secretarial personnel. Currently, many foreign businesses, especially professionals, have to bring in their own managers and secretaries from abroad or from Hong Kong, because there are very few qualified people available domestically. If this situation can be improved, the staffing costs of foreign investors will be lowered and more foreign exchange will be saved by them. This would in turn lessen the domestic unemployment problem.

One way of raising the standard of domestic education is to create a suitable working environment for those in the academic field. Currently, the living standards of faculty members in universities are in general lower than those of staff and workers in factories. Most of the young and

2 Some Chinese economists have asserted that China has opened up too many areas to foreign investors who have used transfer pricing to make profits for themselves at the expense of the Chinese, and that China should reduce the number of areas open to foreign investment and allow a few cities like Guangzhou to operate special policies suitable for foreign investment. See *South China Morning Post*, 27 May 1987, p. BN1.

middle-aged university lecturers do not have conducive living or working environments. Their lives are also harder than those of senior professors, for the latter are not as active in teaching and other academic activities. This is in sharp contrast to the situation in the United States and Japan where the respective educational systems have played a major role in the economic success of these two countries. According to a survey, the wages of those in the academic field in the United States equal approximately the average wage of all other wage earners, while in Japan university professors and teachers are within the top 10% of all wage earners.[3] By national law, the salaries of academic staff in Japan are 10% higher than those of top civil servants. Although it might be wrong to assert that Japan's good educational system is the only reason for its economic success, without this enlightened policy on education, Japan may not have been able to achieve the high level of technology which underscores its importance as a world power. China would do well to learn from Japan in this regard.

Another important measure China should introduce is to raise the legal consciousness of government officials and to improve their ability to implement laws and regulations properly. Over the last few years, there have been many reported cases where government officials regarded their own words as law and thus 'implemented' the relevant laws with substantial deviations. Such behaviour has naturally caused tremendous confusion among foreign investors and given China a bad name. In fact, some foreign commentators have stated openly that 'Chinese law is like a lump of dough. You can stretch it and make noodles, fold it and make dumplings, and roll it up and steam it into bread. And it is all up to the person holding the dough in his hands.'[4] This kind of belief, correct or otherwise, has led foreign businesses to rely on 'China brokers', primarily people from Hong Kong or overseas Chinese, who claim to have good connections with Chinese government officials with regard to business transactions. Such a practice clearly adds to the costs of foreign investors, which may either be passed to the Chinese side or to the consumers, depending on the nature of the transactions concerned. Worse still, foreign investors are sometimes tempted to bribe the Chinese officials in the hope of getting what they want more easily.

In order to prevent abuses of power by government officials and to eradicate purely subjective decision-making by these officials, compulsory legal training should be introduced for officials in charge of foreign economic relations. In future, legislation enacted by the central government should contain sufficiently-detailed rules, so that administrators at various levels will be left with less discretion. In addition, any violation of law, either by Chinese officials or foreigners, must be punished effectively. In this regard, laws should be enacted whereby all recipients of bribes, bribers and accomplices are subject to severe

3 *The Asian Wall Street Journal*, 25 March 1987, p. 6.
4 *China Trade Report*, 13 February 1987, p. 12.

punishment. At the same time, those who expose these 'dirty dealings' should be given rewards. Measures like these will help to inculcate in the public, a strong sense of legal consciousness which will no doubt help towards attracting more foreign investment.

II. Concrete measures

Some further, and more specific, measures need to be taken by the Chinese government at all levels in view of the current state of foreign investment in China. Over the last few years, China has imported thousands of items of advanced technology, but many of these items have not been made full use of in the production process. In other words, the advanced technology has not been absorbed into the domestic economy. In order to save on valuable foreign exchange, the government should ensure that the imported technology and equipment are fully utilized and absorbed. As a supplementary measure, an exchange of personnel, such as engineers and students, between scientific research institutions and manufacturing concerns should be encouraged and expanded.

As discussed earlier, one of major difficulties facing foreign investors is the lack of information and the lack of avenues for consultation. If trade development offices were established in major foreign-investment cities, foreign businesses would face fewer problems when making investments in China. Such offices can provide investment information, and advice on the feasibility of projects and on relevant laws. They can also handle application and registration procedures on behalf of foreign investors. Currently, some cities such as Shanghai and Tianjin have trade development offices which provide similar services to foreign investors. Nevertheless, with the expansion in foreign investment, such offices, run by city governments, may not be able to provide adequate services to foreign investors. To deal with this eventuality, private and collective service companies should be allowed.

With regard to the balancing of foreign exchange accounts, the government's current policy and laws focus on incentives. Export and hi-tech companies are granted more favourable terms in respect of export-import activities, the supply of raw materials and other facilities, and taxation. While these measures have proven to be effective, the central government should consider allocating a certain portion of its foreign exchange to the most important projects under the State plan. By so doing, the foreign investors involved will be spared the discretionary provision of foreign exchange by local government officials. Nevertheless, such projects should be restricted to outstanding advanced technology investments, particularly those for the manufacture of components or intermediate products which cannot be sold in international markets.

In order to provide enterprises producing import-substitutes with foreign exchange or to allow such firms making domestic sales to be paid totally or partially in foreign exchange, the Chinese government is drafting legislation to regulate such transactions. The enactment of specific legal guidelines is urgently required, for otherwise neither the Chinese officials nor the foreign investors would know which type of foreign-investment enterprise should be accorded the privileges and which sectors should be promoted first. This legislation must also take into account at least two obstacles facing domestic sales of import-substitutes. First, in general, the prices of import-substitutes are higher than those of imported products. Secondly, there is a bias among end-users that products produced abroad are of better quality. To overcome these difficulties, foreign-investment enterprises must increase their efficiency and raise the quality of their products. At the same time, domestic end-users should be urged to give priority to products manufactured by foreign-investment enterprises so long as the quality and prices of these products are of international standards. All of the problems highlighted above should be specifically addressed in the new laws concerning import-substitutes.

In conjunction with the balancing of foreign exchange, the prices of domestic raw materials, components and finished products to be sold to foreign-investment enterprises must be adjusted. At present, the regulations of several cities and provinces stipulate that the supply of raw materials, components etc to foreign-investment enterprises must be charged at rates applicable to State-owned enterprises. While these provisions are helpful, there is another issue which must be resolved in order to save foreign exchange for enterprises with foreign participation. The issue is this. Occasionally, finished products or components supplied by domestic enterprises contain imported elements which are subject to import duties for domestic sales. As a result, such domestically-manufactured products or components are more expensive than imported ones, since foreign-investment enterprises enjoy import-duty exemptions in most cases. Thus, unless these products, containing imported elements, are free from import duties, foreign investors will be forced to pay the import duties with foreign exchange. If this issue can be resolved, foreign-investment enterprises will be able to use more domestic materials and products, and save their foreign exchange only for those products and components which need to be imported from abroad.

As an additional measure to balance foreign exchange accounts, the Chinese government should encourage project financing, compensation trade or barter trade. Special departments should then be established at city and provincial levels to handle the increase in these transactions.

In improving the general investment environment, all loop-holes in the existing laws should also be plugged. For instance, there have been reports of export-processing enterprises evading income tax. What happens is this. Such enterprises are required to report to the tax authorities, the prices of raw materials imported by them and the sales prices of the final products against which income tax is levied. Since Chinese tax officials are not familiar with prices in the international market and have no means of verifying the figures given by the enterprises concerned, the latter sometimes inflate the costs of raw materials while lowering the sale prices of the final products, in order to reduce tax duties. In other cases, Chinese subsidiaries of foreign companies artifically raise the management fees chargeable to their parent companies, for the purpose of reducing income in China. Thus, in order to carry out the current open policy effectively, legislative measures must be taken to prevent such abuses.

III. Efforts to be made by foreign investors

The success of a foreign-investment enterprise depends on good long-term planning and sound short-and medium-term decisions by all the parties concerned. Before entering the Chinese market, foreign investors will need to have a relatively clear understanding of the Chinese policy on foreign invesment so that they can work out their strategies. At the same time, foreign investors must understand that the production and distribution of their products will be unavoidably affected by China's political and economic system.

From China's point of view, there is no doubt that long-term investments in the manufacturing sector will be welcomed and accorded preferential treatment. As for short- and medium-term investments, foreign investors must consider the export capacity of the projects in question. When drafting their production plans, they should consider the Chinese government's economic directives and the situation in the domestic market. In addition, they should decide which location will best suit their projects since differences exist among coastal areas, inland provinces and cities with regard to financial and trading systems, social environment and infrastructure. Of course, the selection of the investment project itself is also very important. For instance, foreign investors must be aware that in most cases, the Chinese partner will have to rely on the foreign partner to manage the project. Thus, unless the foreign investor in question is familiar with operating that particular type of business, there will not be very effective cooperation between the parties.

The selection of the appropriate Chinese partner is also crucial. In general, a Chinese concern which satisfies the following criteria should be considered a good potential partner:

(1) It has a strong financial position in terms of Renminbi and foreign exchange;
(2) Its management is familiar with the business and with the market, and is willing to carry out the current open policy;
(3) It has an adequate number of skilled workers, engineers and management personnel;
(4) Its management is familiar with the procedures relating to import and export and to applications for licences;

(5) It has contacts with the institutions in charge of supplying raw materials and distributing products, as well as those dealing with tax, finance, labour and insurance, and auditing authorities, banks and law offices;
(6) It has some experience in conducting economic and technical exchanges with foreign enterprises; and
(7) Its superior department supports Sino-foreign economic cooperation.

It should be remembered, however, that information concerning these matters may not be readily available, but foreign investors should certainly pay ample attention to each of them.

An important way to ensure effective cooperation is to conduct a detailed feasibility study before embarking on a major deal. Nevertheless, the majority of such studies appear to be rather simple estimates of the return on investment, and quite a few projects continue to suffer from the lack of adequate forecasts regarding the supply of energy, raw materials, and so on. Another weakness of such feasibility studies has been the lack of any systematic assessment of the market potential for a particular product or project. On many occasions, the feasibility studies failed to consider the market potential on a 'developing' basis, that is, market demand, and there was no regard to the fact that technology may change while a project is being built. For instance, a given item of technology may have been advanced when the parties concerned started negotiations but, since completion of a project takes several years, at the end of that period, that item of technology may have lost its superiority and competiveness. A potentially promising project may also be defeated by competition from other enterprises or sectors. The glut of hotels in Guangzhou and other cities is a good example.

It is submitted that foreign investors must take extraordinary care when preparing feasibility studies. This is because most of the Chinese parties are not familiar with the process and are quite ignorant of the international market situation. At the same time, all parties must submit accurate statistics and information so that a realistic feasibility study can be prepared. Bearing in mind the current situation in China, it is hoped that greater flexibility would be allowed in the areas of finance and technology transfer.

It should be noted that 'personal' relationships still play an important, at times vital, part in the operations of foreign-investment projects. This situation has led many foreign investors to believe that in China a successful investment does not depend on what you know, but who you know. For short-term and personal (selfish) benefits, foreign businesses occasionally use unlawful means to establish personal relationships with Chinese government officials. It appears that a system of 'investment broking' has been set up by those who claim to have strong connections with the decision-makers in China. These people label themselves as 'China consultants'. They often exaggerate their influence and would have foreign investors believe that, without an introduction by them, they would not be able to penetrate the Chinese market. However, this is not necessarily the case. In the long run, such dubious practices will not only damage China's open policy but will also do tremendous harm to foreign investment. For example, foreign investors will have to increase their expenditures. It is therefore necessary for them to adopt a long-term view and avoid doing anything which may encourage the development of personal relationships. At the same time, the Chinese and foreign parties should strengthen their relationship with each other in a spirit of mutual trust and cooperation.

Appendix one

Provisions of the State Council of the People's Republic of China for the encouragement of foreign investment*

Promulgated by the State Council on 11 October 1986

Article 1. These Provisions are hereby formulated in order to improve the investment environment, facilitate the absorption of foreign investment, introduce advanced technology, improve product quality, expand exports in order to generate foreign exchange income and develop the national economy.

Article 2. The State encourages foreign companies, enterprises and other economic entities or individuals (hereinafter referred to as 'Foreign Investors') to establish Chinese-foreign equity joint ventures, Chinese-foreign cooperative ventures and wholly foreign-owned enterprises (hereinafter referred to as 'Enterprises with Foreign Investment') within the territory of China.

The State grants special preferences to the Enterprises with Foreign Investment listed below:

(1) Productive enterprises whose products are mainly for export, which have a foreign exchange surplus after deducting from their total annual foreign exchange revenues the annual foreign exchange expenditures incurred in production and operation and the foreign exchange needed for the remittance abroad of the profits earned by Foreign Investors (hereinafter referred to as 'Export Enterprises').

(2) Productive enterprises possessing advanced technology supplied by Foreign Investors which are engaged in developing new products and upgrading existing products in order to increase foreign exchange earnings from exports, or in producing import-substitutes (hereinafter referred to as 'Technologically Advanced Enterprises').

Article 3. Export Enterprises and Technologically Advanced Enterprises shall be exempt from payment to the State of all subsidies to staff and workers, except for the payment or allocation of funds for labour insurance, welfare costs and housing subsidies for Chinese staff and workers in accordance with the provisions of the State.

Article 4. The site (land) use fees for Export Enterprises and Technologically Advanced Enterprises, except for those located in busy urban sectors of large cities, shall be computed and charged according to the following standards:

(1) At RMB5 to RMB20 per square meter per year in areas where the development fee and the site use fee are computed and charged together;

(2) At not more than RMB3 per square meter per year in site areas where the development fee is computed and charged on a one-time basis or in

* Based on English translations of the official Chinese text.

areas which are developed by the above-mentioned enterprises themselves.

Exemptions for specified periods of time from the fees provided in the foregoing provision may be granted at the discretion of the local people's governments concerned.

Article 5. Export Enterprises and Technologically Advanced Enterprises shall be given priority in the supply of water and electricity and in the use of transportation services and communication facilities needed for their production and operation. Fees shall be computed and charged in accordance with the standards for local state enterprises.

Article 6. Export Enterprises and Technologically Advanced Enterprises, after examination by the Bank of China, shall be given priority in receiving loans for short-term revolving funds needed for production and distribution, as well as for other types of credit they need.

Article 7. When Foreign Investors in Export Enterprises and Technologically Advanced Enterprises remit abroad profits distributed to them by such enterprises, the amount remitted shall be exempt from income tax.

Article 8. After the expiration of the period allowed for the reduction or exemption of enterprise income tax in accordance with the provisions of the State, Export Enterprises whose exports in the year amount to 70% or more of their respective production, in value terms, for that year, may pay their enterprise income tax at half the rate of the existing tax.

Export Enterprises in the special economic zones and in the economic and technological development zones and other Export Enterprises that have already paid enterprise income tax at a tax rate of 15% and that comply with the foregoing conditions, shall pay enterprise income tax at a rate of 10%

Article 9. After the expiration of the period allowed for reduction or exemption of enterprise income tax in accordance with the provisions of the State, Technologically Advanced Enterprises may enjoy a three-year extension during which enterprise income tax is paid at a reduced rate that is half of the existing rate.

Article 10. Foreign Investors who reinvest the profits distributed to them by their enterprises in order to establish or expand Export Enterprises or Technologically Advanced Enterprises for a operational period of not less than five years, after application to and approval by the tax authorities, shall be refunded the total amount of enterprise income tax already paid on the reinvested portion. If the investment is withdrawn prior to the end of the five-year operational period, the amount of enterprise income tax refunded shall be repaid.

Article 11. Except for crude oil, refined oil and other products subject to special State provisions, export products of Enterprises with Foreign Investment shall be exempt from the Consolidated Industrial and Commercial Tax.

Article 12. Enterprises with Foreign Investment may arrange the export of their products directly or may also export by consignment to agents in accordance with State provisions. For products that require an export licence, in accordance with the annual export plan of the enterprise, an application for an export licence may be made every six months.

Article 13. Machinery and equipment, vehicles used in production, raw materials, fuel, knocked down parts, spare parts, machine component parts and fittings, (including imports restricted by the State) which Enterprises with Foreign investment need to import in order to carry out their export contracts do not require further applications for examination and approval and are exempt from the requirement for import licences. The Customs Department shall exercise supervision and control, and shall inspect and release such imports on the basis of the enterprise contract or the export contract.

The imported materials and items mentioned above are restricted to use by the enterprise and are not to be sold on the domestic market. If they are used in products to be sold domestically, import procedures shall be handled in accordance with the relevant provisions and taxes shall be paid according to the relevant regulations.

Article 14. Under the supervision of the foreign exchange control departments, Enterprises with Foreign Investment may mutually adjust their foreign exchange surpluses and deficiencies among each other as per their respective needs.

The Bank of China and other banks designated by the People's Bank of China may provide cash security services and may grant loans in Renminbi to Enterprises with Foreign Investment.

Article 15. The people's governments at all levels and relevant departments in charge shall guarantee the right of autonomy of Enterprises with Foreign Investment and shall support Enterprises with Foreign Investment in their respective management in accordance with international advanced scientific methods.

Within the scope of their approved contracts, Enterprises with Foreign Investment have the right to independently determine their respective production and operation plans, and to raise and use funds, to purchase production materials and to sell products at their own discretion. Similarly, they have the right to determine their respective wage levels, the forms of wages and bonuses and the allowance system.

Enterprises with Foreign Investment may, in accordance with their production and operation requirements, independently determine their own organizational structure and personnel system, employ or dismiss senior management personnel, increase or dismiss staff and workers. They may recruit and employ technical personnel, managerial personnel and workers in their locality. The unit to which such employed personnel belong shall provide its support and shall permit their transfer. Staff and workers who break the rules and regulations, and thereby cause certain adverse consequences may be subject to differing disciplinary actions up to that of discharge in accordance with the seriousness of the case. Enterprises with Foreign Investment that recruit, employ, dismiss or discharge staff and workers, shall file a report with the local labour and personnel departments for the record.

Article 16. All districts and departments must implement the Circular of the State Council Concerning Firmly Curbing the Indiscriminate Levy of Charges on Enterprises. The people's governments at the provincial level shall formulate specific methods and strengthen supervision and administration thereof.

Enterprises with Foreign Investment that encounter unreasonable charges may refuse to pay and may also appeal to the local economic committees up to the State Economic Commission.

Article 17. The people's governments at all levels and relevant departments in charge shall strengthen the coordination of their work, improve efficiency in handling matters and shall promptly examine and approve matters reported by Enterprises with Foreign Investment that require response and resolution. The agreement, contract, and articles of association of an Enterprise with Foreign Investment shall be examined and approved by the departments in charge under the State Council. The examination and approval authority must within three months from the date of receipt of all documents decide to approve or not to approve them.

Article 18. Export Enterprises and Technologically Advanced Enterprises mentioned in these Provisions shall be confirmed jointly as such by the foreign economic relations and trade departments where such enterprises are located and the relevant departments in accordance with the enterprise contract, and certification shall be issued.

If the actual results of the annual exports of an Export Enterprise are unable to realize the goal of achieving a favorable balance in its foreign exchange revenue and expenditure that is stipulated in the enterprise contract, it is allowed to delay payment until the following year the taxes and fees which have already been reduced or exempted in a given year.

Article 19. Except where these Provisions expressly provide that they are to be applicable to Export Enterprises or Technologically Advanced Enterprises, other articles shall be applicable to all Enterprises with Foreign Investment.

These Provisions apply from the date of implementation to those Enterprises with Foreign Investment that have obtained approval for establishment before the date of implementation of these Provisions and that qualify for the preferential terms of these Provisions.

Article 20. For enterprises invested in and established by companies, enterprises and other economic organizations or individuals from Hongkong, Macau or Taiwan, matters shall be handled by reference to these Provisions.

Article 21. The Ministry of Foreign Economic Relations and Trade shall be responsible for interpreting these Provisions.

Article 22. These Provisions shall go into effect on the date on which they are promulgated.

Appendix two

Rules of the Ministry of Foreign Economic Relations and Trade for the implementation of examination and confirmation of Export Enterprises and Technologically Advanced Enterprises with foreign investment*

Promulgated on 27 January 1987

In accordance with the Provisions of the State Council of the People's Republic of China for the Encouragement of Foreign Investment (hereinafter referred to as the 'Provisions'), the present rules are hereby formulated in order to examine and confirm export enterprises and technologically advanced enterprises with foreign investment.

Article 1. Sino-foreign joint ventures, Sino-foreign cooperative enterprises and wholly foreign-owned enterprises in China which have been established in accordance with the law and conform to Article 2 of the Provisions on export enterprises and technologically advanced enterprises, may enjoy preferential treatment after they are examined and confirmed and obtain relevant certificates.

Article 2. Enterprises with foreign investment which meet simultaneously the following three requirements can be confirmed as export enterprises:

(1) The enterprises should be ones that manufacture products for export;
(2) Their products are mainly for export (including export arranged directly by themselves, arranged by entrusted foreign trade corporations and through other channels), and their annual value of export goods should amount to more than 50% of the total annual production value;
(3) They must balance the annual operating foreign exchange earnings and expenditure or have a foreign exchange surplus (computing method: surplus of foreign exchange revenue and expenditure at the end of year equals to carry-over surplus from previous year plus annual operating foreign exchange revenue minus annual operating foreign exchange expenditure).

Article 3. Export enterprises which conform to Article 2 in the event that their value of export products amounts to more than 70% of their total annual production value, shall enjoy the preferential treatment of Article 8 of the Provisions after being confirmed by the examination.

Article 4. The enterprises that meet the following requirements can be confirmed as technologically advanced enterprises: the technology, production techniques and key facilities of the enterprises with foreign investment should pertain to the projects proclaimed by the State as appropriate and advanced; they should be in short supply on the domestic market; and the products are

* Based on English translations of the official Chinese text.

newly developed or capable of expanding export or substituting import products or upgrading similar domestic products.

Article 5. An enterprise with foreign investment which meets both the requirements of 'export enterprises' and 'technologically advanced enterprises' can choose one of the two categories and enjoy the relevant preferential treatment.

Article 6. The examination and confirmation authorities of export enterprises and technologically advanced enterprises are the departments of foreign economic relations and trade in provinces, autonomous regions, municipalities or cities that have their own plan and national plan, or the people's governments (management committees) of special economic zones. The export enterprises and technologically advanced enterprises that are established by departments and organizations directly under the State Council shall be examined and confirmed by the Ministry of Foreign Economic Relations and Trade.

Enterprises with foreign investment that meet the requirements of Articles 2, 3, 4 of the present rules, can separately submit the following documents to the abovementioned authorities and apply for examination and confirmation:

(1) Application forms of export enterprises and technologically advanced enterprises;
(2) A copy of contract and approval documents;
(3) Feasbility study of project and approval documents.

Article 7. The examination and confirmation authorities at various levels should complete the examination and decide to approve or not to approve them within 30 days from the date of receiving the above-mentioned documents listed in Article 6. The examination and confirmation for technologically advanced enterprises should be handled together with relevant departments in charge.

Article 8. The application forms for export enterprises and technologically advanced enterprises as well as the application forms for confirmation will be formulated in a unified way by the Ministry of Foreign Economic Relations and Trade. The confirmation certificates shall be signed and sealed separately by the above-mentioned examination and confirmation authorities at various levels. The original certificate shall be kept by the application enterprise and the copies of the certificate will be sent to relevant departments at the same level for record. The confirmation authorities at various levels and the application forms submitted by the enterprises should be sent to the Ministry of Foreign Economic Relations and Trade as well as to the State Economic Commission for record.

Article 9. Enterprises with foreign investment should, in accordance with the state provisions concerned, work out their annual export plan, compile regularly statistic report forms and submit them to the original examination and confirmation authorities. They will be the basis for examining export enterprises.

Article 10. The original examination and confirmation authorities should, together with other relevant departments, examine export enterprises and technologically advanced enterprises annually. The enterprises will, in accordance with the requirements in Articles 2, 3, 4 of the present rules and their approved contracts, be examined in export plan, real annual export result, technical index, quality of products and degree of local production content.

Article 11. Examination and confirmation authorities shall compile a list of export enterprises and technologically advanced enterprises which qualify after examination, and circulate a notice of their qualification to relevant departments. These enterprises may continue to enjoy all preferential treatment in the next year. In case of non-qualification found through examination at the end of year, the enterprises shall make up the taxes deducted and exempted as having enjoyed the preferential treatment for export enterprises and technologically advanced enterprises.

In the case of confirmed export enterprises and technologically advanced enterprises which do not qualify after examination for three years running, the original examination and confirmation authorities shall, together with relevant departments in charge, reexamine and revoke the certificate for confirmation of export enterprises and technologically advanced enterprises.

Article 12. Measures for confirmation and examination of the enterprises with foreign investment located in Shenzhen, Zhuhai, Shantou and Xiamen will be formulated by the people's governments (management committees) of the special economic zones in accordance with the present rules and in the light of their actual conditions. They should be submitted to the Ministry of Foreign Economic Relations and Trade for record.

Article 13. The confirmation and examination of export enterprises and technologically advanced enterprises will be implemented in accordance with the present rules from the date of promulgation.

Appendix three

Rules for foreign-investment enterprises applying for import and export licences*

Promulgated by the Ministry of Foreign Economic Relations and Trade on 24 January 1987

Article 1. The said rules are formulated in accordance with the 'Regulations for the Implementation of the Law of the People's Republic of China on Joint Ventures Using Chinese and Foreign Investment' and the 'Provisions of the State Council for the Encouragement of Foreign Investment' to simplify the procedures for application of import and export licences so as to facilitate the business operations of enterprises with foreign investment.

Article 2. Foreign-investment enterprises shall apply for import licences for equipment and other materials, which are imported as investment of the foreign partners and require import licences, in accordance with the list of imported equipment and materials approved for the enterprise concerned. Chinese Customs shall examine the imported goods which do not require import licences in accordance with the approved list of imported equipment and materials.

Article 3. Foreign-investment enterprises may import, without import licences, machinery and other equipment (including those requiring import licences), vehicles to be used in production (trucks for transportation, special vehicles and vehicles for both passenger and cargo transport purposes), raw materials, fuel, spare parts, accessories and components which are needed in their export-oriented production, and the Customs shall supervise and examine them in accordance with the documents approved for the establishment of the enterprises, contracts or import-export contracts. The imported equipment and materials can only be used by the importers for production and cannot be sold or transferred in China. In special cases, if the imported raw materials and parts or the products manufactured with imported raw materials and parts are sold in China, the enterprises shall have to go through the same import formalities in accordance with Article 4 of the present Provisions.

Article 4. Foreign-investment enterprises may apply, within the scope of their approved business operation, for their import licences every six months in accordance with the approved import plan if import licences are required for equipment and vehicles for use in production raw materials, fuel, spare parts, accessories and components these enterprises need to import for the purpose of producing goods for domestic sales and business transactions on the domestic market. The Customs shall examine the import of those items that are not under the import licence plan in accordance with documents and contracts approved for the establishment of the enterprises.

Article 5. Import licences are to be issued by the provincial-level departments of foreign economic relations and trade for the imports of reasonable amounts

* Based on English translations of the official Chinese text.

of those non-production goods needed for the foreign-investment enterprises' own use (if such imports require import licences).

Article 6. If export licences are required for exporting those products the foreign-investment enterprises produce, the enterprises shall apply for export licences every six months in accordance with their approved annual export plan.

Article 7. If foreign-investment enterprises export the products they produce and the exports do not need export licences, the Customs shall examine them in accordance with signed export contracts and other relevant documents.

Article 8. If foreign-investment enterprises export products, which are not produced by themselves, in order to solve their foreign-exchange balancing problem, export licences will be issued in accordance with approved documents (if their products are under the export licence plan). The Customs will examine the products, (if the products are not under the export licence plan), only in accordance with signed export contracts.

Article 9. Enterprises with foreign investment may apply for import and export licences to the relevant authorities in charge of the issuing of licences in accordance with the licence categories announced by the Ministry of Foreign Economic Relations and Trade.

Article 10. The said rules come into force on the day of promulgation.

Appendix four

Provisions on the purchase and export of domestic products by foreign-investment enterprises to balance foreign exchange accounts

Promulgated by the Ministry of Foreign Economic Relàtions and Trade on 20 January 1987

Article 1. These provisions are hereby formulated in accordance with the relevant regulations of the State Council for the purpose of facilitating enterprises with foreign investment to balance their foreign exchange accounts. Subject to approval of their application, these enterprises are allowed to purchase and export products from other local sources (hereinafter referred to as 'non-resultant products') to make up for the shortfall in their foreign exchange - accounts.

Article 2. In principle, these enterprises should balance their foreign exchange accounts by exporting the resultant products of their respective enterprises. But those enterprises that have run into temporary difficulties in this regard may apply, within a certain period of time, for the purchase and export of non-resultant domestic products (except those subject to unified State Control) so as to balance their foreign exchange accounts.

Article 3. An enterprise with foreign investment which complies with Article 2 of the provisions and which needs to purchase and export non-resultant domestic products to balance its foreign exchange accounts should first apply to the local provincial department of foreign economic relations and trade, stating the amount of foreign exchange and the corresponding amount of Renminbi needed in the current year to purchase domestic products for export, and their names, specifications and quantities and their export channels.

Article 4. The approved quantity of non-resultant domestic products to be purchased by a foreign-investment enterprise should be limited to the amount of foreign exchange needed to cover the short fall in its production and operation, the foreign investor's profit repatriation, or remittance of capital upon its termination and liquidation.

Article 5. Foreign-investment enterprises which are approved to purchase and export non-resultant domestic products to balance their foreign exchange accounts should mainly purchase products manufactured in the province, autonomous region or municipality where they are located. If they need to purchase them from other provinces, they should first have the approval of the provincial-level department of the foreign economic relations and trade of the relevant province, autonomous region or municipality.

Article 6. The domestic products purchased by an enterprise with foreign investment for export in order to balance its foreign exchange account must be shipped out of China and sold abroad, and must not be re-sold within China.

* Based on English translations of the official Chinese text.

Article 7. Enterprises with foreign investment which are approved to purchase non-resultant domestic products to balance their foreign exchange accounts may export the products by themselves or by China's foreign trade corporations as their agents.

Article 8. Apart from approving enterprises with foreign investment to purchase domestic products for export, the people's governments of all provinces, autonomous regions, municipalities and cities with independent plans may, with the aim of fulfilling State export targets, organize export of their local product through specialized foreign trade companies. Of the foreign exchange thus earned and locally retained in accordance with the relevant State regulations, part of the retained portion will go to the suppliers of the products according to the stipulated ratios and the remainder may be used by local people's governments to balance the foreign exchange accounts among the enterprises with foreign investment under the supervision of the local foreign exchange control departments.

Article 9. With regard to the products to be purchased and exported by enterprises with foreign investment as mentioned in Article 3 of the provisions, and those to be exported by people's governments of provinces, autonomous regions, municipalities and cities with independent plans as mentioned in Article 8, the purchase and export of those commodities which require State export licences or are subject to export quotas should be approved by the Ministry of Foreign Economic Relations and Trade. That of other commodities should be approved by provincial-level departments of foreign economic relations and trade and then be submitted to the Ministry of Foreign Economic Relations and the Trade for the record.

The above-mentioned approval authorities (departments) should give replies to the respective applications within one month beginning from the date of their receipt. Among the approved export products, the export licences required for those that should be exported with licences should be issued in accordance with the procedures of the Ministry of Foreign Economic Relations and Trade on applying of export and import licences by foreign-investment enterprises.

Article 10. These provisions shall go into effect on the date of issue.

Appendix five

Provisions of the Ministry of Labour and Personnel of the People's Republic of China on the right of autonomy of enterprises with foreign investment in the hiring of personnel and on wages, insurance and welfare expenses of staff and workers*

Promulgated by the Ministry of Labour and Personnel on 28 November 1986

The following provisions are hereby formulated in order to implement the Provisions of the State Council for the Encouragement of Foreign Investment, guarantee the right of autonomy of Enterprises with Foreign Investment in the hiring of personnel, and to appropriately determine the wages and insurance and welfare expenses for staff and workers from the Chinese party:

(1) On the Right of Autonomy of Enterprises with Foreign Investment in the Hiring of Personnel

(a) An Enterprise with Foreign Investment may, in accordance with its production and operation requirements, determine on its own the organizational structure and personnel system, and, with the assistance of the labour and personnel department in its locality, recruit and employ staff and workers on its own through an examination and selection process in which only the best (qualified) are hired. In the event that engineering and technical personnel or operation and management personnel needed by the Enterprise with Foreign Investment are not available in the locality, the Enterprise with Foreign Investment may, after the labour and personnel department in the province, autonomous region or municipality directly under the Central Government where it is located has consulted with and obtained the consent of the labour and personnel department in the district concerned, recruit outside the locality.

(b) With respect to the engineering and technical personnel, operation and management personnel and technical workers whom Enterprises with Foreign Investment have decided to hire after examination, the original units of which such personnel are in employment shall actively give their support and permit their transfer. In the event of any dispute, the labour and personnel department in their locality shall adjudicate.

(c) Senior management personnel designated by the Chinese party to work in Enterprises with Foreign Investment should be persons who are well oriented in existing policies, technically competent, know how to manage, ready to accept new challenges and who can cooperate and work together with the foreign investors. The relevant departments shall support them in their work and generally shall not transfer them to other jobs during their term of office. In the event

* Based on English translations of the official Chinese text.

that they must be transferred, the consent of the Board of Directors should be obtained.

(d) With regard to personnel who are not qualified for their posts after having completed the prescribed probationary or training period, and personnel who have become redundant as a result of changes in the production or technical conditions of the Enterprise with Foreign Investment, the enterprise may dismiss them. Staff and workers who have violated the rules and regulations of the enterprise and thereby caused certain bad consequences can, in accordance with the seriousness of the case, be given different penalties up to that of discharge.

(2) On the Wages, Insurance and Welfare Expenses of Staff and Workers

(a) The wage levels of the staff and workers in an Enterprise with Foreign Investment will be determined by the Board of Directors on the principle that it should not less than 120% of the average wages of the staff and workers of State-owned enterprises with similar conditions, of the same trade and in the same locality; such levels shall be adjusted gradually according to the economic performance of the enterprise. Enterprises with good economic performance may give bigger wage raises; those with poor economic performance may give smaller or no raises.

(b) An Enterprise with Foreign Investment shall make payments to the retirement and pension fund and unemployment insurance fund for staff and workers from the Chinese party in accordance with the stipulations of the people's government in the locality. The insurance and welfare benefits of staff and workers during their employment shall be made in accordance with relevant stipulations of the Chinese Government concerning State-owned enterprises; expenses required therefor shall be disbursed from the costs and expenses of the enterprise strictly in accordance with the facts.

(c) Enterprises with Foreign Investment shall make payments to the housing subsidy fund in accordance with the stipulations of the people's government in the locality. The Chinese party to the enterprise shall use such fund to subsidize the costs of the building and purchase of housing for staff and workers.

Appendix six

Rules for the implementation of relevant articles concerning preferential tax terms stipulated in the Provisions of the State Council for the encouragement of foreign investment*

Promulgated by the Finance Ministry on 30 January 1987

The following rules are formulated for the purpose of implementing the relevant articles concerning preferential tax terms stipulated in the Provisions of the State Council of the People's Republic of China for the Encouragement of Foreign Investment (hereinafter referred to as 'the Provisions').

I. Article 7 of the Provisions reads: 'When foreign investors in export enterprises and technologically advanced enterprises remit abroad profits distributed to them by such enterprises, the amount remitted shall be exempt from income tax.' This means that when foreign partners in Sino-foreign export enterprises and technologically advanced enterprises remit abroad profits distributed to them in the fiscal year 1986 and the following fiscal years, the amount remitted shall be exempt from income tax which is 10% of the amount remitted. When foreign partners in such enterprises remit abroad profits distributed to them in advance by such enterprises and they have paid their income tax prior to the date when the Provisions are published, the amount of paid income tax should be refunded to the foreign partners. The original rules on the income tax of the amount remitted hold effective if the foreign partners in such enterprises remitted abroad profits distributed to them prior to the fiscal year 1986.

II. Article 8 of the Provisions reads: 'After the expiration of the period for the reduction or exemption of enterprise income tax in accordance with the Provisions of the State, export enterprises, whose value of export in that year amounts to 70% or more of the value of their products for that year, may pay enterprise income tax at one half the rate of the present tax.' This applies to export enterprises with or without a period for the reduction or exemption of enterprise income tax in accordance with the Provisions of existing tax laws and relevant regulations.

(1) The above-mentioned export enterprises, whose value of export products in that year amounts to 70% or more of the value of the total products for the same year, may enjoy the 50% tax reduction or exemption for the year in accordance with the present tax rates only after they present certificates issued by approving and confirming organs and examined and confirmed by local tax authorities.
(2) For those export enterprises which have been confirmed and have paid enterprise income tax in advance on a quarterly basis in 1986, they may balance it when they pay the 1986 annual enterprise income tax.
(3) The above-mentioned export enterprises pay their income tax at a rate of 10% if their tax rate is lower than 10% after a 50% reduction.

III. Article 9 of the Provisions reads: 'After the expiration of the period of reduction or exemption of enterprise income tax in accordance with the

* Based on English translations of the official Chinese text.

Provisions of the State, technologically advanced enterprises may extend for three years the payment of enterprise income tax at a rate reduced by one half.' This applies to technologically advanced enterprises with or without a period for the reduction or exemption of enterprise income tax in accordance with the existing tax laws and relevant regulations.

(1) If the period is not expired for the reduction or exemption of the enterprise income tax in line with the existing tax laws and relevant regulations, the above-mentioned technologically advanced enterprises may pay their enterprise income tax at a rate reduced by 50% in the first three years after the expiration of the period for the enterprise income tax reduction or exemption. If the period for enterprise income tax reduction or exemption expires or the above-mentioned technologically advanced enterprises do not have such a period in line with the existing tax laws and relevant regulations, the enterprises which may be confirmed as technologically advanced enterprises may pay their enterprise income tax at a rate reduced by 50% in the first three years beginning from the year when they are confirmed as technologically advanced. Those that are newly established after 1986 and do not have the period for enterprise income tax reduction or exemption in line with the existing tax laws and relevant regulations, may from their first profit-making year pay their enterprise income tax at a rate reduced by 50% for the first three years.

(2) The above-mentioned technologically advanced enterprises which have paid in advance their quarterly enterprise income tax for 1986, may balance their payment of the quarterly enterprise income tax when they pay the 1986 annual income tax.

(3) The above-mentioned technologically advanced enterprises pay enterprise income tax at a rate of 10% if their tax rate is lower than 10 percent after a 50% reduction.

IV. Article 10 of the Provisions reads: 'Foreign investors who reinvest the profits distributed to them by their enterprises in order to establish or expand export enterprises or technologically advanced enterprises for a period of operation of not less than five years, after application to and approval by the tax authorities, shall be refunded the total amount of enterprise income tax already paid on the reinvested portion.' This means that when foreign investors reinvest the profits distributed to them by their enterprises in order to establish or expand export enterprises or technologically advanced enterprises, the profits must be those which are distributed to them in 1986 and the following years. The original Provisions hold effective in this regard for those foreign investors who reinvest the profits distributed to them preceding the year 1986.

V. If a foreign-investment enterprise is approved to be an export enterprise and a technologically advanced enterprise by the examining and confirming authorities in the same year, it may be allowed to choose to enjoy the preferential terms stated in Article 8 or Article 9 of the Provisions, but cannot enjoy at the same time the preferential terms in both articles. After the expiration of the period of three years and a half for the 50% reduction of enterprise income tax, a technologically advanced enterprise may enjoy the preferential terms as stipulated in Article 8 if it accords with the requirements set in this article.

VI. The preferential tax terms stipulated in the Provisions do not apply to Sino-foreign enterprises which are engaged in the exploration and development of such resources as oil and precious metals.

VII. All the areas and departments must abide by the said detailed rules in implementing the preferential tax policy as set in the Provisions.

Appendix seven

Regulations governing the application of Renminbi loans mortgaged by foreign exchange*

Promulgated by the People's Bank of China, effective on 12 December 1986

The Regulations are formulated to meet the needs of Renminbi loans mortgaged by foreign exchange (hereinafter referred to as 'mortgage Renminbi loans').

Article 1. Eligibility. All registered enterprises in the People's Republic of China including State-owned enterprises, collective enterprises, Sino-foreign joint venture enterprises, Sino-foreign cooperative enterprises and wholly owned foreign enterprises are eligible to apply for Renminbi loans mortgaged by their foreign exchange (including foreign exchange borrowed from abroad).

Article 2. Usage. Mortgage Renminbi loans can be used to cover working capital needs or for investment in fixed assets depending on the source of the foreign exchange mortgaged by the applicant. Those to be used for fixed asset investment must be brought in line with the State or the regional fixed asset investment plan.

Article 3. Variety and maturity. Mortgage Renminbi loans can be categorized into two kinds of loans: short-term as well as medium-term loans. The maturities of short-term loans are three months, six months and one year. The medium-term loans carry maturities from one year up to five years.

Article 4. Variety of foreign currency accepted. At present, the foreign currencies that can be used as mortgages are limited to the US dollar, Japanese yen, Hongkong dollar, deutsche mark and pound sterling.

Article 5. Roles of banks. Mortgage Renminbi loans shall be extended by the Bank of China and other financial institutions that are authorized by the PBOC, except in the Special Economic Zones (SEZs). The Renminbi funds for mortgage loans will be provided by the PBOC and the Renminbi funds recovered upon maturity of the loans shall be returned to the PBOC. All Renminbi funds shall be under the unified management of the head office of the PBOC.

Article 6. Application and examination. Applicants for mortgage Renminbi loans shall declare to the State Administration of Exchange Control or its branches the sources and amounts of their foreign exchange for examination. After their reports are verified, they can go through the application formalities with a designated bank authorized by the PBOC. If the foreign exchange to be mortgaged by the applicants is borrowed from abroad, the applicants shall submit the original loans contract (of the foreign exchange) and the debt repayment plan (including both principal and interest) for the application. Matters that are beyond the designated bank's authority shall be submitted to the PBOC for examination after the designated bank has examined the application and verified it to be in line with the present Regulations.

* Based on English translations of the official Chinese text.

Article 7. Approval. PBOC branches in various provinces, autonomous regions, municipalities directly under the jurisdiction of the Central Government and Shenzhen (hereinafter referred to as 'provincial, regional and municipal PBOC branches') shall prepare their annual mortgage Renminbi loan plans. They shall enjoy the autonomy to examine and approve loans applications within the limits of the Renminbi funds allocated by the PBOC head office. The branches of the State Administration of Exchange Control shall keep in close touch with the planning and the capital management departments of the PBOC so that co-ordination between the foreign exchange mortgaged and the Renminbi funds to be loaned out can be handled properly in the approval and examination process. Under the authorization of the provincial, regional and municipal PBOC branches, designated banks can approve loan applications of small amounts.

Article 8. Disbursement. After approval of the application by a designated bank, the applicant (or the applying unit) shall sign a borrowing contract (see the sample contract below) with the authorized bank. The borrowing contract will be in triplicate: one will be used by the designated bank for the disbursement of loans; one will be submitted to the branch of the State Administration of Exchange Control for record; and one will be kept by the applicant (or the applying unit).

Commissions for the designated bank shall be paid by the applicant (or the applying unit) in accordance with the unified regulations of the PBOC head office.

Article 9. Repayment. Upon maturity, the borrower shall repay the same amount of Renminbi funds he/she has borrowed in exchange for the return of the mortgaged amount of foreign exchange. The repayment shall not be subject to changes in exchange rates. The borrower shall not redeem the foreign exchange he/she has mortgaged before maturity. The mortgaged foreign exchange shall be turned over to the PBOC if the borrower fails to repay the mortgage Renminbi loans upon maturity. In cases where the mortgaged foreign exchange is borrowed from abroad, the borrower shall continue to be liable to the creditor for the repayment of the principal and interest for the foreign exchange he/she has borrowed.

Article 10. Calculation of the Renminbi loans. The maximum amount of the Renminbi loans that the designated bank can extend to the borrower shall not exceed the amount of mortgaged foreign exchange calculated according to the exchange rate (buying rate) as announced by the State Administration of Exchange Control on the day the loan is made.

Article 11. Interest. No interest will be charged or paid on the Renminbi funds and the mortgaged foreign exchange.

Article 12. Management of mortgaged foreign exchange. The mortgaged foreign exchange will be put under the unified management of the State Administration of Exchange Control. Branches of the State Administration of Exchange Control in various localities shall deposit their mortgaged foreign exchange in special accounts with the Bank of China branches in their respective localities. Interest paid on these deposits shall be handed over to the Bank of China head office in a unified and coordinated way after the payment has been certified by the PBOC. The interest will be credited to the PBOC's special foreign exchange account with the Bank of China. Upon receipt of the interest notice from the local branch of the Bank of China, the PBOC shall in turn mail the notice to the accounting department of the PBOC head office.

Article 13. Allocation and payment. The PBOC shall allocate and pay the Renminbi funds to the designated banks according to the actual amount of the mortgage Renminbi loans. The renminbi funds recovered upon maturity of the issued loans shall be turned over to the PBOC no later than the next day after the Renminbi funds are recovered.

Article 14. Statistic. A 'Renminbi Loan Using Foreign Exchange as Mortgage' statistics item will be created. Figures originally entered under '0234' and '0329' shall be under the newly created item. The newly created item will have the code number '94' for the purpose of reporting to a higher authority. Branches of the State Administration of Exchange Control shall report their mortgaged foreign exchange to the higher authorities under either the item called 'Mortgaged Foreign Exchange Income' or the item 'Mortgaged Foreign Exchange Expenses'.

Article 15. Supplementary guidelines. Provincial, regional and municipal PBOC branches shall rely on the present Regulations to prepare their own supplementary guidelines. They shall submit their prepared guidelines to the PBOC head office for record.

Article 16. Interpretation. The PBOC shall retain the right to interpret the present Regulations.

Article 17. Effective date. The Regulations go into effect on the date of promulgation.

Sample Contract for Mortgage Renminbi Loans

(1) Debtor and Creditor:
  (a) Debtor: ______
    Licence issued by the Ministry for Industry and Commerce: ______
    Nature of the Enterprise: ______
    Address: ______
    Telephone: ______
    The Bank with Which It Opens Account: ______
    Account Number: ______ RMB: ______
    Foreign Exchange: ______
  (b) Creditor: ______
    Foreign Exchange Account Number: ______
(2) Borrowed Amount: (according to the buying rate of the day) ______
  RMB (to be spelled out): ______
(3) Use of the Loan: ______
(4) Loan Duration: Starting from day month year
  to day month year
(5) Mortgaged Foreign Exchange Currency: ______
  Sum: (to be spelled out) ______
(6) Source of the Mortgaged Foreign Exchange: ______
(7) Repayment of the Loan. The right to use the mortgaged foreign exchange is vested with the creditor when the contract comes into force and the borrower shall not redeem the mortgaged foreign exchange before the expiration of the duration of the loan. When the mortgage duration expires, the borrower shall return all borrowed Renminbi funds in exchange for the return of the corresponding amount of the mortgaged foreign exchange and the exchange shall not be affected by the fluctuation of exchange rate. In case the borrower fails to redeem the foreign exchange due, the creditor is entitled to dispose of the mortgaged foreign exchange one way or the other to make good the loan the borrower fails to redeem and the borrower shall not raise any objection.

(8) In case the foreign exchange is borrowed from abroad, the borrower shall continue to be liable to repay the foreign exchange principal and interest to the original creditor.

(9) No interest shall accrue from the Renminbi loan and the mortgaged foreign exchange.

(10) Supervision of the Loan: The creditor has the right to know, supervise and check on the use of the loan the borrower has borrowed.

The borrower shall actively cooperate with and provide convenience to the creditor. If the borrower fails to honor the contract, the creditor is entitled to call the loan before maturity or to impose an interest-penalty on the borrower.

(11) Term of Validity: The contract is valid from the day it is signed to the day the loan is repaid.

Both the borrower and the creditor shall honor the contract term as soon as both sides affix their seals and signatures on this contract.

Borrower (unit designation) (official seal)	Creditor (name of the bank) (official seal)
Legal Representative (post and name) (signature and seal)	Legal Representative (post and name) (signature and seal) ____ day ____ month ______ year

Appendix eight

Procedures of the Customs of the People's Republic of China for the administration of materials and parts that enterprises with foreign investment need to import in order to perform product export contracts*

Promulgated by the General Administration of Customs of China on 24 November 1986 and effective on 1 December 1986

Article 1. These Procedures are formulated in accordance with the Provisional Customs Law of the People's Republic of China and relevant Provisions of the State Council for the Encouragement of Foreign Investment in order to encourage the re-export of products that are processed (manufactured) by enterprises with foreign investment for which materials and parts need to be imported to perform their export contracts and to expand exports to generate foreign exchange earnings.

Article 2. Enterprises with foreign investment shall, in accordance with the provisions of these Procedures, enjoy preferential treatment and perform the obligations in customs clearance and the paying of taxes. The goods imported and exported by them shall be declared to the Customs strictly according to the facts. Machinery and equipment, vehicles used in production and raw materials, fuel, knock-down parts, spare parts, components, sets of parts, auxiliary materials and packaging materials (hereinafter referred to as 'Materials and Parts') that need to be imported by these enterprises for the execution of their export contracts shall be categorized as bonded warehouse goods and shall be subject to supervision and control by the Customs.

Article 3. The imported machinery, equipment, vehicles used in production, and Materials and Parts referred to in Article 2 of these Procedures shall be exempted from the requirement of obtaining import licences. The Customs shall inspect and release such imports on the strength of the concerned enterprise's contract(s) or the import-export contract(s).

For products that are processed from Materials and Parts imported by enterprises with foreign investment and then re-exported, the Customs shall, at the time of re-export, handle the inspection and release of such products in accordance with the provisions of the Procedures of the Ministry of Foreign Economic Relations and Trade Concerning the Application of Import and Export Licences by Enterprises with Foreign Investment.

If imported Materials and Parts are used in products to be sold domestically, the enterprise with foreign investment in question shall have to go through the import procedures retroactively in accordance with the relevant provisions of the State.

Where such products belong to the category of commodities subject to the control of import licensing control, import licences for the said imported goods shall be submitted to and inspected by the Customs.

* Based on English translations of the official Chinese text.

Article 4. As regards the imported Materials and Parts referred to in Article 2 of these Procedures, exemption from import duties and the consolidated industrial and commercial tax applies only to that part of the imported Materials and Parts that is actually consumed in the processing of products for export.

The tax-free Materials and Parts referred to above shall include reasonable quantities of imported catalysts, catalytic agents, abrasives and fuel that are directly used in the processing of products for export and that are consumed in the production process.

Imported Materials and Parts shall be restricted to use by the enterprise that processes products for export and such products may not be sold on the domestic market. For those products that are, for one reason or another, approved for domestic disposal (sale), the imported Materials and Parts that are used for their manufacture shall be taxed retroactively in accordance with the relevant regulations. Taxes may be reduced or exempted for substandard and defective products and scrap materials that are left over in the course of production on the basis of their use value as the case may be.

Article 5. Materials and Parts that enterprises with foreign investment need to import in order to manufacture products that are included in the List of Products to Substitute Imports approved by the department in charge as stipulated by the State shall, in the light of these Procedures, be treated as bonded warehouse goods over which the Customs shall exercise supervision and control, thus obviating the need to go through the procedures for the payment of taxes at the time of import. When the products referred to above are supplied to domestic users, import duties and the consolidated industrial and commercial tax on the imported Materials and Parts used shall be paid to the Customs, and the import procedures required shall be completed retroactively in accordance with the relevant regulations.

If domestic users import similar types of products from abroad, they may enjoy preferential tax reduction or exemption. When enterprises with foreign investment supply the products referred to above to these users, preferential tax reduction or exemption may also be granted, provided that they shall, in accordance with the relevant provisions of the State, submit for inspection the certificate of tax reduction or exemption that has been approved by the department in charge.

Article 6. Materials and Parts that are purchased by enterprises with foreign investment from the bonded warehouses of the relevant departments or are imported by other enterprises in the capacity of agents of the said enterprises with foreign investment shall be likewise treated as those imported by the enterprises with foreign investment themselves, hence similarly subject to the relevant provisions of these Procedures.

Article 7. Enterprises with foreign investment that are engaged in processing operations for which materials must be imported must complete the registration procedures with the Customs in the locality (or the appropriate administrative division of Customs) for the record, for which their relevant contracts must be submitted, and, upon examination by the Customs, a Manual of the Customs of the People's Republic of China for the Registration of Materials and Parts Needed to be Imported for Processing and Re-export by Enterprises with Foreign Investment In Order to Perform Product Export Contracts (hereinafter referred to as the 'Registration Manual') shall be issued to the said enterprises with foreign investment. Those enterprises which qualify, upon verification by Customs in the locality, may be dealt with in accordance with the administrative provisions of the Customs for bonded factories that import materials for processing operations.

When the above-mentioned Materials and Parts are imported and, after processing, the finished products are exported, an enterprise with foreign investment shall make declarations to the Customs at the place of entry and exit by submitting the Registration Manual, three copies of the customs declaration form for imported and exported goods, the invoice for the goods, packing lists and other relevant lists and certificates. The Customs shall make annotations and comments, and then affix a seal on the Registration Handbook, which shall then be returned to the enterprises with foreign investment, which shall use this to complete the verification and cancellation procedures at the Customs in the locality (or the appropriate administrative division of the Customs).

Article 8. In respect of imported Materials and Parts imported under the items of each import contract, within two months after completing the execution (performance) of the relevant contracts, enterprises with foreign investment shall submit the Registration Manual, the customs declaration form for imported and exported goods and other relevant documents to Customs to complete the verification and cancellation procedures.

A record of the import, storage and care, allocation for use and passing on to factories for processing of Materials and Parts, and the storage, export and domestic sales of the finished products after processing, must be kept by enterprises with foreign investment in specialized account books and quarterly statements must be submitted to the Customs for examination. As for products that require a long production period, upon the verification and approval of the Customs, such statements may be submitted every six months.

Article 9. If products processed from imported and tax-exempted Materials and Parts are, upon approval, sold domestically, the enterprise with foreign investment concerned shall, within one month of the date of approval, pay retroactively to the competent Customs the customs duties and consolidated industrial and commercial tax on the imported Materials and Parts that were originally exempted from tax.

Article 10. Except where the Customs has given approval because of special reasons, enterprises with foreign investment shall, within one year of the date of import of the tax-exempted imported Materials and Parts, process them into finished products and perform the relevant contracts.

Article 11. When imported Materials and Parts, after being processed into finished products, are not exported directly but instead are transferred to another production enterprise, which also does processing on imported materials for re-export, for reprocessing and assembly, the enterprise that imported the Materials and Parts shall, together with this other production enterprise, complete the procedures with the Customs as regards transfer and verification and cancellation, for which the purchase and sales contract or production and processing contract signed by the two parties and other relevant documents must be submitted. Such production enterprise that carries on the business of reprocessing of imported materials for re-export shall, in accordance with the stipulations of these Procedures, apply for a new Registration Manual, and shall comply with the relevant stipulations of these Procedures, subject to the supervision and control of Customs.

Article 12. In case of any alteration, transfer, suspension or cancellation of contracts that occurs after the importation of Materials and Parts, the enterprise with foreign investment concerned shall complete as soon as possible the required procedures with the Customs for the said alteration, transfer, or cancellation.

Article 13. In order to facilitate the business activities of carrying out processing and export by enterprises with foreign investment and by production enterprises that do reprocessing of imported materials for re-export, the Customs may, based on the actual situation, dispatch Customs officers to be stationed at the factories to carry out actual supervision and control, and may examine the relevant account books. The enterprises referred to above shall provide offices and the necessary facilities.

Article 14. Enterprises with foreign investment may not, without authorization, transfer or sell domestically imported Materials and Parts and their processed products that are bonded warehouse goods. If an enterprise concerned is found to have made a transfer, or to have sold domestically without authorization, or to have acted illegally in violation of the stipulations of these Procedures, the matter shall be dealt with by the Customs in accordance with customs law and the relevant decrees and regulations of the State.

Article 15. These Procedures shall be implemented as from 1 December 1986.

Appendix nine

A practical guide to investing in China

An awareness of the appropriate procedures relating to the approval, registration and implementation of investment projects in China, as in any other countries, will no doubt encourage international cooperation. When we consider that China is a vast country whose economic and legal systems are still in a state of flux, and that a good number of governmental bodies are involved in foreign-investment matters (see the diagram on page 254), foreign investors should as a general rule, wherever possible, rely on their Chinese partners to secure the necessary governmental approvals. This does not mean, however, that foreign investors need not make any effort to understand and master the rules and procedures concerning investment matters in China. The purpose of this Guide is to summarize, for the benefit of first-time overseas investors, the basic rules on setting up and carrying on business operations in China.

Discovering investment opportunities in China

There are several ways to find out what investment opportunities are available in China. Although overseas investors may prefer to make a trip to China to get first-hand information regarding investment projects there, it is advisable and cost-effective for such investors to do some homework before they leave for China. They should first decide which province or city they wish to make an investment in and then have a basic understanding of the local environment, such as transportation, communications, level of industrialization etc. This information can be gathered in a variety of ways, for example, from various China yearbooks or by contacting the relevant Chinese embassies, consulates and commercial institutions. Inquiries may also be made to international investment firms or law offices which are familiar with the investment climate in China. As far as identification of available investment opportunities is concerned, the best source is *China Economic News* which publishes regularly a list of projects for which various local Chinese governments are seeking foreign investment: Overseas investors may also learn of China's foreign-investment interests by attending conferences and exhibitions sponsored either within or without China. In addition, foreign-investment service centres have been established in several major Chinese cities. They provide foreign-investment information and other relevant services to overseas investors.

Entry and stay in China

A foreigner visiting China must obtain, in advance, an entry visa from the Chinese embassy or consulate in his country. This rule applies to all non-Chinese citizens regardless of the length of their visit. In exceptional cases, such as emergencies, visas can be issued at the Chinese customs. Such visas are issued only when the applicants can prove the exceptional nature of their cases.

There are currently multiple-entry and single-entry visas available to foreign businessmen. Multiple-entry visas are issued for stays of three or six months. Before such a visa can be issued, a letter from a Chinese sponsor or superior department stating the necessity for such a visa is required. As a matter of fact,

CENTRAL GOVERNMENT AUTHORITIES INVOLVED IN INVESTMENT

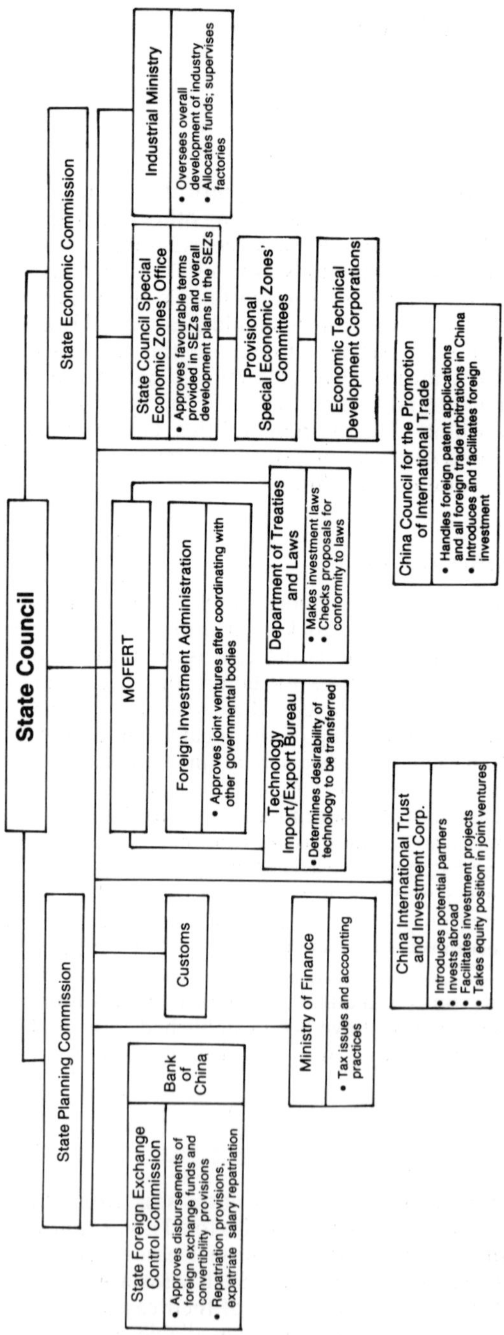

LOCAL GOVERNMENT AUTHORITIES INVOLVED IN INVESTMENT PROJECTS

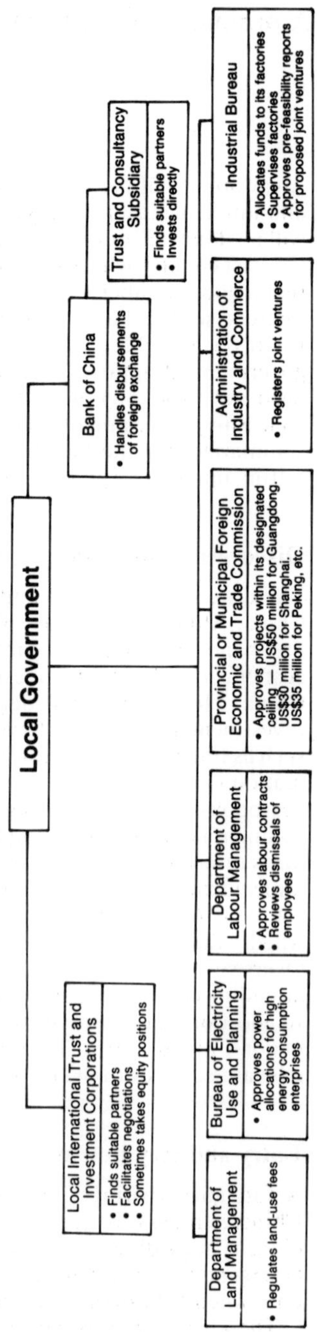

Source: *China Trade Report*, 13 February 1987.

overseas representative offices of the Chinese government require visa applicants to present a letter or telex from their Chinese contacts before a visa, for either a single or multiple-entry, is issued. Where such a letter or telex cannot be obtained for whatever reason, foreign businessmen may obtain a tourist visa from a Chinese travel agency. Such agencies do not require any supporting documents from the Chinese side but will charge a fee for their assistance. Visas secured through travel agencies are tourist visas. Since Chinese law makes no distinction between tourist visas and other visas, this alternative may serve as a valuable back-up to the usual channels for obtaining visas.

Holders of valid visas are allowed to travel in most of the major cities, a number of counties as well as the countryside areas which are identified by the Chinese government as 'open areas'. For those who wish to travel beyond such areas, a special travel permit issued by the local public security bureau is required.

Foreign citizens who wish to stay in China for a longer period are required to obtain an alien-residence permit from the local public security bureau. An alien-residence permit is generally valid for a year and is renewable upon request. It is good for studying, teaching, working or any other purposes, for there is no work-permit system in China. Like Chinese citizens, holders of alien-residence permits are required to register the details of their households, for example, their residential addresses and the names of members of their households, with the local public security bureau. Upon their departure, such foreign nationals must de-register with the bureau.

Approval of contracts

Under the current Chinese system, all commercial or economic transactions involving foreign businesses require approvals from Chinese authorities either at central or local government level, depending on the nature of the transaction and the amount involved. As a general rule, contracts involving large amounts need to be approved by the Ministry of Foreign Economic Relations and Trade ('MOFERT'). A technology transfer contract is one such example. Technology transfer or licensing contracts are governed by the Regulations of the People's Republic of China for the Administration of Technology Import Contracts, promulgated by the State Council on 24 May 1985 (the 'Technology Contract Regulations'), as well as the Foreign Economic Contract Law which regulates the formation and implementation of contracts involving foreign businesses.

According to the Technology Contract Regulations, the Chinese party to the contract is required, within 30 days after the execution of the contract, to submit an application to the MOFERT or its entrusted agencies for examination and approval. Article 10 of the Technology Contract Regulations provides that the application should include:

(1) a written request;
(2) a duplicate copy of the contract together with a Chinese translation thereof if the contract is in foreign language; and
(3) documents concerning the legal status of the parties involved.

Under the Procedures for Examination and Approval of Technology Import Contracts, which were approved by the State Council on 26 August 1985 and promulgated by the MOFERT on 1 October 1985 ('the Technology Contract Approval Procedures'), all contracts for the transfer of industrial property rights or know-how and for technical services, or involving a transfer of technology pursuant to the purchase by Chinese parties of machinery, equipment or goods, must go through the formalities of governmental examination and approval. (Article 2, Technology Contract Approval Procedures.) In summary, technology contracts must be examined and approved as follows (Article 4):

(1) In accordance with the authorization (in terms of investment amount involved) of governments at different levels, the contracts for all projects whose feasibility study reports have been approved by the State Planning Commission must be examined and approved by the MOFERT;
(2) The contracts for all projects whose feasibility study reports have been approved by the responsible departments or bureaus directly under the control of the State Council must be examined and approved by the MOFERT or the responsible department or bureau under the direct control of the State Council appointed by the MOFERT;
(3) The contracts for all projects whose feasibility study reports have been approved by a provincial level government, a special economic zone or a coastal open city must be examined and approved by the respective Department of Foreign Economic Relations and Trade of the province or city. The contracts for all projects whose feasibility study reports have been approved by a city or county government must also be examined and approved by these local departments.

The relevant approving authority for technology contracts must complete its examination and approval within 60 days from the date of receipt of the application (Article 7). Once a contract is examined and approved, an approval certificate, printed and numbered pursuant to the uniform system of the MOFERT, will be issued by the approving authority. If an application is denied, the authority will be required to give reasons for its decision.

In order to facilitate the approval process, it is advisable for the Chinese party to consult the relevant approving authority on the major points of the contract in question or on articles in the contract, before or during the negotiations, in order to seek the authority's opinion on a particular point, or even to submit the drafts of the contract to the authority for preliminary examination.

Representative offices

Occasionally, business concerns prefer to set up representative offices in China before embarking on full-scale cooperative arrangements. The establishment and operation of a foreign representative office are governed by several pieces of legislation. These are the Interim Regulations of the People's Republic of China Concerning the Control of Resident Offices of Foreign Enterprises, promulgated by the State Council on 30 October 1980 (the 'Interim Regulations'), Notice of the General Bureau of Industrial and Commercial Administration of the People's Republic of China Concerning Registration of Resident Offices of Foreign Enterprises, promulgated on 8 December 1980, Procedures of the People's Bank of China for the Establishment of Representative Offices in China by Overseas Chinese and Foreign Financial Institutions, issued on 1 February 1983 (the 'People's Bank Procedures'), and the Procedures of the State Administration for Industry and Commerce of the People's Republic of China for the Registration and Administration of Resident Representative Offices of Foreign Enterprises, approved by the State Council on 5 March 1983 and promulgated by the State Administration for Industry and Commerce ('SAIC') on 15 March 1983. While the People's Bank Procedures apply exclusively to the establishment of representative offices by foreign banks and financial institutions, the other three statutes form the legal regime regulating the activities of foreign representative offices in China. In addition, a number of local governments have promulgated their own rules in respect of the establishment of representative offices in their localities by foreign enterprises.

A foreign enterprise wishing to establish a resident representative office must first apply to the relevant Chinese authorities for permission and then, after obtaining approval, go through the registration procedures. (Article 2, Interim Regulations). Without such approval and completion of registration procedures, no foreign enterprise will be allowed to carry on any of the business activities of a resident representative office. Under Article 4 of the Interim Regulations, foreign enterprises should apply to one of the following Chinese authorities, depending on the nature of their business:

(1) A trader, manufacturer or shipping agent should apply to the MOFERT;
(2) A maritime shipping operator or a maritime shipping agent should apply to the Ministry of Communications;
(3) An air transport enterprise should apply to the General Administration of the Civil Aviation of China; and
(4) Enterprises outside these lines of activity (except banking or insurance institutions) should, according to the nature of their operations, apply to the proper commissions, ministries or bureaus under the Chinese government.

Article 3 sets out some of the documents and materials which must be submitted with the application:

(1) An application form signed by the chairman of the board of directors or the general manager of the foreign enterprise concerned. The application should contain details such as the nature and scope of the resident office to be set up;
(2) The legal documents attesting to the legal status of the foreign enterprise;
(3) Confirmation of credit-standing issued by the banking institutions which have business contacts with the enterprise; and
(4) Detailed information about the members of the resident office.

As a general rule, the establishment of a foreign representative office in China must involve one of the local Chinese institutions which have direct business contacts with foreign companies. What this Chinese institution does is that it acts as a sponsor for the foreign applicant and submits the application documents to the Chinese government on its behalf and also liaises between it and the Chinese authorities.

Once an application for the establishment of a foreign representative office is approved by the relevant Chinese authority, a certificate of approval will be issued to the applicant. Within 30 days from the date of the approval, the foreign enterprise must register with the local SAIC (Article 5, Interim Regulations). The original approval document will be recalled if the enterprise fails to register within the prescribed deadline.

The registration procedures involve filling in the registration form, paying the registration fee and submitting the approval certificate. Once the registration procedures are completed, a registration certificate will be issued to the foreign representative office (Article 5, Interim Regulations).

As soon as the registration certificate is issued, the representative office in question is allowed to carry on economic or commercial activities. It is important to note, however, that a foreign representative office must also comply with other requirements such as opening a bank account with the Bank of China, and registering with the public security bureau, customs administration and tax bureau. More information in this regard will be outlined later in this Guide.

Joint ventures and cooperative ventures

As discussed earlier in this book, the formal legal status of cooperative ventures has yet to be prescribed by Chinese law. Many of the rules and regulations which are applicable to joint ventures, such as registration and approval procedures, are in practice, depending on their format, applicable to cooperative ventures.

Under Chinese law, joint ventures must be approved by the MOFERT or other authorities which are entrusted by the MOFERT with this responsibility. In general, a proposal for the establishment of a joint venture should include the following documents:

(1) An application for the establishment of a joint venture;
(2) A feasibility study report;
(3) The joint venture agreement, contract and articles of association;
(4) A list of candidates for chairman, vice chairman and directors, appointed by the parties to the venture; and
(5) Written opinions from the Chinese joint venture party's superior department and the provincial level government where the joint venture is located, with regard to the establishment of the joint venture. (See Article 9 of the Regulations for the Implementation of the Joint Venture Law of China, promulgated by the State Council on 20 December 1983)

The examining and approving authorities are required to complete their decision-making process within three months from the date of receipt of the above application documents, and notify the parties of their final decision.

Sino-foreign joint ventures and contractual ventures are required to register with the local SAIC within one month from the date of receipt of the certificate of approval (Article 11, Joint Venture Regulations). Upon registration, a business licence will be issued and the joint venture acquires a formal legal status with effect from the date of issuance.

Currently, the registration procedures for joint ventures are governed by the Regulations of the People's Republic of China on the Registration of Joint Ventures Using Chinese and Foreign Investment, promulgated by the State Council on 26 July 1980, and the Provisional Regulations of the General Bureau of Industrial and Commercial Administration of the People's Republic of China on the Standards of Registration Fees to be paid by Joint Ventures Using Chinese and Foreign Investment, promulgated on 7 February 1982. Under these regulations, joint ventures with a registered capital of RMB10m or less are required to pay a fee equal to 0.1% of the registered capital. For ventures with a larger registered capital, the portion exceeding the RMB10m level is to be assessed at a rate of 0.05%. If a joint venture intends to increase its capital after registration, the registration fees will be recalculated on the basis of the total sum of capital. In other words, the joint venture will then be required to pay additional registration fees.

Wholly foreign-owned enterprises

Procedures for the establishment of wholly foreign-owned enterprises have not yet been set up by law in China. In practice, applications for the incorporation of such ventures are examined and reviewed by the MOFERT which is required to approve or reject the applications within 90 days. Upon approval, the applicant must apply for registration with the local SAIC and secure a business licence within 30 days from the date of receipt of the certificate of approval.

In general, the establishment of a wholly foreign-owned enterprise requires the assistance of a Chinese entity which is to be appointed by the foreign enterprise and which agrees to offer the needed support in respect of the application process. If the Chinese entity agrees to be the sponsor, it will be responsible for making arrangements for various operational matters such as land use, employment, supply of water, power, communications facilities and other infrastructural items, supply of raw materials and components etc. In addition, the foreign applicant must prepare a feasibility study and draft a project proposal. These two items are, as a common practice, to be submitted to the local authorities where the project is to be located for consideration. Only after the local authorities have approved the proposed projects can the foreign applicant submit to the MOFERT or its entrusted bodies for approval, a formal application together with other relevant documents such as the feasibility study report, articles of association, names of the appointed directors and managers of the company, and other relevant documents.

Advantages and disadvantages of various forms of economic cooperation

The comparative advantages and disadvantages of each form of cooperation depend on the objectives of the foreign investors and the nature of the projects concerned. For instance, if a given foreign investor is interested in an investment project which requires the continuous assistance of a Chinese partner, an equity joint venture format may be best. Furthermore, since Sino-foreign joint ventures enjoy preferential tax terms, foreign investors who are keen on tax reductions may find this format a good choice. At the same time, the legal regime governing equity joint ventures is relatively complete and it may provide foreign investors with more certainty. On the other hand, the cooperative venture format is the most flexible. Here the parties to the venture can decide for themselves, subject to the approval of the relevant Chinese authorities, the constitution of the venture and the organization of management etc. However, as far as control is concerned, the wholly foreign-owned enterprise format provides investors with the most freedom in decision-making.

Issues concerning business operations

In general, any permanent establishment set up by a foreign investor, such as a representative office, equity joint venture, cooperative venture or wholly foreign-owned enterprise, will, upon receipt of the certificate of approval and the business licence, need to register with the local tax bureaus and local customs administration, and open an account with the Bank of China. The purpose of registration with the tax bureaus is basically to provide business information, that is, setting out in detail the nature and scope of the business activities involved. Customs registration is by definition for import-export purposes, especially for the importation of equipment, materials and other items for both production and personal use by the foreign-investment enterprises and their employees.

In addition, each such enterprise will have to contact the local land management department, and the bureaus in charge of infrastructure and labour management department, so as to secure the requisite land use rights, power, water and communications facilities and employment assistance. At present, there are supply companies in several major cities which provide assistance to foreign investors with regard to procurement and marketing. In cities without such companies, foreign investors may go to the State Materials Administrative Department and other relevant agencies to seek procurement and marketing assistance. The Chinese government encourages foreign investors to use local raw materials and components and to market their products abroad.

As regards other matters involving Chinese law or policies, it is advisable for foreign investors to seek direct consultations with the Chinese governmental bodies or law offices which are authorized to practise Chinese law. In addition, these investors may go to the various service centres established by the local governments in several major Chinese cities. If they should come across situations which were not foreseen or are unforeseeable, it is always advisable for them to bring the matter to the Chinese partners or local institutions with the aim of resolving the issues in an amicable and cooperative manner.

Appendix ten

Arbitration in China*

China has a tradition and a preference for solving disputes through means other than litigation which is used only occasionally. The Chinese people regard litigation as unfriendly and only use it as the last resort. This attitude prevails in China's foreign economic exchanges. Chinese negotiators were even reluctant at least for some time, to have a dispute settlement clause in contracts. Currently, almost all sales contracts, investment contracts and other agreements concerning foreign economic transactions include a dispute resolution provision. It usually provides that disputes must be settled first through friendly negotiation or consultation, then conciliation and arbitration and lastly through litigation. Even at the arbitration and litigation stages, disputing parties are encouraged to settle through consultation or conciliation. Indeed, the disputing parties are free to withdraw from arbitration or litigation proceedings and to resolve their dispute by other methods. This article will briefly discuss several features of arbitration in China.

Institutions for arbitration

There are currently three institutions which are qualified to handle arbitrations involving foreign business concerns in China: the Foreign Economic and Trade Arbitration Commission (the FETAC), formerly the Foreign Trade Arbitration Commission, the Maritime Arbitration Commission, and the arbitral tribunal in the Shenzhen Special Economic Zone. The FETAC and the Maritime Arbitration Commission were established under the auspices of the China Council for the Promotion of International Trade in 1956 and 1958 respectively. The Shenzhen arbitration tribunal, established in April, 1984, is a subdivision of the FETAC, which is in charge of handling disputes arising in Shenzhen and nearby regions. This tribunal has a list of 15 arbitrators, 8 of whom are from Hong Kong.

In general, the Maritime Arbitration Commission takes cognisance of disputes arising from salvage services, collisions at sea, charterparties, agency services, carriage by sea and marine insurance. The FETAC exercises jurisdiction for the arbitration of disputes arising from contracts and transactions in foreign trade, the implementation of agreements and contracts using foreign funds, Sino-foreign joint ventures, technology transfer pacts, coproduction arrangements by Chinese and foreign firms, compensation trade, etc. The FETAC enjoys by far the most popularity in China. It has a total number of 65 arbitrators (Intertrade, November 1984, p.60) and handles almost all disputes concerning foreign economic transactions except maritime ones.

Arbitration proceedings and selection of arbitrators

Under the current Chinese system, arbitration proceedings can only be conducted when an arbitration arrangement has been made between the disputing parties prior or subsequent to the dispute. For instance, the parties may have concluded a contract in which arbitration is provided as a means of dispute

* This article appeared in Butterworths Journal of International Banking and Financial Law, April 1987.

resolution or, after the occurence of the dispute, the parties enter into an agreement to arbitrate. An arbitration arrangement must be in writing. A typical arbitration clause in contracts between a Chinese and foreign party is as follows:

> 'Any dispute arising from the execution of or in connection with this contract shall be first settled amicably through friendly consultation. In case no settlement can be reached through consultation, the dispute shall be submitted to the Foreign Economic and Trade Arbitration Commission of the China Council for the Promotion of International Trade, Beijing, for arbitration in accordance with its Provisional Rules of Procedure. The arbitral award is final and binding upon both parties.'

In starting arbitration proceedings with the FETAC, a written application containing the following must be submitted, usually by the plaintiff: name and address of both disputing parties, statement of facts, the claim and facts and evidence upon which it is made, and name of an arbitrator chosen by the plaintiff or an authorisation allowing the chairman of the FETAC to appoint an arbitrator. Other documents such as contracts, arbitration agreement, correspondence, etc. should be attached as appendices in support of the application and claim. In addition, the plaintiff must deposit with the FETAC an abitration fee equivalent to 0.5% of the claim. In practice, it must not exceed 1% of the claim: the losing party must pay the winning party's costs. The compensation, however, must not exceed 5% of the total arbitration award.

Each disputing party is entitled to choose an arbitrator from the members of the FETAC which so far consists only of Chinese nationals. For Shenzhen arbitral tribunal, however, a disputing party may choose a Hong Kong arbitrator. The arbitrators so chosen should jointly select a presiding arbitrator from the members of the FETAC. These three arbitrators form a tribunal to hear the case. The disputing parties may agree to select a sole arbitrator (also from the FETAC) to arbitrate. If one of the parties fails to select an arbitrator within the prescribed time limit, the chairman of the FETAC should, upon request of the other party, appoint an arbitrator on the former's behalf. If the arbitrators cannot agree on the choice of the presiding arbitrator within a certain time, the chairman of the FETAC must appoint an arbitrator for it. If both parties have given such an authorisation, the chairman may, with the consent of both parties, appoint a sole arbitrator to hear the case.

The arbitrators are required to examine and hear the case independently and impartially. None of them should have any bias towards or represent any particular party's interests. If an arbitrator's qualifications or the arbitration agreement is challenged by a disputing party, the FETAC 'may rule on it'.

Arbitration is usually held at the FETAC's office in Beijing, China, unless the parties to a dispute prefer it to be conducted elsewhere. The date of hearing is fixed by the chairman of the FETAC in consultation with the presiding arbitrator.

Arbitration awards are decided by a majority vote of the tribunal. Dissenting opinion may be made in writing and kept on file. All arbitration awards must be made in writing. An arbitration tribunal may render, instead of a final award, a provisional or partial award. The reasons for making the award must be included in the award. Once a case is decided by an arbitration tribunal, it is final and may not be appealed to any court or institution.

Rules, policies and laws applied by arbitral tribunals

Chinese arbitrators are tireless in emphasising that an arbitration is not only aimed at obtaining a settlement of disputes but also 'to help enhance friendship and promote cooperation' between the disputing parties through such settlement. Accordingly, Chinese arbitrators always urge the disputing parties to solve their problem through friendly consultation. Although China has begun to pay more attention to both arbitration and litigation than in the past, Chinese arbitration tribunals have continued to make awards in accordance with the rules of procedure only when the dispute cannot be settled through consultation or conciliation. Conciliation is regarded as the second stage following consultation. If either party insists on avoiding consultation or conciliation and moving directly on to arbitration, this is permissible, if it does not violate a compulsory conciliation clause in the contract concerned. But this procedure is not recommended by the Chinese.

In China, contracting parties are free to choose the rules of procedure applicable to arbitration. Mostly, when an arbitration institution is authorised to proceed, the contract with a Chinese party usually provides for the rules of procedure of that institution to apply. If the arbitration is to be conducted by the FETAC, the Provisional Rules of Procedure of the Foreign Trade Arbitration Commission of the China Council for the Promotion of International Trade adopted on 31 March, 1956 (the 'Provisional Rules') will apply.

In deciding a case, the FETAC is to follow the principle of independence and pursue the policy of equality and mutual benefit and refer to international practice. Contracting parties may specify in the contact the applicable substantive law. Otherwise, the FETAC will apply the law most closely related to the contract in question. Nevertheless, disputes involving Sino-foreign joint ventures. wholly foreign-owned enterprises established in China, Sino-foreign cooperative ventures and foreign enterprises engaging in the development of natural resoures in China must be arbitrated in accordance with the relevant Chinese substantive law.

When Chinese substantive law applies, the FETAC studies and analyses relevant issues in accordance with Chinese provisions, customs and other principles and policies in China.

Apparently, the Chinese arbitral tribunal relies heavily on agreements or contracts between the disputing parties. As far as international practice is concerned, the FETAC only refers to those practices that are 'proved in the long run of world trade favourable to the development of international trade' and economic relations.

Appointment of attorneys

Article 18 of the Provisional Rules (currently in effect) provides that 'A disputing party may confer with the Arbitration Commission on matters relating to the proceedings either in person or by attorney agents.' Such attorneys may be citizens of the People's Republic of China or foreign citizens. The attorneys referred to above may 'defend the interests (of a disputing party) during proceedings of a case before the Arbitration Commission'. Article 1 of the Provisional Rules seems to conflict with China's Provisional Regulations on Lawyers effective on 1 January, 1982, which imply that only Chinese citizens are qualified to practice law in China. Article 191 of the Law of Civil Procedure provisionally adopted on 8 March, 1982 clarifies this matter, at least to some extent, by providing that 'when foreign nationals, people without nationality, foreign enterprises and foreign organisations entrust lawyers to represent them to take legal procedures, and to answer to legal procedures at the people's courts, the lawyers of the PRC must be entrusted'. The silence of this provision on arbitration may be interpreted as allowing some exception for arbitrations. This view is in accordance with recent arbitration practice by the FETAC. Disputing parties may still confer with the FETAC on matters relating to arbitration proceedings in person or by attorney. 'Such attorneys may be citizens of the PRC or a foreign citizen.' (Intertrade, November 1984, p. 62).

Arbitration clause in courts

China's preference for non-judical rather than judical procedure in dispute resolution is reflected in both Chinese law and policy. The Law of Civil Procedure stipulates that disputes arising from foreign trade and economic transactions may be resolved through arbitration or litigation (Article 192). It provides that cases which have been arbitrated by the PRC foreign affairs arbitration organs shall not be submitted to the people's court for legal procedures. (Article 193)

These provisions of the Law of Civil Procedure give rise to quite a few questions. First, what is a foreign affairs organisation? Apparently only the FETAC, the Maritime Arbitration Commission and the Shenzhen arbitration subdivision are qualified in China. But what if a given dispute is arbitrated by an arbitration tribunal outside China? Does it also prevent a Chinese court from accepting the case? The logical answer would be 'yes'. Secondly, at what stage of arbitration should a case be regarded as arbitrated? Chinese practice shows that if a dispute occurs in connection with a contract, which contains an arbitration clause, the Chinese courts cannot handle the case, unless the disputing parties agree otherwise. Where disputing parties agree to submit their dispute to arbitration after the dispute occurs, to withdraw from the arbitration requires mutual consent of the parties. The role of courts in dispute settlement is limited to implementation of arbitration awards. When one disputing party refuses or fails to carry out an arbitration award, the other party may resort to the courts for implementation.

Other devices

Two other methods of dispute settlement are also used in China, ie a combination of arbitration and joint conciliation. Under the combination or integration, as it is sometimes called, arbitration and conciliation are conducted simultaneously. Conciliation is also conducted on a voluntary basis with the consent of both parties. Its purpose is to distinguish 'right from wrong' and to assess liabilities. The disputing parties are free at any time to reach agreement through conciliation before an award is made.

Joint conciliation is peculiar to China. In joint conciliations, the Chinese party applies to the FETAC and the foreign party to a corresponding arbitral body in his own country. On receiving the request, the FETAC and the foreign arbitral body each appoints one or more conciliators of equal number. If no agreement is reached by the parties through such joint conciliation, the dispute is submitted to arbitration in accordance with the arbitration clause in the contract.

With the development of China's policy of opening up to the outside world and the rapid expansion of Sino-foreign economic exchanges, the use of arbitration in settling disputes involving Chinese and foreign parties has become quite common. The FETAC has to handle some 90 cases at a time, while the Maritime Arbitration Commission takes an additional 30. The recent accession by China to the United Nation's Convention on the Recognition and Enforcement of Foreign Arbitral Awards will further strengthen the position of Chinese arbitral organisations at international level. It will ensure the enforcement of arbitral awards by Chinese and foreign arbitral tribunals both inside and outside China.

Index

G

Z